The Southern Front

Segui il tuo corso,
e lascia dir le genti.

—*Dante*

The Southern Front

History and Politics in the Cultural War

Eugene D. Genovese

University of Missouri Press / Columbia and London

Library of Congress Cataloging-in-Publication Data
Genovese, Eugene D., 1930–
    The southern front : history and politics in the cultural war /
Eugene D. Genovese.
        p.   cm.
    Includes bibliographical references and index.
    ISBN 0-8262-1001-5
    1. Southern States—History—1775–1865—Historiography.
    2. Slavery—Southern States—Historiography.   3. Southern States—
Historiography.   4. Afro-American—Historiography.   5. Christianity and
politics.   I. Title.
F213.S65   1995
975′.0072—dc20   94-48718
                                                                            CIP

∞ This paper meets the requirements of the
American National Standard for Permanence of Paper
for Printed Library Materials, Z39.48, 1984.

Designer: Kristie Lee
Typesetter: BOOKCOMP
Printer and binder: Thomson-Shore, Inc.
Typefaces: Giovanni Book, Giovanni Black, Poster
    Bodoni Compressed

For

Josephine & Robert Genovese
Rebecca Fox & William Scott Green

—con amore

Contents

Culture and Politics

Epilogue

Preface

This volume brings together essays, addresses, and reviews written from the mid-1980s to 1994, some of which appear here in print for the first time. I have excluded a number of papers that might seem appropriate in a book that highlights the South, most notably those on religious life and economic theory in the Old South, for they will, in effect, be recast as part of a forthcoming book of another order. The Epilogue will, I hope, convey something of the political temper of the times in which the essays were written.

Since the book is a collection some repetition has been unavoidable. I have tried to keep it to a minimum by pruning each chapter. The coherence of the discrete pieces required some repetition, and I admit to having risked a bit more in order to establish emphasis. I have revised each chapter with a view toward improving the style but have resisted the temptation to do more with the substance than minor adjustments to effect greater clarity.

Wherever words appear in italics, the emphasis is from the original texts quoted.

With the partial exception of Chapter 6, I have removed the citations and other footnotes as pointless encumbrances, but I have added notes to the Epilogue. Those who wish to check the sources may consult the versions that appeared previously. I am grateful to the publishers who have given permission to reprint earlier versions of the chapters. The specifics of previous publication are provided in the Bibliographical Notes preceding the Index.

My personal debts are large, for many people offered criticism of each piece at the time it was written. Here, I can only offer my thanks in a general way and hope that they know how much I

---

have appreciated and learned from their efforts. But I owe a special debt to Louis A. Ferleger and Robert L. Paquette, who read almost all of the pieces as they were written and then read the manuscript of this book. Elizabeth Fox-Genovese performed her usual wifely duty in criticizing each piece through each draft, as well as the final manuscript as a whole. She also graciously agreed to let me include the essay on Lewis P. Simpson and the brief tribute to M. E. Bradford appended to Chapter 20, both of which we wrote jointly. I am indebted to Beverly Jarrett and Jane Lago of the University of Missouri Press for their support and editing.

The Southern Front

In Lieu of an Introduction

Personal Reflections

The philosophy of every man is contained in his politics.

—*Antonio Gramsci*

1

Marxism, Christianity, and Bias in the Study of Southern Slave Society

Those who pretend to write an objective, value-free history charge those who frankly espouse a worldview with having blind prejudice and contempt for evidence, but the charge itself betrays prejudice and contempt. Until recently, we primarily had to contend with the illusion that a historian could proceed without a worldview and attendant political bias and somehow arrive at an objectivity that one might have thought only God capable of.

That illusion stemmed from a narrow reading of such calls for objectivity as might be found in, say, Max Weber's plea for ethical neutrality in the social sciences. Weber spoke out boldly on politics in appropriate forums, while he advocated analytical rigor in specifically scientific work. He argued that a social scientist who wished to study syndicalism, for example, had to analyze its ideas and practices independent of a judgment on the validity of syndicalism itself. We may reply that it is impossible to keep value judgments from distorting our most determined efforts at objective analysis. And we may suspect that Weber knew as much and primarily intended a warning. Our reply should itself warn us against our own biases and admonish us to try to hold the inevitable distortions to a minimum. Weber may well have exaggerated the possibilities for objectivity, but he was right to insist that we must rein in our prejudices if we wish to do honest scientific work.

We cannot escape the intrusion of a worldview into our work as historians. Whether that worldview is Marxist, Christian, liberal, conservative, fascist, or other, the label tells us little. Giovanni Gentile, Italian fascism's ablest theorist, advanced a philosophy and even political policies that proved anathema to many prominent fascist intellectuals and party activists. Similarly, Christian interpretations of history that derive from the theology of Calvin or Arminius, Schleiermacher or Hodge, Barth or Tillich are likely to diverge widely, and it would be extraordinarily presumptuous to declare all but one's favorite interpretation to be un-Christian.

Among Marxists no quarrels are drearier and less productive than those which focus on "what Marx really meant." As the Marxist historian Eric Hobsbawm has long insisted, there have been "many Marxisms," for, in truth, Marx, like all great thinkers, left an ambiguous legacy, and mutually exclusive lines of thought may legitimately be developed from his many-sided work. It was, as I recall, Che Guevara, of all people, who demolished much nonsense when asked if he was a Marxist. We call ourselves scientific socialists, he replied. Well then, would you ask a physicist if he considered himself a Newtonian?

A quarter century ago I wrote an essay entitled "Marxian Interpretations of the Slave South," which led off with two quotations that identified my own stance. The first was from Alfred North Whitehead: "A science which hesitates to forget its founders is lost." The second was from Karl Marx: *"Je ne suis pas un marxiste."* My interest in the Old South began when I was an undergraduate. As a committed Marxist, I naturally began by pondering Marx's writing on the subject and quickly decided that he did not know what he was talking about. He had clearly extrapolated from his limited reading on the slave societies of the Caribbean and mechanistically applied his conclusions to the slave society of the Old South. Marx relied heavily on Frederick Law Olmsted's travelogues and on the economic analysis of John E. Cairnes, who himself had engaged in dubious extrapolation from Caribbean sources. I therefore had to ask myself why I should pay attention to an analysis that was not being borne out by the empirical work I had begun to do.

Simultaneously, I saw much in Marx's *Capital* and *Theories of Surplus Value*—in his interpretation of history and political

economy—that was heuristically arresting. I concluded that anyone who sought to construct a sound Marxist interpretation of
the Old South had to begin by rejecting Marx's specific analysis
of a subject with which he had only superficial acquaintance and,
instead, proceed in accordance with Marx's own admonition to
eschew ideological impositions on historical data and to reject
attempts to construct a suprahistorical theory of human experience. Marx practiced what he preached, at least when he worked
as a historian in such works as *The Eighteenth Brumaire of Louis
Bonaparte* and in the great historical passages of *Capital* on the
origins and development of capitalism.

Here we come directly to politics. When today's radicals, in sharp
contradistinction to Marx himself, condemn Western civilization
and Christianity for racism, slavery, sexism, and imperialism without mentioning the slavery, racism, sexism, and imperialism of
non-Western peoples, they promote massive lies that can only
lead to grave political errors. Among other things, radicals, many
of whom call themselves Marxists, forget Marx's oft-made observation that Western imperialism spurred the only genuine social
revolutions that Asia had ever experienced. Indeed, not necessarily
to his credit, Marx notoriously supported the United States in its
war on Mexico for that very reason. In any case, only the Christian West extruded a profound theoretical opposition to those
enormities, challenging their moral foundations and raising mass
movements against them. It requires no genius to see that a politics based on mendacity will end badly.

The Left has repeatedly ruined its prospects by such opportunism. For the moment I shall restrict myself to one observation. All sections of the Left claim that the people are constantly
deceived by the ideological manipulations of their oppressors
and that, therefore, the unveiling of the unvarnished truth about
social, economic, and political relations constitutes the principal
educational and ideological task of those who would fight for
a more just and humane society. In its own way it proclaims:
Know the truth, and the truth will make you free. That should
mean that since the people's cause is just, they must face any
amount of evidence of their own weaknesses and errors, so as

to be able to correct them and steel themselves for battle. The people can safely rest their case on the balance of the evidence in a telling of the whole story of domination and subordination in social relations. Conversely, if the struggle against injustice proceeds with lies, distortions, and swindles, who is so stupid as to think that a new society could emerge as anything except rotten to its core? The current game of denying the very possibility of objective truth or of the necessity to approximate it as closely as possible thus reveals itself as contempt for the people—for the allegedly oppressed—who apparently are incapable of facing unpleasantness and evidence of their own failings and who aspire to nothing better than to do unto others the horrors that have been done unto them. The self-proclaimed anti-elitists who sing such songs are practicing elitism with a vengeance.

Today we face the dangerous irrationality of a self-styled post-modernism. It is more dangerous than the pretense of ethical neutrality in social science and historical scholarship because, despite all pretense, it quickly passes into nihilism. Normally, cynicism and fanaticism combat each other and represent, as it were, opposing heresies. Yet, marvelous to say, they now march in lockstep. We are being told that since objectivity rests only with a God who does not exist, we should scorn it as the ideology of oppressors.

Those who denounce objectivity as a fraud in the service of oppression are offering flagrant mendacity as a Higher Law. And since just about everyone, except non-Hispanic, heterosexual, white males, is today a victim of oppression, we are invited to present our subjectivity—our "feelings," which usually appear as hatreds—as a substitute for a nonexistent truth. I make no apology for the harshness of these remarks. In accordance with the fashion of parading one's feelings as a contribution to every discussion of every subject, I shall admit to being outraged at hearing endless whines about oppression from American intellectuals—black as well as white, female as well as male. For since they (we) rank among the top one or two percent of the world's most privileged people, the whines may fairly be judged obscene. But then, I suppose I am merely revealing my own status as an oppressor by invoking an untenable standard of statistical objectivity, when I should be demonstrating my sensitivity to the precious feelings of the insulted and the injured. Unfortunately, never having met a human being who did not feel insulted and injured in this vale of tears, my capacity for compassion has been badly stunted. Atheist that I am, I learned that much from Christian teaching on original sin and human depravity, which has been confirmed by all historical experience of which I am aware, even if it is no longer in fashion in mainstream Christian churches.

For a particularly destructive illustration of the consequences of fudging the political implications of historical scholarship, consider the relation of the admirable work on slave life to the problem of black nationalism. For the last few decades a large number of fine scholars, black and white, have investigated slave life (religion, folklore, family, material conditions, resistance) and have unanimously concluded that the slaves forged a vibrant culture under conditions of extreme adversity. Most have also acknowledged the centrality of religion to that achievement and demonstrated the unique features of the black religious experience. Taken as a whole, this work reveals a distinct Afro-American culture without analogue in the experience of any other ethnic group. Yet, with the exception of George Rawick, Sterling Stuckey, and only a few others, the scholars who have made these admirable contributions have remained silent on the political implications, which clearly support the black-nationalist interpretation of the black experience in the United States and, at the least, call for serious qualification of the rival liberal-integrationist interpretation. We are entitled to suspect that the scholars whose work is supporting essential black-nationalist contentions are themselves integrationists who are unwilling to face the political consequences of their own scholarship. As a result, the notion that black nationalism ought to be viewed as pathological rather than historically authentic remains widespread and inhibits frank discussion of the most pressing political problems.

Yes, our scholarly work, especially on subjects as explosive as slavery and racism, has inescapable political implications, some of which may, however, contradict our intentions. Yes, a historian has the duty to make those implications clear. But, simultaneously, he has the duty to resist the imposition of his politics on the empirical record. Or to put it another way: It is one thing to lay bare the political implications of our analyses; it is quite another to whore in some ostensible worthy cause.

Some years ago I devoted a decade of work to what became *Roll, Jordan, Roll: The World the Slaves Made*, a book on slave life. That work constituted a detour in my lifelong special project—the history of the slaveholders and the slave society of the Old South over which they exercised hegemony. I embarked upon that detour not because of the emerging struggle against racial segregation, however much that struggle may have influenced my work, but because I found that I could not understand the slaveholders without understanding the slaves. Specifically, I had to evaluate the slaveholders' perception of slave life and consciousness in the light of the reality of that life and consciousness or as much of it as would prove amenable to empirical investigation.

The empirical investigations disturbed a historian with the biases of an atheist and a historical materialist who had always assumed, however mindlessly, that religion should be understood as no more than a corrosive ideology at the service of ruling classes. If, at the beginning, someone had told me that religion would emerge as a positive force in my book—indeed, as the centerpiece—I would have laughed and referred him to a psychiatrist. In the end, the evidence proved overwhelming, and I had to eat my biases, although not my Marxism. For while much went into the making of the heroic black struggle for survival under extreme adversity, nothing loomed so large as the religious faith of the slaves. The very religion that their masters sought to impose on them in the interest of social control carried an extraordinarily powerful message of liberation in this world as well as the next.

The slaves interpreted the Word and experienced the Holy Spirit in their own way, and yet they did no violence to Christianity itself. True, they injected a strong dose of traditional African religion and Afro-American folk culture into their interpretation. But, as every historian knows, so did the peoples of Europe and the rest of the world. The vitality of Christianity—its very sense of being in accord with Word and Spirit—has depended upon the ability of the churches to respond to the positive elements in folk life while resisting heretical tendencies. Recall that the decision of the early church in favor of the Trinity registered popular opposition to an intellectual elite that found irrational the concept of a triune God. The church, in effect, found the Holy Spirit in the consciousness of the faithful. I find puzzling the decision of Nancey Murphy, in her remarkable book, *Theology in the Age of Scientific Reasoning,* to bypass this history, which would seem to lend vital support to her principal thesis that theology has firm claims to rank as a science in accordance with the test of probability theory.

Be that as it may, these musings bring us face-to-face with two questions: Can, in fact, a nonbeliever contribute anything of value to Christian thought? and can a confrontation with Christian thought and experience lead a Marxist or other nonbeliever to deepen his own worldview and help purge it of untenable features? Obviously, I would be the last person to be able to answer the first question with reference to my own work. But let me indicate what I tried to do, the conclusions toward which I was led, and some problems that that work may pose for believers.

To begin with, the overpowering evidence of religious faith aroused in me a skepticism about the reigning tendency in Academia to, as it were, sociologize faith out of religion—to deny the reality of spirituality. That debilitating tendency may be observed even among scholars who profess Christianity but espouse an extreme theological liberalism that leads toward a denial of any claim Christianity may have to being not one religion among many but the Way and the Truth. I would not presume to tell Christians how to be Christians, but I must confess that I cannot understand how Christians, without ceasing to be Christians, can retreat one inch from a belief that Jesus is the second person of a triune God, the Christ, the redeemer. If other religions offer equally valid ways to salvation and if Christianity itself may be understood solely as a code of morals and ethics, then we may as well all become Buddhists or, better, atheists. I intend no offense, but it takes one to know one. And when I read much Protestant theology and religious history today, I have the warm feeling that I am in the company of fellow nonbelievers.

Theories derived from the sociology of religion proved indispensable to my own work, and I am sure that the influence of Max Weber and Ernst Troeltsch, among others, will appear obvious to anyone who reads it. For that matter, the Freudian bias in the psychological dimension of that work has probably not been lost on discerning readers. But no such theory or combination of theories could suffice to explain the power of the folk religion, as manifested, for example, in the spirituals. Mechal Sobel has criticized me for slighting the spiritual dimension of the slaves' experience, and she may well be right. But if so, the error arose from a deficiency of talent, not of intention. For nothing could be clearer than that the slaves' successful struggle for survival as a people was more readily spiritual than physical. Christians are entitled to chide materialists with their inability to account for that dimension, for we have done poorly in response to the challenge.

Contrary to much current practice, the histories of the slaves and the slaveholders cannot be written independent of each other. It would have been astonishing if godless slaveholders had been able to introduce their slaves to Christianity. The hard truth is that the slaveholders, or at least the decisive figures among them, genuinely qualified as believers. Their belief contributed immeasurably to their social power and thereby lent itself to a sociological analysis of the ideological and political functions of religion. But we must still confront the ample evidence of piety among a considerable portion of the slaveholders. Probably half of all the proslavery and antislavery tracts written during the nineteenth century were written by ministers, and a large portion of the rest invoked scriptural arguments. That the Bible proved the principal terrain of ideological struggle over the slavery question demonstrates the centrality of religious thought to the American experience, both northern and southern.

In defending slavery as a Christian social system, the proslavery divines and even the secular theorists appealed to Scripture. Regrettably, such formidable southern theologians as James Henley

Thornwell and Robert L. Dabney—to say nothing of conservative antislavery northern theologians like Charles Hodge, who voted for Lincoln—sustained themselves in scriptural exegesis with the abolitionists. Orthodox theologians demonstrated that neither the Old nor the New Testament condemned slavery as sinful. The abolitionists, displaying no small amount of intellectual dishonesty, never succeeded in making the Word say what they said it did, and eventually they had to spurn the Word for the Spirit. In consequence, they virtually reduced the Holy Spirit to the spirit (the conscience) of individuals. I do not say that an antislavery Christian theology remains an impossibility. I am prepared to hear that, say, the implications of Karl Barth's theology and Nancey Murphy's methodological work could yield an antislavery theology. But as a historian, I do insist that the abolitionists failed to construct one and that, so far as I know, no one has yet improved upon their performance. Note, for example, that Paul Tillich, in his *Systematic Theology*, introduces slavery only to assume its incompatibility with Christianity, thereby assuming precisely what he needs to demonstrate.

I undertook another task in *Roll, Jordan, Roll* and in my subsequent work on the religion of the slaveholders, and here my early training as a Marxist came to the fore. It is remarkable how little attention is paid to theology in most current work on religion. Today, most historians of religion, believers or no, proceed as if theology were the special province of a small portion of a well-educated elite. They thereby separate the religion of the elite from the religion of the common people, apparently on the assumption that only a handful of theologians and sophisticated ministers and laymen know or care about theology. I proceeded on the contrary assumption—that even folk religion, the religion of the least sophisticated, necessarily had a theological content with ideas of God, sin, soul, and salvation, and that the historian's task was to extract those ideas from the mass of the seemingly incoherent beliefs inevitably found in the thoughts of everyman. For if, as I believe with Gramsci, "the philosophy of every man is contained in his politics," so is his theology, which is no less contained in his philosophy.

I may have gotten the answers wrong for the slaves—that remains a matter for further empirical investigation—but I stand by the validity of the assumption. And similarly for the slaveholders. Historians who posit a chasm between the "high culture" of the theologians and the "popular culture" of the least educated of the southern whites run into a serious problem. For the principal themes and ideas of the theologians, including their defense of slavery and a hierarchical natural and social order, clearly resonated through the country preachers and their flocks. In few if any modern societies has the intelligentsia, clerical and lay, been so clearly in harmony with the common people.

The political ramifications of southern Christian theology were enormous. For at the very moment that the northern churches, albeit with stiff internal resistance, were embracing theological liberalism and abandoning the Word for a Spirit increasingly reduced to personal subjectivity, the southern churches were holding the line for Christian orthodoxy, whether in Arminian or Calvinist form. Not for nothing was Thornwell called "the Calhoun of the Church." He, as well as Calhoun, recognized, indeed proclaimed, that the southern insistence upon the Word of the Bible had its direct counterpart in the southern insistence upon the word of the United States Constitution. In politics, as in theology, the overwhelming majority of southerners were strict constructionists.

The study of the religious life of both slaves and slaveholders thus encourages an atheist to hope that he can contribute something to a subject generally slighted by his ideology and can even position him to challenge Christians to clarify their theology. By extension, it encourages a Marxist to reexamine fundamental tenets of his own interpretation of history. Let us proceed, *arguendo*, to accept the idea that social relations lie at the core of historical development. Marx died before he could write all but a few introductory lines on social classes for the final chapter of the third volume of *Capital*. Many Marxists could therefore be excused for having relied on a few sweeping generalizations in *The Critique of Political Economy* and other works and viewing social classes as economic entities. Yet Marx himself did no such thing in his own historical writing, most notably in his analyses of the emergence of capitalism and his studies of the class struggles in nineteenth-century France. One thing is clear: As every serious Marxist has understood, Marx was not an economic determinist.

During the twentieth century, Marxists, especially those influenced by Antonio Gramsci, have discarded the mechanistic dichotomy of a social base and a derivative ideological superstructure. Two grave weaknesses nonetheless continue to plague Marxist thought: an underestimation of nationalism and of religion. These are big subjects, and I can only touch upon the second here. The study of religion in the Old South reveals that the churches largely succeeded in binding social classes to each other, most impressively among the whites. But neither Marxism nor any other historical or sociological theory can fully account for the dynamics—for the alacrity with which the well-to-do and the lowly accepted the "good news" about Jesus.

We can no longer close our eyes to the centrality of the Christian message to the formation of the slaveholding class, as well as of the yeomanry, and to the bond it created between them. Marxists, then, are compelled to reconsider their very notion of social class—or more broadly, of social relations—to include much more than the economic relations that undoubtedly loomed large. Slaveholders may have been slaveholders and yeomen may have been yeomen in the sense that all such classes have much in common with their equivalents elsewhere. But the Protestant slaveholders and yeomen of the Old South may be equated with their Catholic counterparts in Brazil only at the risk of misunderstanding the essentials of their history.

For the political Left there is an especially dark side to the question of ideological bias and its attendant contempt for religion. Conservatives have long charged us with the espousal of Christian heresy. Most tellingly, Eric Voegelin has identified our worldview as a modern gnosticism. There is too much truth for comfort in the charge. Having substituted what may fairly be called a gnostic vision for Christianity and scoffed at the moral baseline of the Ten Commandments and the Sermon on the Mount, we ended a seventy-year experiment with socialism with little more to our credit than tens of millions of corpses. The bourgeois

slave-traders of Europe and New England and the slaveholders of
the South committed terrible atrocities and have much to answer
for, especially to their black victims. But did they overmatch our
own atrocities? For that matter, has a radical-egalitarian party ever
come to power on a significant scale and not plunged into mass
murder and the establishment of tyranny? On this ground alone,
we can no longer postpone a reconsideration of the Christian idea
of justice and equality before God and of our own blood-drenched
romance with the utopia of a man-made heaven here on earth.

As we are tirelessly reminded these days, the history of Christianity has been strewn with blood, but, as we are rarely reminded,
that same history has contributed a body of teaching that has
made possible a line of resistance and counter-attack. If Christianity, in the days in which it took itself seriously, stressed human
depravity and capacity for evil, it also insisted on an element of
divinity in everyman. Secular liberals, invoking Locke's blank slate,
like to say that man is neither beast nor angel. It would seem safer
to say, in the spirit of Christian orthodoxy, that man is both beast
and angel. Christianity therefore denies the right of any individual
or state to treat human beings as objects of social engineering
rather than as discrete personalities sacred in the sight of God.
Until nonbelievers can match that performance they would do
well to temper their criticism and to look to their own moral
responsibilities.

For myself, I have no idea whether I have been able to contribute
anything of value to the study of religion. I do know that the effort
to come to terms with the history of Christianity has contributed
much to my understanding of what my preferred political movement and ideology have been and what they must become if we
are to contribute to the more just and humane world we have
devoted our lives to fighting for.

2

Hans Rosenberg at Brooklyn College

A Communist Student's Recollections of the
Classroom as War Zone

"I shall teach this course as a stiff graduate course, and if you
don't like it, get out now." The words came with a pronounced
German accent, which somehow made them all the scarier to a
college junior. Having taken two semesters of European economic
history with this professor, I had no illusions. He meant what
he said. For those of us who had naively considered his "baby"
courses in economic history draconian, his words were all the
scarier. What the devil were we in for on this round? Whether
anyone "did not like it," I have no idea, but no one dropped.

At the outset the course on the rise of the national state proved
a Hans Rosenberg production. He assigned us Max Weber's essays
on "Politics as a Vocation" and "Bureaucracy" and Ernest Barker's
book on national-state administration. He expected us to be ready
to discuss the assignment by the end of the week, and he was not
a man who took well to excuses. As usual for his courses, some of
the best students in and out of the history department had signed
on, including his favorites, Helen Leibel and Phil Leider, who went
on to fine careers in history and art history, respectively. They had
earned the right to qualify as his favorites. Helen gave every indi-
cation of already being a professional historian, and Phil, a real
charmer if slightly crazy, was everyone's candidate for the most
brilliant mind around. Between the learned, demanding, caustic

professor and an array of tough-minded, hardworking students, class could easily become a nightmare for those who cut corners. But those who cut corners stayed away from Rosenberg's courses.

Brooklyn College was an extraordinary place in the late 1940s, although few of us knew it at the time. I was not alone among Brooklynites in going there because it charged no tuition, and one could live at home. Many of us could never have gone to college under other circumstances, not even the Jews, who made up the overwhelming majority of the student body. Jews, as every one knows, are rich. What everyone knows somehow eluded the Jewish students, most of whom, like the rest of us, came from working-class and lower-middle-class families and had to work hard for what they expected to get out of life.

So, Brooklyn College was just a place we happened to be at. If it was special, how were we supposed to know? At a fresh-man orientation, President Harry Gideonse proudly announced that Brooklyn College ranked third in the country in placing stu-dents in graduate and professional schools. Were we supposed to be impressed? Some of us did not even know what a graduate school was. For myself, I had never even heard of the Ivy League. The history professors included Arthur C. Cole, among the most distinguished historians of nineteenth-century America; Samuel Hurwitz, whose publications never quite revealed the breadth of his knowledge and insights; and Irving Mark, a fine American his-torian and an exceptionally able, if astonishingly dry, teacher who would get fired during the McCarthy purges. That Mark was dry as dust as a lecturer made no impression: You did not go to Brooklyn College to be entertained. There were other historians no less no-table with whom I did not have the chance or the wit to study, and other departments boasted no few outstanding scholars and teach-ers. Like many other students, I had little sense of the privilege that was being bestowed upon me. I recognized it only when I went to graduate school at Columbia and found eminent professors who lived up to their reputations and taught me much, but who were no more gifted than the professors I had already experienced.

Brooklyn College and especially Hans Rosenberg forcibly came back to me recently, when *The New Republic* asked me to review

Dinesh D'Souza's controversial book on the current grand doings in Academia, and I reflected on my own career not so much as a professor but as a participant in the historical associations and in academic politics generally. What was making me so angry? Having been a young Communist during the McCarthy era, I have been gagging on the neo-McCarthyism of those who now, with bittersweet irony, are justly being accused of promoting "political correctness," but that is not the whole story. Like many others, most of whom unfortunately still remain silent, I have especially been gagging on the cult of "sensitivity" that has been betraying our students, especially black students, and I have found myself wishing that they now had the honor and privilege of confronting Hans Rosenberg, who, by going standards, would never have scored well on a sensitivity chart.

At Brooklyn College in the late 1940s you are one of some two hundred members of the Communist Party in a student body of eight thousand—card-carrying party members, mind you, and not to be confused with the eight hundred or so fellow-travelers. Obviously, you have to take courses in European economic history. It is too bad that the professor is a German refugee who, while learned and intellectually formidable, detests Marxism and has a special aversion to Communists. The class struggle must be carried into the classroom, and Marx has to be defended against this enemy of the people. Besides, in how many courses would you have a legitimate excuse to read Maurice Dobb and the other Marxist economic historians you need time to catch up with?

There are about thirty students in the course, at least a third of whom are Marxists and other political radicals, including about a half dozen party comrades and a few of those detestable Trotskyists. Rosenberg delights in denigrating Marx's scholarship and outraging the sensibilities of his leftwing students. He never says that only a fool could fall for that nonsense—his manners are much too traditional for that—but, in his own way, he lets you know. He comes to class ready for a shoot-out, and we are ready too.

The room itself resembles a battlefield. In the front row sit, among others, the Trotskyists—or "Trotskyites," as we insist upon calling them derisively. And not only are they Trotskyites, they are Shachtmanites, the most foul kind of Trotskyites. The rows behind are occupied by "ordinary" students who may or may not notice the barricades before and behind them. The Stalinists sit in the last row. Apart from me, they are Jews, but, in inter-ethnic Brooklyn, they have absorbed the Sicilian principle of keeping your back to the wall at all times, well positioned to see everything in front of you and to avoid being shot in the back. Still, we need not be apprehensive. Rosenberg, an honorable man, always aims for between the eyes.

Rosenberg teaches a subject he obviously loves passionately and is not to be confused with some ideological proselytizer. But neither is he to be confused with those who pretend that the history they teach does not have political implications and consequences. Hence, while he demands evidence for everything and has little patience with dogmatic extrapolations, he makes his social and political views clear when appropriate.

He must be ready for our assaults. True, we are the Old Left, not the New, and our classroom manners pass muster by the standards of New York City. We would face severe criticism if we embarrassed the Party by outraging our fellow students' sense of decency. That stuff is for petty-bourgeois exhibitionists. But we are expected to be relentless and to expose our bourgeois professors for what they really are.

The battles usually take place not over the lecture Rosenberg just gave, but over the one he gave during the previous class meeting. For after each class, one or two comrades are assigned to go to the library to check out his facts and sources. When class next meets, we demand to know how he could have said what he said about, say, the condition of the British yeomanry in the light of so-and-so's definitive study, which says the opposite. Once in a while we actually catch him out. Most of the time, he smashes us. Occasionally, we suspect him of dirty pool. What, after all, are we supposed to say when he cites some new work in one of the languages he reads fluently and we do not read at all?

Rosenberg is courteous enough, if under the rubric of courtesy you can absorb his withering sarcasm and a sardonic smile that suggests you are a dogmatic ass who is making a fool of yourself. He shows genuine interest in what even Communists think, when they have done their work and come to class well prepared. He shows no interest in what you "feel" about anything. He never descends to insult or personal humiliation, but he gets rough when you do not know what you are talking about. He knows the difference—and makes sure you do too—between insulting a student and letting him know when he is faking. Ferocious as he is, he does not appreciate cruelty, as I find out one day.

Rosenberg assigns only two books to the first-semester course on European economic history from the Middle Ages to the Industrial Revolution: a textbook he treats with contempt but tells us to read for the chronology and nuts and bolts; and Henri Pirenne's challenging interpretive study of the origins of capitalism. He hands out reading lists, lots of reading lists. We are supposed to pick the books and articles that interest us most and, in effect, construct our own bibliography. Each week we hand in a three-by-five index card on which we tell him what we have read. He never rebukes anyone for not handing in a card, and only he and God know what he is thinking.

It has to happen, and it does. Mr. X, one of the bright lights of the Shachtmanite running-dogs-of-world-fascism, hands in a card on which he claims to have read Max Weber's *The Protestant Ethic and the Spirit of Capitalism*, a Rosenberg favorite. Sure enough, at the appropriate moment, Rosenberg opens a discussion of the relation of Protestantism to capitalism with a glowing and seemingly endless introduction of Mr. X, who will enlighten us on the Weber Thesis. Poor Mr. X has faked it and has nothing to say. Looking as if he would like to crawl into a hole, he incoherently mumbles generalities. Rosenberg, perhaps pretending, seems unwilling to believe that a student of his would lie. He proceeds as if Mr. X is merely a bit intimidated and needs reassurance. Thereupon follow more excruciating minutes of Rosenberg's trying to help him out. Most of the class is aghast. The Stalinists are delighted, none more so than I.

My comrades get away with smirking since we are sitting in the back of the room and no one except Rosenberg can see them.

I, however, laugh, thereby causing Mr. X visible pain. Rosenberg delivers no lecture on civility. Instead, upset as he is over Mr. X's gaffe, his lips curl into his patented sardonic nonsmile. *"Ja, vell . . ."*—his German accent gets decidedly thicker as he glares at me, and I know I am in trouble. "Now, Mr. Genovese, you will help your colleague out, no?" I protest. I did not claim to have read Max Weber. Besides, I am a materialist and know nothing about spirits! "So you have not read Max Weber. Does that mean you have not thought about this serious problem in our course work? Try using your historical imagination, for God's sake. You have one, don't you?"

I do believe that my classroom manners improved markedly in the event.

Rosenberg's constant assault on his Marxist, especially Communist, students never gets personal or petty. It is true that we are convinced that he has a policy of never giving a party member a grade higher than B, although he never savages us either. Probably, only one of our comrades deserves an A for the course, and even he writes so badly that he may not be showing up well on his tests. Still, Rosenberg just about gives himself away one day—with me. In the end, I would fall down on the final examination and have no complaint about my B for the course. But my midterm . . . ?

What could Rosenberg possibly ask on a midterm examination in a course without a list of required readings? When the dreaded day comes, he hands out blue books and, thickening his German accent for the occasion, announces: "You will decide upon an important question pertinent to the material covered so far in the course, and you will answer your own question." At that point he laughs, a bit sadistically it seems to me, and adds, "And I shall judge you as much by the question as by the answer." A week later he returns the papers, directing me to read mine to the class. When I finish, he remarks, "Now that is what a first-class midterm looks like." I am, needless to say, proud and pleased, notwithstanding my getting a B and noticing that a number of students who had gotten an A were looking perplexed. "What grade did you give him?" shouts a comrade from the last row. "B," comes the poker-faced reply. Then a quick and hearty laugh: "Well, in this case, maybe we'll make it a B+."

Those classrooms were war zones, as both students and professors understood. The blows on either side were not personal. Personal was when Rosenberg called me into his office after my so-so final examination. I do not know whether he would have given me an A for an A performance. I do know that he had expected an A performance and wanted to know, as he went over the examination page by page, if I had just had a bad day or if something was seriously wrong.

Year after year the comrades took his courses *con amore*, marching out of each class session with an oath to settle accounts when we came to power. I do not recall a single serious Communist student who did not intersperse his curses with words of respect. He was a great teacher, and we knew it. Rosenberg was not alone at Brooklyn College in being a slave-driver, in having an instinct for the jugular, and in flaunting his disregard for his students' most deeply held prejudices and sensitivities. He may, however, have been in a class by himself in the richness of his sense of humor.

We saw little of our professors outside of class. They taught five courses, five days a week, and the whole department of history shared one office. We would have been appalled at the thought of bothering them. They had too many students and no teaching assistants to grade papers for them. How they managed to write the excellent books and articles many of them did write remains a mystery. Besides, when were we supposed to find time to see them? Some of us worked full-time at whatever jobs we could find. (I learned firsthand about the media's ethics and skill in inventing and suppressing news while working as a copyboy on the night shift of an eminently respectable newspaper in New York City.) Many others, maybe most, worked part-time. Almost every student had his hands full, and no one wanted to hear about another's problems—unless there was something tangible he could do to help. And so with our professors. We never assumed that they did not care. And we never assumed that our troubles were their concern.

Rosenberg cared. But he intervened only when he could make a difference. We were young men and women, not "kids," and he made no pretense of being our social worker, psychotherapist, or surrogate father. In my case, he bears responsibility for my having devoted my subsequent life to the study of the Old South. By the time I graduated I had learned about graduate school and had decided to become a historian. Rosenberg, to my great surprise, invited me to his home to talk about it. He mentioned a senior honors paper on the slaveholders that I had written for Arthur Cole. You will, he said, of course continue to study the slaveholders and make them your life's work. I thought he had lost his mind. I demurred politely but thought: Sure, a working-class Sicilian American from Brooklyn, who has never so much as seen a mule or a cotton field, is chomping at the bit to spend his life in a study of the Chivalry and a bunch of rednecks. He flashed that sardonic smile. "Well, I have studied the Junkers, who rose to power more or less at a definite time and went kaput in 1945. Your slaveholders also rose to power more or less at a definite time and went kaput in 1865. Where could you find anything so close to a laboratory in which to study how a ruling class really rules? Why don't you test those crazy Marxist theories of yours?" He did not say, "Put up or shut up," but I got the message.

Rosenberg taught history with a combination of cold objectivity and hot passion that carried its own lessons about scholarship, intellectual work, politics, life. And he did it without sermons. He could be rough on his students. Certainly, he was demanding. He thereby showed us respect. And respect required that he challenge our every prejudice, feeling, and cherished ideal—that he defy our very sensibility. A model of the modern "insensitive professor," Hans Rosenberg was everything a college professor must be.

Representative Carolinians

Aristocracies often commit very
tyrannical and very inhuman actions;
but they rarely entertain grovelling
thoughts; and they show a kind of
haughty contempt of little pleasures,
even whilst they indulge in them. The
effect is greatly to raise the general
pitch of society. In aristocratic ages
vast ideas are commonly entertained
of the dignity, the power, and the
greatness of man.

—*Alexis de Tocqueville*

3

James Johnston Pettigrew

Even in these dreariest of days in Academia, when American history has largely become a plaything for canting ideologues, the Old South continues to attract outstanding talent. Despite the pressure of a kind of Gresham's Law, fine books and articles continue to appear, as Clyde Wilson's *Carolina Cavalier* attests. Our times call for a correct ideological line, which at its increasingly popular extreme regards the Old South as a rehearsal for Nazi Germany and calls for eradication of all traces of the conservative voices that have loomed so large in southern history. And in our leading professional associations and their journals and in the classrooms of our most prestigious colleges and universities the correct line prevails.

The continued interest in the Old South proceeds from the worst and best of reasons. The worst includes the step-by-step domination of departments of history in our southern as well as northern universities by those who regard what Richard Weaver aptly called the Southern Tradition and all its works as an evil past to be exorcised by all means, fair and foul. It is no longer enough to reject slavery, segregation, and racism. Every positive feature of the mainstream southern experience must also be rejected by those who would rather not face charges of indulging in racist and proslavery apologetics. We are being entertained lavishly by a new philosophy of history that has the supreme merit of reducibility to four words: "Black, good; white, bad."

The prevalence of this view in the North need not agitate us, for it has ever been thus. Its prevalence in the South is another matter, about which prudence dictates silence from carpetbaggers like myself. Since prudence has never been my strongest suit, I shall risk the suggestion that my fellow carpetbaggers, who today inundate southern universities with generally unfortunate consequences, have less to answer for than do the scalawags who feel called upon to repudiate their own great, if deeply flawed, regional culture. That such a repudiation could only flow from a pathetic loss of identity and attendant self-hatred does not deter them. Nor do they seem to understand that self-hatred, no matter how flamboyantly presented as a high-minded search for a new and more progressive identity, is no more attractive in white Southerners than in Jews, blacks, Sicilians, or anyone else.

The best of reasons for continued interest in the Old South includes not only a perennial quest for the origins of the War that remains our greatest national trauma—and drama—but a strong sense that there is much to be learned here about the tragic nature of the historical dimension of the human condition. Honest historians, whatever their specific viewpoint, cannot avoid a confrontation with that tragic dimension, for there is abundant evidence of a hegemonic slaveholding class that, notwithstanding a full measure of ogres and timeservers, boasted a host of extraordinary men and women: God-fearing, courageous, socially and morally responsible—and tough. Historians, that is, cannot avoid a confrontation with the lives of the slaveholders who embodied those qualities and yet proved to be the agents of the greatest enormity of the age—men and women who, whatever their virtues, were constantly driven to the acts of savagery toward black people required for their very survival as owners of human flesh.

The coexistence of qualities that defined the slaveholders and many of the yeomen who accepted the slave society into which they were born manifested itself differently in accordance with region, income, social status, and personal character and temperament. Still, in one manifestation or another, those qualities repeatedly surfaced. The elite slaveholders of the Virginia tidewater or the Carolina low country might not qualify as "typical," but they did embody the best and worst characteristics of the southern slaveholders as a class. And notwithstanding the gross categories that currently obsess social historians, certain figures emerge as representative—as worthy of study both as impressive individuals and as men whose lives illuminate the course of southern civilization.

James Johnston Pettigrew, born into the elite of the North Carolina low country and subsequently a resident of Charleston, was one of those representative men. Remembered primarily, if at all, as a minor Confederate military commander, he displayed exemplary courage at Gettysburg and elsewhere, only to have his reputation posthumously sullied by unfair criticism. Pettigrew was barely thirty-five years old when he fell during a skirmish on the Potomac in 1863, but during his short life he made a decided impact on all who knew him, including his kinsman and legal mentor, James L. Petigru, South Carolina's celebrated intransigent unionist and reputedly the greatest lawyer in a state famous for its legal talent.

Pettigrew had to wait a long time for a biographer, but he could not have hoped to find a better one than Clyde Wilson. A professor of history at the University of South Carolina, Wilson is best known to historians as the superb editor of the multivolume *Papers of John C. Calhoun* and to the general public as a contributor to *Chronicles* and other journals and as editor of that stimulating manifesto of southern conservatism, *Why the South Will Survive* (1981). A careful scholar who has thought hard and deep about his beloved South, he displays an unusually strong "feel" for the society of the Old South as it existed rather than as it is presented by historians who read the conditions and perspectives of the twentieth century back into it. Wilson is, in short, an exemplary historian who, in this book, displays his formidable talent.

Wilson writes gracefully and well, unfolding, so far as possible, his narrative in a manner that carries its own interpretation. But when, as happens from time to time, an interpretive set piece is required, he rises to the challenge. Thus he treats us to strong and fresh, if brief, discussions of southern concepts of chivalry and the gentleman, the nature of a much misunderstood southern unionism, and the relation of planters to yeomen. For good measure, he provides an incisive analysis of the psyche of a fascinating man. In all, Wilson tells the story of an arresting life and, in so doing, offers the public an invaluable introduction to essential aspects of life in the old South and offers specialists a no less invaluable consideration of long disputed topics.

In this first-rate study of a man, his world, and his times, Wilson recounts Pettigrew's active if sadly foreshortened life as a product of one of North Carolina's prominent families; as a young resident on a particularly interesting plantation; as a gifted student at the justly celebrated Bingham Academy and at the University of North Carolina; as an observer of society in Charleston, where he practiced law; as a member of the South Carolina legislature who helped lead the fight against the movement to reopen the African slave trade; as a critic of Robert Barnwell Rhett and the fire-eaters and also of the political legacy of John C. Calhoun; as a unionist who finally crossed over and supported secession; and as a student, traveler, and penetrating observer in Europe. In each case Wilson unobtrusively delineates Pettigrew's unique qualities and individual performance in a manner that reveals the ways in which, and the extent to which, he deserves to rank as a representative man. In each case Wilson sheds light on the society and the times: on education and religion, on ideological currents and political battles, on legal, political, and literary life.

Pettigrew's influence far transcended his efforts as a lawyer, state legislator, and author. One of the more curious, telling, and little appreciated aspects of life in the Old South was the intellectual vigor displayed by a generally well-educated slaveholding class. A surprising number of prominent slaveholders scorned the lime-light and the lure of fame, which, to be sure attracted many others. Pettigrew, like no few of his peers, restricted his sphere of influence to those privy to the example set by his everyday life. Another largely forgotten man, William H. Trescot, the father of American diplomatic history and an impressive social theorist, said in his eulogy that Pettigrew's achievements could not begin to reveal the depth and breadth of his influence on his contemporaries: "The influence was in himself. . . . He was a man who desired to be, not to seem." Trescot could easily have been describing Langdon

Cheves, John Belton O'Neall, Louisa Susanna McCord, William Campbell Preston, James Henley Thornwell, or any number of other Carolinians.

Pettigrew deserves to be remembered for much more than his professional and military careers. Among other accomplishments, he was the author of a marvelous book, *Notes on Spain and the Spaniards in the Summer of 1859, with a Glance at Sardinia.* Unfortunately, Pettigrew had the rotten luck to bring the book out in 1861, when southerners as well as northerners were preoccupied. Understandably, it went virtually unread. It has remained virtually unread, even by southern historians, who can hardly plead preoccupation. It nonetheless deserves to be republished and read carefully for its insights into the culture of Spain and the Italian *Mezzogiorno* and its reflections on the American South, as well as for the sheer pleasure it imparts.

Wilson provides a well-crafted examination of *Spain and the Spaniards.* As he shows, Pettigrew not only wrote a splendid travelogue; he seized the opportunity to reflect, more deeply than most men were capable of doing, on the strengths and weaknesses of southern civilization in relation to the divergent tendencies among various European peoples. Reading that book, we may only lament that Pettigrew did not live to write his projected history of the Moors in Spain, for which he, a talented linguist, had prepared himself by adding Arabic and Hebrew to his knowledge of Greek, Latin, French, German, Italian, and Spanish. In the end, Wilson's account of *Spain and the Spaniards* provides, as does that book itself, a picture of a man and a southern people who saw themselves as the heirs of a great Western Christian civilization and yet who found themselves in opposition to the secular, industrializing, and philosophically and politically radical turn it was taking.

On one issue I must part company with Wilson. I refer to a big quarrel not only with him but with an outstanding coterie of southern conservative interpreters of the Old South—Allen Tate, Richard Weaver, and M. E. Bradford, to name only some of the most illustrious. Wilson is here defending the Southern Tradition in politics and social theory: its critique of egalitarianism and radical democracy; its defense of family-based social order; its commitment to a classical republican polity. His accounts of Pettigrew's biting criticism of industrial capitalism and of his devotion to southern—and southern European—traditions make especially thought-provoking reading.

But Wilson, like his fellow southern conservatives, pays dearly for his philosophical idealism. Hostile to slavery and racism, he seeks to root the positive qualities he finds in the life of the Old South in an older Christian civilization and transatlantic republicanism. Too good a historian to treat slavery as a bagatelle, he nonetheless underestimates its effect on the formation of southern culture, ideals, and character.

Lurking below the surface is an interpretation that stresses the yeomanry and that thereby implicitly treats the slaveholders as, as it were, wealthy and privileged extensions of yeomen and as men for whom slaveholding proved a disagreeable necessity. This will not do. Europeans spread the kind of Christian culture and conservative values that Wilson champions to all parts of North America, but they sank deep roots only in the South and at the very moment when they were, on Wilson's own showing, striking bedrock in the North. How, then, could we explain the dogged resistance to the kind of modernity that the transatlantic bourgeoisie was vigorously promoting if we discount the organic, rather than cash-nexus, basis of southern social relations? I do not believe that we could, and if I read Pettigrew and his compeers correctly, they did not believe it either.

This is a big subject for another day, properly pursued in a full discussion of what is living and what is dead in the Southern Tradition. For the moment, however disconcerting Wilson's questionable judgment on this matter, it detracts little from an admirable book.

4

James Henley Thornwell

The God-fearing, Bible-reading, hymn-singing Confederate army grew out of a southern soil well cultivated during the long struggle of countless, if largely unsung, preachers to civilize a harsh and violent frontier. Personal piety and Bible-centered family circles bolstered the churches in a successful effort to shape the regional culture. The churches assumed responsibility for the education and moral instruction of the people, high and low. To a degree rarely appreciated, they set the terms for a vast consensus on the proper foundations of the social order. Let there be no mistake: A firm commitment to slavery lay at the heart of that consensus, but few dared to enter public discussion of slavery's character and consequences without being prepared to ground their views in Scripture. For unlike the North, the South resisted the rising pressure to slight the Word and reduce the Spirit to philosophical speculation. In helping to forge that conservative sensibility, the most humble preachers stood with the most sophisticated theologians. Much like the leading secular intellectuals, most of whom also invoked religious sanction, they did not suffer the acute alienation of the intellectuals of the North and, indeed, of the whole of transatlantic bourgeois society.

The southern intellectuals, clerical and lay, have for the most part been swept into that famous Dustbin of History, to which those who back losing causes are routinely consigned. With a few honorable exceptions, our historians assure us that the Old South had no intellectual life worthy of the name and scarcely any intellectuals worth reading today. It would take little effort to expose these assertions as rubbish, but let me settle for the observation that the southern theologians easily held their own with the northern and that in James Henley Thornwell of South Carolina (1822–1862) the South had a brain second to none.

The son of a particularly successful up-country overseer and a devoutly Calvinistic Baptist mother, Thornwell had opportunities uncommon for his class. Bright and disciplined, he seized them. His widowed mother found patrons to sponsor his education, and he received some private tutoring to supplement time in an old field school and an academy. He was graduated with highest distinction from South Carolina College (now the University of South Carolina) and within a few years returned there to teach. Thornwell's entry into the ministry surprised his college mates for he had not been especially pious as a student and had been expected to plunge into a political career.

Thornwell rose to become one of the foremost leaders of a state that burst with outstanding men. Calhoun considered him a giant among men, notwithstanding political differences over nullification and much else. He served with distinction as president of South Carolina College, the finest institution of higher learning in the Lower South and one of the finest in the United States. He edited the prestigious and intellectually impressive *Southern Presbyterian Review* and served as pastor of the socially and politically powerful Presbyterian congregation in Columbia. A staunch advocate of *jure divino*, he was widely recognized as a premier ecclesiologist even by his adversaries, northern and southern. His impact upon the most eminent southern divines—Benjamin Palmer, John Adger, John Girardeau, among others—could hardly be exaggerated. Among other accomplishments, his contributions to the theory and practice of education could be read with profit today for the light they throw on current concerns. And by common consent, he emerged as the greatest theologian in the South and among the greatest in the United States.

With regret I must here pass lightly over his theology, for his sermons and discourses on the Trinity, the nature and attributes of God, the personality of the Holy Ghost, and other subjects have much to teach about the human condition and our prospects. Our immediate concern is with his social and political thought, and much of his best efforts in defense of Calvinist orthodoxy remain beside the point. For while it is true, and of capital importance, that he grounded his worldview in theology, the portions of his work relevant to social theory pertain less to Calvinist specifics than to those doctrines he shared even with the Arminian Methodists. Had it not been so, not merely for Thornwell but for the southern divines in general, the Old South's discernibly conservative view of the social order and its Christian defense of slavery could never have achieved consensus. To put it another way, a particular doctrine of the Fall, original sin, and the Atonement undergirded his social theory, but it did so at the most general level to which all Christians might subscribe. The Methodist Bishop George Foster Pierce, the Baptist Reverend Thornton Stringfellow, the New School Presbyterian Reverend Frederick A. Ross, the Episcopal bishops Levi Silliman Ives and Leonides Polk, and the Roman Catholic Bishop John England disagreed among themselves on the ways of salvation but agreed on a defense of slavery that derived from their common Christian principles.

Thornwell identified as the foundation of all Christian thought the personality of God and His readiness to condescend to commune with His creatures. He insisted that the Word alone could not save us, for it constituted the means, not the source, of life: "The Spirit *and* the Bible, this is the great principle of Protestant Christianity." But, unlike the liberal theologians and heterodox Calvinists who were sweeping the North and increasingly espousing abolitionism, Thornwell rejected the invocation of the Spirit when it became an excuse to slight the Word. For without the supremacy of the Word in the popular mind, "the most enormous crimes" would be committed in the name of religion. Hence, we cannot expect to know the Word unless infused by the Holy Spirit, for "faith is an intuition awakened by the Holy Ghost." With that intuition "the Bible becomes no longer a dead letter, but a spirit, and religion is not a tradition, but a life." In consequence, the "true principle, the only infallible source and measure of religious truth is the Word of God . . . [revealed in] the sacred Scriptures."

From these few, firm, general principles Thornwell derived his view of the church and human affairs. But as with his view of the natural world, he left ample space for the natural and social sciences and made signal contributions to the campaign, spear-headed by the Old School Presbyterians, to establish true science as being in harmony with Scripture. The attempted reconciliation, promoted through advocacy of the Baconian inductive method, ultimately ended in a disaster for the churches, but in the South it fared well before the War. Thornwell's scripturally grounded sociopolitical views took full account of the generally accepted political economy and sociology of his day and were by no means lazy extrapolations from selected sacred texts.

Thornwell's contemporaries, intending a compliment, often referred to him as "the Calhoun of the Church," and historians, not all of whom have intended a compliment, have followed suit. No doubt he was, but we might pause to reflect that no one has ever called Calhoun "the Thornwell of the state." As a no-quarter defender of *jure divino* and the foremost exponent of the republican nature of scripturally sanctioned church polity, Thornwell did in fact parallel Calhoun's efforts in political theory, as both of them appreciated. Yet there is a danger in the compliment, which his Christian contemporaries should have seen in the first instance, and which critical historians have seen all too well. For it suggests that Thornwell's orthodox theology represented a grand apologetic for the political ideology inherent in his views of church and state, considered separately and in their interrelation. To the contrary, his views of church polity and of social order, including his subtle defense of slavery, derived from his theology, for he was concerned, first and foremost, with God and salvation. With undoubted sincerity he declared that if southern Christians could be convinced of the sinfulness of slavery, they would—or should—waste no time in putting it on the road to extinction.

Here and elsewhere Thornwell put his finger on an essential feature of the unfolding tragedy of the South: The God-fearing southern people turned to the Bible to justify slavery, and the Bible did not disappoint them. Their theologians rent the abolitionists, at least on the essentials, in their war of biblical exegesis.

Increasingly, the abolitionists had to retreat to arguments from the Spirit rather than the Word—a procedure that served them well among many northerners for whom the Word was becoming something of a nuisance, but a procedure that ruined them among the country people of the South, who resisted theological liberalism, however nicely repackaged in New England as neo-Calvinism.

Thornwell's sermons and essays on slavery passed into an extraordinary critique of the condition of the modern world and represent a peak moment in the development of southern thought, but they contain deeply disquieting implications for southern conservatives and for all others who seek an accurate understanding of a conflicted—or, if you prefer, sinful—world.

Thornwell had a taste for polemics and a reputation for swinging hard. We might say of him what he said about his friend the Reverend Dr. Robert J. Breckenridge of Kentucky: "What he does, he does with his might. Where he loves, he loves with his whole soul; when he hates, he hates with equal cordiality; and when he fights, he wants a clear field and nothing to do but fight." Normally, Thornwell restrained himself in a manner appropriate to a southern gentleman, but he had bad moments, as in his denunciation of Charles Hodge, the doyen of Princeton Theological Seminary. Poor Hodge. There Hodge was the joy of the Old School Presbyterians in the North, much as Thornwell was in the South; Thornwell's powerful ally against the New School and against all opponents of orthodoxy; and an outspoken defender of southern rights and the scriptural justification for slavery. Yet when Hodge took a conciliatory position on questions of church polity, Thornwell went for his jugular: "Hodge's argument is utterly rotten." And that was for openers.

Thornwell was not a man to take lightly questions that others might treat as mere matters of tactics or administration. The struggle concerned church boards and the rights and powers of the ruling elders. Beneath the specifics lay the question of power and authority—of the relation of the elders to the laity and of the church to the world. Thornwell took high church ground. Hodge, an ultra-conservative in the North, looked like a liberal temporizer in South Carolina. Allegedly, his concessions to the laity had two defects: They broke with Scripture and, however inadvertently, they opened a wedge to the democratic radicalism that was threatening to inundate church and state. The struggle for order in the church thus combined an intransigent view of scriptural authority with a deep commitment to social stratification. For Thornwell the power of the church "is solely ministerial and declarative. . . . Whatever is not commanded [in the Bible], expressly or implicitly, is unlawful." Conversely, he condemned the notion that whatever is not forbidden is allowable. The silence of Scripture constituted a prohibition.

The analogy to Calhoun's constitutional theory could hardly be missed, but Thornwell left nothing to chance: "The Church, like the Government of the United States, is a positive institution, with positive grants of power, and whatever is not given, is *withheld.*" The scripturally sanctioned rulers of the church "stand in the same relation to the church that the rulers of the United States sustain to the people. . . . The ideal of the freest, noblest government under heaven, which Milton so rapturously sketched, corresponds, without an exception, to our Presbyterian representative republic."

Moving from church to state—significantly, in a sermon on "The Christian Doctrine of Slavery"—he denounced the political radicalism of the age and upheld "representative, republican government against the despotism of the masses on the one hand, and the supremacy of a single will on the other." In this sermon, as in others, Thornwell assailed the abolitionists for waging war not merely on slavery as a peculiar form of property and on southern rights, which constituted the bastion of the Constitution, but on the very principle of social order. Implicitly, sometimes explicitly, the abolitionists were attacking all class distinctions and legitimate authority. Indeed, they were attacking Christianity itself since the Bible commanded social stratification in the wake of the Fall. Thornwell charged that the abolitionist argument "fully and legitimately carried out, would condemn every arrangement of society, which did not secure to its members an absolute equality of position." It was, he concluded, "the very spirit of socialism and communism." And in one of his fiercest polemical outbursts, he added, "The parties in this conflict are not merely Abolitionists and Slaveholders; they are Atheists, Socialists, Communists, Red republicans, Jacobins on the one side, and the friends of order and regulated freedom on the other. In one word, the world is the battle ground. Christianity and Atheism are the combatants, and the progress of humanity is the stake."

Thornwell and his fellow southern divines argued—and, I regret to say, demonstrated—that the Old Testament established slavery as ordained of God and that Jesus, who spoke not one word against it and did not exclude slaveholders from the church, reaffirmed the sanction. But many of the divines, with Thornwell at their head, went further and subsumed slavery under the general principle of social subordination. Thus they forcefully associated the subordination of slaves to masters with the prior subordination of women to men. Thornwell denounced all equality other than spiritual as contrary to God's law and, in effect, made slavery a special case in the general subordination of the laboring classes to the propertied. Note it well: He did not take racial ground on the essential issue, although he did regard blacks as an inferior race destined to be among the hewers of wood and drawers of water.

Had Thornwell merely peddled the myth of Ham, according to which blacks lay under a special curse, as many lesser minds and weaker scholars did, his defense of slavery and his social thought would be much less interesting and would—or should—constitute an embarrassment to his admirers. But, like other able southern divines, albeit with greater learning, clarity, and depth, he recognized that the Bible sanctioned slavery in general—"in the abstract," as his contemporaries put it—not black slavery in particular. For God had ordained slavery among the ancient Israelites without regard to race, as "race" came to be understood. Thornwell knew, and modern scholarship confirms, that members of all races, including the Caucasian, were subject to lawful enslavement and that slavery was established as a special case in a wider social subordination. Thornwell, while holding blacks to be culturally inferior, assailed the scientific racism according to which they constituted a separate species, and he held a cautiously hopeful view of the future of the race. The pseudoscientific theories of race popular at Harvard and elsewhere in the North he denounced as unscriptural. To bring blacks into the church, he bravely stood against a hostile demonstration in Charleston and declared, "We are not ashamed to call [the black man] our brother."

For Thornwell the essential problem remained that of a proper Christian social order. With George Fitzhugh and no few others, he considered the alleged racial inferiority a regionally specific complication of a worldwide problem. He pointed to the deepening crisis of European society, which he observed firsthand in his travels, and expressed horror at the condition of the British poor. He concluded that Europe was already facing, and the North would soon face, all-out class war and revolutionary turmoil. Consequently, he projected slavery as the Christian solution to "the Social Question," as the hostile relation of capital and labor was then usually called. In the bluntest possible language, he predicted that the capitalist countries would have to institute a labor system so close to southern slavery as to be indistinguishable from it.

Thornwell had studied political economy and did not challenge its reigning Ricardian and Malthusian laws. He could not, however, rest comfortably with its callous disregard of the human misery inherent in capitalist economic development. He must surely have gagged on the analysis made by George Tucker, Virginia's outstanding political economist, according to which slavery would disappear as the cost of free labor fell below that of slave. For stripped of the complacent, not to say cold-blooded, celebration of economic progress, the analysis pointed toward the immiseration of the laboring classes, white and black. Thornwell acknowledged that those economic laws, if left to work themselves out in a marketplace society, would generate the result, but he had the wit to know that economic laws alone do not direct the course of man. He expected the suffering laborers to rise with revolutionary violence against so monstrous a system, and he sought a solution that would be conservative in its insistence that the privileged classes accept responsibility for the well-being of their inferiors. He found that solution in the personal subordination of the laborer to some form of slavery or industrial serfdom. That such a solution would have impeded economic progress he surely knew, but we may doubt that he lost much sleep over it.

Thornwell marched at the head of a swelling army of southern divines of all denominations and in tandem with the secular theorists. Indeed, twenty years earlier the great Thomas Roderick Dew, notwithstanding his devotion to the Manchester School and his enthusiasm for capitalist progress, gloomily predicted, and accepted the necessity for, a worldwide proslavery reaction. Yet in one sense Thornwell was no friend to slavery at all. Like many southern divines he ruthlessly criticized its evils and demanded such sweeping reforms as the legal sanction of slave marriages, repeal of the laws against slave literacy, and effective measures to punish cruel masters. In short, he demanded that southern slavery be made to conform to biblical standards. On the eve of secession he even flirted with the idea of proposing gradual emancipation.

But what did Thornwell understand by emancipation? This, after all, was the same man who, at that very moment, was recommending slavery as a solution to Europe's Social Question. He meant the raising of blacks out of chattel slavery into some kind of industrial serfdom or "warranteeism," as Henry Hughes of Mississippi called it—that is, the raising of blacks, with requisite racial qualification, to the level of the white laboring classes that were on their way to the same fate. He envisioned a system that would subordinate all laborers to personal masters while it guaranteed not only cradle-to-grave security but respect for the individual and the family beyond that which the existing system as yet provided.

Shortly before his death Thornwell went further. Cautiously, in his "Sermon on National Sins," preached on the eve of the War, and boldly in a remarkable paper on "Relation of the State to Christ," prepared for the Presbyterian Church as a memorial to be sent to the Confederate Congress, he called upon the South to dedicate itself to Christ. He criticized the American Founding Fathers for having forgotten God and for having opened the Republic to the will of the majority. "A foundation was thus laid for the worst of all possible forms of government—a democratic absolutism." To the extent to which the state is a moral person, he insisted, "it must needs be under moral obligation, and moral obligation without reference to a superior will is a flat contradiction in terms. Thornwell demanded that the new Constitution be amended to declare the Confederacy in submission to Jesus, for "to Jesus Christ all power in heaven and earth is committed." Vague recognition of God would not do. The State must recognize the triune God of the Bible—the Father, Son, and Holy Ghost.

Thornwell made clear that he wanted neither an established church nor religious tests. The state must guarantee liberty of conscience for all. "He may be an Atheist, Deist, Infidel, Turk, or Pagan: It is no concern of the State so long as he walks orderly." Could a Jew become chief magistrate? Certainly, so long as he does nothing in office "inconsistent with the Christian religion." At issue lay the moral basis of society, which, Thornwell argued, had to be informed by one religious system and, therefore, in the Protestant South, by Christianity. I cannot prove that T. S. Eliot read Thornwell's essay, although I suspect as much, but I would invite a comparison of "Relation of the State to Christ" with Eliot's celebrated essay "The Idea3 of a Christian Society."

Thornwell's foray had a sharply critical edge. He warned, in the sternest terms his Calvinist soul could muster, that God was testing his people; that their victory would depend upon repentance; that, specifically, they must be prepared to do justice to the slaves and all others placed in their charge:

> God is the ruler among the nations; and the people who refuse Him their allegiance shall be broken with a road of iron, or dashed in pieces like a potter's vessel. Our republic [the Confederate States of America] will perish like the Pagan republics of Greece and Rome, unless we baptize it into the name of Christ. . . . We long to see, what the world has never yet beheld, a truly Christian Republic, and we humbly hope that God has reserved it for the people of these Confederate States to realize the grand and glorious idea. God has wooed us by extraordinary goodness; He is now tempering us by gentle chastisements. Let the issue be the penitent submission of this great people at the footstool of His Son.

Thornwell's theology and ecclesiology are not much in fashion today, but, then, fashions have a way of waning and returning.

And the proslavery specifics of his social thought are, let us pray, interred with him. But it would hardly be wise to discount his larger views, which contain valuable insights into the problem of reconciling democracy with freedom as well as penetrating explorations of human psychology and its political ramifications— explorations I have only been able to hint at. Unbiased study of his work ought to enlighten anyone, from any part of the political spectrum, who reflects on his heroic attempt to envision a Christian society that could reconcile, so far as possible in a world haunted by evil, the conflicting claims of social order with social justice and of both with the freedom and dignity of the individual.

I should not presume to tell southern conservatives where to place Thornwell in their tradition, but, surely, a straight line runs from him to the Agrarians, who, astonishingly, virtually ignored the thought of the antebellum theologians. That straight line runs counter to any romance with the ideals and practices of the marketplace, which today entrance much of the Reaganite coalition and other refurbished nineteenth-century liberals. For if southern conservatives, in contradistinction to people who call themselves conservatives and live in the South, have a tradition to appeal to—and I believe they have a great one—it is a tradition that has resisted bourgeois society, its atomistic culture, and its marketplace morality.

Evaluating that tradition and Thornwell's place in it, I might be told, is the concern of southern conservatives and none of my business. But the enormities of our century and our common fate in a world of nuclear weapons and a technological capacity for unprecedented assaults on human dignity and the human spirit compel me to risk the presumption. For the questions that that great man raised, the brave if often unacceptable answers he proposed, and the insights into ourselves he offered continue to speak to all honest and sane men.

5

Thomas B. Chaplin

The southern slaveholders proudly presided over the greatest enormity of the age. As deeply believing Christians, they fearlessly said *Amen!* to Paul's celebrated warning to the Galatians, "Whatsoever a man soweth, that he shall also reap," and pronounced slavery ordained of God. Theodore Rosengarten reminds us that we know much more about the masters than about their slaves, for they left vast quantities of diaries, journals, account books, family letters, and other public and private papers. Those sources reveal the people who presided over the enormity as, more often than not, admirable men and women who struggled heroically to build a Christian civilization.

The slaveholders carved out plantations that served as homes and extended households for their "families, white and black," built churches and schools under conditions difficult even by the standards of a rapidly developing country, and raised towns that brought civility, culture, and order to an atomized frontier. And they created an array of supporting, caring, loyal personal and family relations that our own age might envy. They were, above all, God-fearing people, whose faith sustained them through the ever threatening deaths of their children and the constant sorrows that beset their lives in a dangerous and violent world. They qualified, by any reasonable standard, as good and decent people who tried to live decently with their slaves. But they were doomed to fail, for, at bottom, their relations with their slaves rested on injustice and violence. Therein lay the tragedy that has made them, individually and as a class, the most arresting of Americans.

The slaveholders of the low country of the Carolinas and Georgia forged a society close to the plantation legend, and St. Helena Island in the Beaufort district of South Carolina may serve as a microcosm. Devoid of white family farms, St. Helena was home to between eight thousand and nine thousand souls throughout the antebellum period, with a black–white ratio of about seven to one. Its dominant class was wealthy, cultured, and inbred. Thomas B. Chaplin, like no few others, had a plantation bounded on three sides by the property of relatives.

Here on St. Helena and throughout the low country the planters styled themselves "the Chivalry"—pronounced Chiv-al'-ry in South Carolina, where to this day folks pronounce their names as no one else would. Although they differed markedly from the planters of the South Carolina up country, not to mention the western cotton states, they left a deep mark across the South. Complex economic processes encouraged and compelled a considerable shift of South Carolinians to the slave states of the Old Southwest. The Chivalry contributed substantially to the taming of that initially barbarous country, and a low-country gentleman would in time be at home and at ease in, say, Huntsville, Alabama, or Port Gibson, Mississippi. Together with the tidewater Virginians—so different and yet so similar—the high-toned ladies and gentlemen of the low country set the standards everywhere they went. The rough but rising interior planters chafed under the easterners' pretensions and often punished them politically, but they emulated them in ways that brought increasing coherence to the slaveholding class of the South.

Theodore Rosengarten's many admirers can stop asking what, after *All God's Dangers: The Life of Nate Shaw*, he would do for an encore. In that earlier book the gifted Rosengarten combined meticulous research, a powerful historical imagination, and a deep human sensitivity to tell the story of a modern black sharecropper. Here, he does the same for a antebellum white planter. *Tombee* consists of a fine full-length biography of Thomas Chaplin and several hundred pages of the journal he kept from 1845 to 1858 and to which he returned in later years. It is a measure of Rosengarten's craftsmanship that he offers the journal, which on its own offers engrossing reading, as a check upon his own interpretations.

Tombee presents a rich portrait of the aristocratic South Carolina low country.—its agriculture, work routines, elite social life, mores, and much more. But nonspecialists need not fear. Rosengarten writes gracefully and lays out the details of planting and cotton picking, for example, in a manner technically accurate yet always readable and enjoyable. By deftly combining the inner world of an individual, the performance of a social class, and the material conditions of community life, Rosengarten bares a society that is long gone but still haunts a racially rent America.

Thomas Benjamin Chaplin (1822–1890), the master of Tombee Plantation, might have had it all. The heir to a fortune in slaves and land, he married a wealthy woman who turned out to be a devoted wife and mother. In 1845 he owned enough land to rank among the top third of St. Helena's planters. He fell into the bottom third by 1860, having had to sell more than half his slaves during the depressed late 1840s. The journal reveals him in constant struggle to hold his own, to pay for his children's education, even to feed his family properly. Part of Chaplin's misfortune resulted from the falling cotton prices and profits that beset the low country. But the economy recovered, whereas Chaplin did not. Drinking heavily, he handled his business badly, tormented his wife, and squandered much of the family fortune. He indulged in the typical pleasures and vices of the low-country slavocracy: hunting and fishing, expensive dining, champagne parties, hospitality he could neither refuse nor afford. But unlike his more successful neighbors, he did not compensate by managing his plantation efficiently. A poor manager, he steadily drifted toward bankruptcy, rescued if barely by his mother.

Periodically, Chaplin threw himself into plantation work. In fact, he craved it after his own fashion. Unfortunately, his fashion meant little more than keeping himself busy by keeping his slaves busy. "I am," he moaned, "head over heels in work." That is, he was scrambling about, giving orders. The actual management of the plantation fell, for better or worse, to his black foreman, who was much better than Chaplin but apparently not good enough. Rosengarten acidly observes, "The hands had no time to lose. *He* could not relax, thinking of all they had to do." In this respect, Chaplin was a typical southern planter. Almost every master, mistress, and even overseer routinely commented, "I repaired the fences" or "I worked my garden," when they meant that their slaves had done so. What made Chaplin special was not his presumption but his incompetence.

Chaplin had manly qualities, as his physical courage and coolness under fire during the War for Southern Independence demonstrated, but he had a large share of weaknesses, manifested most blatantly in his prewar alcoholism and his postwar opium addiction. As Rosengarten remarked in an interview with the *New York Times*, Chaplin was "likable and contemptible by turns." Chaplin moved in elite circles with a fifth-generation pedigree but without the ease expected of a scion of the Chivalry. As his fortune deteriorated, he characteristically indulged in a self-fulfilling prophecy by narrowing his circle of intimates, certain that others would no longer want his company. In good times and bad, he carried himself like some petty bourgeois or precariously perched arriviste. "He worried," Rosengarten writes, "that people did not appreciate him for his company, but only wanted him along because he would supply the champagne for dinner, the dogs for hunting, or the Negroes for rowing."

Chaplin had good reason to worry about his outlays for dinners at the Agricultural Society or the other endless expenditures required by station and custom. Rosengarten notes, "He seldom had ten dollars in his pocket, and would resort to selling fish for pin money." Yet we may doubt that cash flow was the main problem, for throughout the South it plagued rich slaveholders, who somehow worked around it. The main problem was his unsteadiness and declining fortunes and, perhaps especially, his pride, which closed him off from the usual sources of credit, big and small. Chaplin could not bring himself to do what many others did—borrow twenty-five dollars or so at one courthouse day, to be repaid at the next.

Before the War, Chaplin, apparently without much reflection, followed the states' rights radicals into advocacy of secession.

After the War, with much belated reflection, he rued the day. The War destroyed the remains of his fortune, and he never recovered. He taught black children for a while, and, when the white supremacists rode to power in 1877, he was appointed a trial justice—a post that paid enough to keep him afloat but not much more. Most of his children died young, and his remaining sons disappointed and rejected him. He looked back on the War as a catastrophe for all concerned, especially for the blacks, whom he saw as the primary victims of the marketplace society that had destroyed an organic community.

Rosengarten, in one of his few weak analyses, argues that Chaplin had never seen blacks as humans. I find this reading contradicted by the evidence in the journal, although Chaplin's views—and silences—do lend themselves to alternate readings. Indeed, as Rosengarten more plausibly said in his interview with the *New York Times*, "This idea that black people were *people* kept breaking in on his consciousness." In any case, Chaplin's "black family" disappeared along with his sons, and only a staunch and caring second wife remained to comfort him.

Chaplin had recurring moments of self-pity, and, as Rosengarten writes, "The record shows he was vain, obtuse, abrasive. It also shows he had the qualities of an ordinary, decent person." If, even at the end, he had trouble in forgiving those who trespassed against him—and in his own mind their number was legion—he at least slowly gained a perspective that accorded with his better nature.

More than at first he could acknowledge, he had been sustained by the love and forbearance of his first wife, Mary. As she approached death, he came to learn as much and, to his credit, he never forgot what he had learned. Mary, concerned with his peace of mind during her final moments, pleaded that he not blame himself for her pain: "I only reap punishment due to my own weaknesses, believe me *you* are one of the best of husbands. I can only hope you will not long be troubled by a wife so frail, weak, and suffering." Luckier by far than most men, he ended his life married to Sophy, Mary's sister, who had long been a second mother to his children and who gave him as much as Mary had.

He did not take his luck for granted and tried hard to do better by her than he felt he had done by Mary.

Sophy's companionship tempered the bitterness of his declining years. If he could not entirely shake the sense of having lost the world, he found in his life with her a fragment worth living for— a grace he could recognize as God's mercy on a poor sinner. Unsure and hesitating, he had become a better Christian than he feared he was. And at least in this one respect, he proved representative of his class and, more generally, of the country people of the South. For he had recklessly supported the low-country radicals in their plunge into secession, believing that a southern Confederacy would provide the necessary foundation for the better life he sought for himself, his children, and his community. In time—the terrible time of invasion, defeat, humiliation, and expropriation—he would come to understand that he had participated willingly in a generation which had complacently proclaimed as God-ordained its insular world and its own power therein. In the loneliness of the decades left to him, he would recall the Preacher of *Ecclesiastes* and pronounce all to be vanity.

And if I read correctly Chaplin's melancholy yet sober postwar reflections, he learned late, but not too late, that, like the Pharisees and Sadducees of old, his generation and he himself had cried out for a sign without being able to read the signs of the times. We can only speculate, but the memory of Mary and the presence of Sophy seem to have prepared him to find consolation in the fearful answer given that older generation by Jesus: "And there shall no sign be given unto it, but the sign of the prophet Jonas."

Southern Slave Society

Paradoxically the moment Virginia
entered into modernity was also the
moment when Virginia began to
evolve into a uniquely reactionary
community. It would eventually,
together with other Southern
colonies to be established, enter
into a compact to share with the
Northern colonies emancipated
from England by the Revolution
a federal government. But by this
time Virginia and the other Southern
states were beginning to offer a
strong resistance to modernity,
imagining themselves—idealizing
themselves—as a providential and
chosen community struggling against
dispossession by modern history.
Shortly this community would be
destroyed as apostate to modern
history.

—Lewis P. Simpson

6

The Culture of the Old South

With Elizabeth Fox-Genovese

Whoever undertakes to write the much needed comprehensive cultural history of the Old South will have to build on the seminal work of Lewis P. Simpson. Simpson interprets southern letters as a distinct tradition in critical tension with the transatlantic bourgeois tradition that spawned it, and a comparable tension informs his own project. For, as our premier interpreter of southern letters, Simpson appears to cherish the unrooted—more charitably, the universal—"Republic of Letters" that stands as the preeminent identification of what he calls the modern mind. Withal, he peerlessly delineates the ways in which the antebellum southern mind differed from its bourgeois counterpart.[1]

Simpson's preoccupations with the relation between tradition and modernity and with southern distinctiveness have rendered him uncommonly sensitive to the nature and character of antebellum southern society. Never nostalgic, he rejects the easy view that

1. The development of Simpson's interpretation of the Old South may be traced most conveniently through three of his books: *The Man of Letters in New England and the South: Essays on the Literary Vocation in America* (Baton Rouge: Louisiana State University Press, 1973); *The Dispossessed Garden: Pastoral and History in Southern Literature* (Athens: University of Georgia Press, 1975); and *The Brazen Face of History: Studies in the Literary Consciousness in America* (Baton Rouge: Louisiana State University Press, 1980).

51

the South embodied some form of traditional or seigneurial social relations and the corollary that southerners espoused unmediated traditional values. Instead, he eloquently argues, most notably in *The Dispossessed Garden*, that the Old South represented something new under the sun: a slave society inscribed in a modern (capitalist) world that had extruded but could not control it. Simpson has rejected the interpretation of the Old South as in some way residually feudal, but he has also rejected the much more popular interpretation of it as "middle-class." The Old South, he insists, must be understood as a novel slave society under the aegis of a master class. *Middle class* alone designates nothing. Small and middling slaveholders and propertied nonslaveholders lived in a society based upon slave property and did not constitute the same kind of middle class or classes that small and middling property holders did in a society based upon bourgeois property. The middle-class interpretation could only make sense if by *middle class* were meant "bourgeois," but those who wish to view the Old South as "middle class" eschew the term *bourgeois*. For the substitution of *bourgeois* for the less precise *middle class* would come perilously close to exposing the interpretation as implausible. The South did have a modest bourgeoisie, and more important, it could never fully isolate itself from the conquering bourgeois ideology and, more broadly, the culture of the larger transatlantic world. The South remained a battleground for warring tendencies, but, as Simpson stresses, a battleground increasingly dominated during the eighteenth and nineteenth centuries by a master class with overwhelming power over material production and human reproduction—a master class that commanded the regional political economy.

According to Simpson, the southern intellectuals' participation in this distinct society alienated them from the international Republic of Letters to which they aspired and from which they sought recognition. For Simpson, this Republic of Letters amounts to the transnational polity of mind that has, at least since Petrarch, ostensibly embraced "free" intellectuals. From Petrarch and the Renaissance humanists to Sir Francis Bacon, on to the luminaries of the Enlightenment and beyond, Western civilization has enjoyed—some might say suffered—the emergence and expansion of an intellectual elite that has proclaimed itself independent of and superior to the time-honored realms of church and state, which it has aimed to supersede. This Third Realm sees itself as the carrier of a Golden Age of the future and has always tried to render unto Mind—in short to itself—the things previously rendered unto Caesar and unto God.

Simpson's concept of Mind, which merits more extended discussion than we can provide here, in essence emphasizes—and even distills into archetypical form—the transition in Western thought from a view of truth as inscribed in the mind of God and only partially and episodically revealed to man to a view of truth as the product of the human mind itself. The men of the premodern world institutionalized access to God's Mind in church and state. Their modern, not to mention postmodern, successors, lacking the conviction of an absolute, transcendental, or prior truth, also cast doubt on the authority of institutions that could only draw their legitimacy from their custodianship of transcendent Mind. In this perspective, the Republic of Letters emerges as their quintessential institution, without enforceable boundaries or laws and especially without authority. For pretensions to higher standards notwithstanding, the laws of the Republic of Letters, bereft of roots in particular societies, reduce to opinion and fashion. Thus the Republic of Letters has mocked traditional institutions, which it has also dismissed as arbitrary, and it has elevated the alienation of the individual to its own privileged version of citizenship. Simpson understands as much and can be acutely critical, but he also displays deep sympathy with the tradition of enlightened and combative alienation.

In *The Man of Letters in New England and the South*, Simpson cogently argues that southern men of letters differed from their New England counterparts because of their relation to their own qualitatively different society. Southern slave society differed from New England society and from all other nascent bourgeois societies by resisting the tendencies toward the universalism—the rootlessness—that defined those societies' distinct character. The very logic of the triumph of the mind of man over the mind of God dictated alienation as the condition of the intellectual. Southern intellectuals also participated in that logic, but they did so as men and women firmly committed to the society in which they lived—a society imbued with particularism, not as nostalgia but as practice.

New England transcendentalism, Simpson observes, shared with the growing philosophies of skepticism an alienation from "the homeland of man and the community of men who make the world a household."[2] Simpson does not elaborate on the household metaphor he introduces, but it should be clear from his discussions of the southern pastoral that slavery engendered a formidable myth of the South as a world of extended households. That myth was no idle creation of self-serving proslavery ideologues. It arose from the essential nature of the political economy, which counterpoised the organic social relations of its interior life to the market relations of its exterior connection to the world market and the transatlantic bourgeois world.[3] The southern intellectuals could not follow Emerson and other Yankees into a celebration of Self, no matter how "individualistic" they were in their own way. Referring to Emerson and others, Simpson writes, "Family, friends, and servants all fade as the Self in the flow of the currents of the Universal Being becomes part and parcel of God. The flow of being is away from the human community and the world, never toward it." The moral imperatives of a modern slave society grounded in extended plantation households demanded the reverse. As the slaveholders' ethos matured, it became steadily more communitarian.[4]

2. Simpson, *Man of Letters*, 83.

3. For an elaboration see Elizabeth Fox-Genovese and Eugene D. Genovese, *Fruits of Merchant Capital: Slavery and Bourgeois Property in the Rise and Expansion of Capitalism* (New York: Oxford University Press, 1983), and Elizabeth Fox-Genovese, *Within the Plantation Household: Black and White Women of the Old South* (Chapel Hill: University of North Carolina Press, 1988).

4. Simpson, *Man of Letters*, 83. This emergent communitarianism is analyzed with respect to legal theory and practice in Mark V. Tushnet, *The*

Southern writers lost their capacity for ironic detachment and disaffection, for the crisis of the literary order in the transatlantic world never reached the South. "Literary pastoralism," Simpson writes, "became devoted wholly to the defense of slavery instead of the defense of poetry. . . . The literary realm virtually disappeared."[5] Simpson is referring to the literary realm strictly defined. As he acknowledges, the Old South had a considerable number of impressive intellectuals who doubtless considered themselves men of letters: theologians, social theorists, historians, political scientists, political economists. The political economists are especially instructive, for several ranked among the ablest in the United States. George Tucker, perhaps best known today for his novel *The Valley of the Shenandoah*, made significant contributions to the theory of economic development and to economic statistics. Jacob N. Cardozo displayed an unusually high level of technical sophistication in his studies of rent, international trade, and related subjects. Among others, Thomas Cooper, Louisa Susanna McCord, J. D. B. DeBow, and especially Thomas Roderick Dew did work worthy of respect. All, with the controversial exception of Tucker, strongly supported slavery while espousing the political economy of Adam Smith and his successors.[6]

American Law of Slavery, 1810–1860: Considerations of Humanity and Interest (Princeton: Princeton University Press, 1981).

5. Simpson, *Man of Letters*, 239.

6. George Tucker's contributions to economic analysis were among the very few by antebellum Americans praised or even noticed in Joseph A. Schumpeter's magisterial *History of Economic Analysis* (New York: Oxford University Press, 1954), 519, 521–22, 714. For divergent interpretations of Tucker's attitude toward slavery see Robert Colin McClean, *George Tucker: Moral Philosopher as Man of Letters* (Chapel Hill: University of North Carolina Press, 1961), and Tipton R. Snavely, *George Tucker as Political Economist* (Charlottesville: University Press of Virginia), 1964. For our interpretation of the course of early southern political economy see Eugene D. Genovese and Elizabeth Fox-Genovese, "Slavery, Economic Development, and the Law: The Dilemma of Southern Political Economists, 1800–1860," *Washington and Lee Law Review* 41 (1984): 1–29.

Therein lay the problem, for the logic of their political economy, worked out splendidly by Tucker, led them to project the eventual demise of slavery and the advance of free labor and bourgeois social relations or, alternatively, to project the gradual restriction of slavery to specified geographic areas on the periphery of a world economy based on free labor. Any moral or philosophical defense of slavery they may have wished to make had to end, even in the no-quarter polemics of the redoubtable Louisa McCord, as a gratuitous superimposition on their political economy. They might, that is, flirt with criticism of slavery itself without suffering ostracism, for their essential loyalty to the South remained unquestioned. But their specific economic writings faded into the background of southern intellectual life when the proslavery intellectuals moved to the high ground of a positive defense of slavery as the necessary and proper basis for civilized society. During the 1850s, the moral and social philosophers and those who began to call themselves sociologists effectively assumed the task of defending slavery and of speaking for the South in its ideological war with the North.

Simpson plausibly dates the beginning of the image of the South as a dispossessed world from John Randolph of Roanoke. We should recall that while Randolph defended southern institutions and values passionately, he was no friend to slavery. Men of his generation were the last who could admire and defend the world the slaveholders were making while they considered slavery itself a problem, a misfortune, a curse. With few exception, those who followed, including Randolph's half-brother Nathaniel Beverley Tucker, had to face the hard truth that slavery itself provided the social basis for the interests, institutions, and values that Randolph had courageously and eloquently espoused throughout his life. Thomas Jefferson may well have seen the light, for how else can we explain the last years of the author of the *Notes on the State of Virginia*? Having penned a searing indictment of slavery, he recoiled at the implications of the Missouri debate, fell silent on emancipation, and ended his life staunchly defending the South against alleged northern aggression. The men of 1830–1860 shed Jefferson's qualms and retreated from his vision of a democratic republic of freeholders. Their republicanism, closer in spirit to Randolph's proud identification with aristocracy, accepted as essential the subordination of the laboring classes in a stratified society and celebrated slavery as the proper foundation of moral as well as social order.

The proslavery intellectuals knew perfectly well that the South was not a "traditional society" and that its slave society had been spawned by the expansion of capitalism and fueled by the industrial revolution. George Fitzhugh's invocation of Ecclesiastes notwithstanding, they even seemed to glimpse that southern slave society was a new thing under the sun. Their intellectual effort, especially their literary effort, constituted a massive attempt to "create" the missing tradition by relating the plantation community to the organic communities of premodern Europe. They struggled to create a culture that would stand as a worthy heir to the best in the Western Christian tradition and prove a bulwark against the disintegrating tendencies of the modern world. They perceived their project not as reactionary or restorationist but as progressive—as a morally superior, socially cohesive, alternate road to modernity. Their defense of traditional values and their assertion of continuity with the organic European community of earlier times ranked not as bad faith, as superficial critics often charged, but as a heroic if deeply contradictory attempt to build what Simpson has wryly called "a plantation on a hill."

The dream of the plantation as the encompassing model of social order, like the New Englanders' dream of the ideal city of two centuries earlier, had an inescapably utopian and reactionary cast. Above all, it opposed—even tried to deny—the countervailing forces that threatened to engulf it from without and erode it from within. It left, as Simpson maintains, little room for an unfolding of the Third Realm—for the expansion of autonomous Mind. In this respect, social relations and intellectual tradition converged. The consolidation of southern slave society in opposition to northern bourgeois society occurred during the early years of the republic, when southern intellectuals were suppressing their doubts about slavery. During the late eighteenth century, attacks on slavery had gained wide currency in the Third Realm, less because of intellectuals' deep concern with the condition of laboring people than because of their deep concern with their own status as individuals. Slavery represented the absolute antithesis of the freedom of being for which they fought for themselves. Slavery in this respect constituted an existential rather than a material condition. Yet in the decades after the Revolution, material conditions regained their paramount role as guarantors of the life of Mind.

Northerners, having cast their material lot with free labor, found ample justification for their continuing, indeed growing, preoccupation with the freedom of the Self. Southerners, having cast theirs with slavery, retreated from what they would increasingly call the antisocial and irresponsible claims of that Self. The northern way, like the bourgeois way in general, permitted, even invited, a simultaneously narrower and broader view of the Self and its claims than anything the world had previously known or anything southerners could accept. The Self of Mind Triumphant joined the narrowly personal to the broadly abstract and universal. Arrogantly subjective and rationalistic, that Self could claim uniqueness and universality for its own experience, could claim absolute authority both for its discrete perceptions and its universalizing rational powers. In so doing, it abstracted itself from time, place, and society. Hence it perceived itself as everywhere and always alienated. Southern slave society left little room for that alienation and its critical distance on its social system.

Yet if the South left little room for a Third Realm, it also left little for a First or Second. As Simpson suggests, "Church, State, and Letters were all three absorbed by a class convinced that its existence depended on fostering a solid order centered in 'only one opinion and one interest.' "[7] There is much to be said for this formulation, if properly qualified, but its starkness risks distortion. The Old South was by no means a totalitarian or a "closed" society, and it is surprising to find Simpson, here and elsewhere,

---

7. Simpson, *Man of Letters*, 240.

conceding so much ground to this shibboleth of liberal criticism. The hegemony of the master class presupposed a wide range of shared culture with the yeomanry but also exhibited deep strains of class antagonism. The cotton states and even substantial parts of the border states did close on the slavery question, but they remained remarkably tolerant of heterodoxy in religion, politics, and philosophy. If southern poets and novelists were suffocated by their commitment to slavery, the reasons lay elsewhere than in censorship or self-censorship.

We might project a loss of critical nerve, but if we do, the question may arise whether any society that attaches its intellectuals to its social relations and primary institutions and values could possibly produce a great literature. And then we should have to explain away Elizabethan England and seventeenth-century France. And suppose that society and its social relations, institutions, and values deserve adherence? On what grounds could we condemn the result? Simpson's remarks on the cultural exigencies of the master class remain heuristically valuable and contain more than a grain of truth, but they say too much, for it could be argued that the "alienation" of northern and other bourgeois intellectuals wondrously conformed to the exigencies of their own societies, however much they whined about the consequences.

Public opinion did not prevent southern writers from criticizing the realities of southern life from the vantage point of its highest professed ideals. Eminent jurists and legal scholars like John Belton O'Neall of South Carolina and Thomas R. R. Cobb of Georgia did just that in demanding reform of the slave codes. The theologians peppered their communicants with calls for higher Christian standards and with slashing attacks on the un-Christian personal and social behavior of all too many slaveholders. Agricultural, industrial, and political reformers preached long and hard against the cultural backwardness of the master class as well as the people at large. In most cases they failed to effect the desired reforms, and slavery did lie at the root of their failure. For in most respects slavery as a social system prevented deep structural reform and sooner or later discouraged critical thought or, as with the political economists, swept it aside.

Simpson, of all people, does not need the brittle formulation
of an incipient totalitarian society; much less does he need to
comfort those who find totalitarianism wherever they encounter
a broad social consensus. He has advanced further than anyone—
and by a good deal—in laying bare the specific contradictions
into which a commitment to slavery plunged southern writers.
Throughout his work, especially in his extraordinary book, *The
Dispossessed Garden*, he has analyzed their dilemma. Their alienation from the world of industrial capitalism led them into a
reassertion of the pastoral, which at first glance looks like no
more than a regional variation of the transatlantic conservative
critique of marketplace values. But they lived in and supported
an alternate social system, which flowered in the wake of the rise
of the world market and yet extruded a plantation society that
in material interests and spirit and ideals counterpoised to the
marketplace a system of extended households and organic social
relations. Perhaps Simpson's own sympathy for the highest ideals
of the Third Realm has encouraged his too-ready toleration of the
view of the South as incipiently totalitarian, but such a view in the
end is of a piece with the spurious concept of the human mind
as transcendentally free.

Southern writers' use of the pastoral simultaneously reveals their
kinship to and their differences with the discourses of the Third
Realm. As early as William Byrd of Virginia, they could invoke
the pastoral and proclaim the South a garden. Yet, as Simpson
insists, that pastoral image imperfectly masked its dark underside:
The master of the garden was no gardener. Nor did that role
fall to sturdy yeomen or to loyal dependent peasants. Rather, it
fell to degraded beings who were legally classified as chattel. The
moral justification for assigning the labor of the garden to slaves
proclaimed their moral as well as intellectual and even physical
inferiority, but, in so doing, it threatened to render preposterous
the southern version of the myth of the garden:

> If virtue is rural, if it stems from labor in the earth, then the slave
> should be as virtuous as the master—acting in some sense as the
> peasant was imagined to act in the capacity of an intermediary
> between the virtue conferred by the direct contact with the soil

and the lord's supervision of his labor and his life. But the slave
was a chattel, in brutal economic terms, a thing.[8]

The contradiction haunted the intellectuals of the Old South
and led some of them to question, if feebly, the perpetuity of
chattel slavery. But in daring to question, they only succeeded
in deepening their dilemma. Simpson astutely assesses the
southern intellectuals' effort as directed toward the creation of
a worldview—philosophy, social theory, ethos—appropriate to a
slave society and appropriate as a standard for a worldwide Christian renewal. He dissects, as no one else has, the betrayal of Mind
toward which the southern intellectuals were inexorably led. For
their commitment to property in man arose within a transatlantic
culture that was establishing a Third Realm firmly and necessarily
committed to the antagonistic principle of property in oneself.

In this context Simpson delineates and elaborates the way in
which the southern intellectuals separated themselves from the
Republic of Letters and condemned themselves to a measure of
literary paralysis at the very moment in which, and by the very
process through which, they were impressively struggling to create
an alternate road to modernity. Indeed, Simpson goes further and
suggests that, had the War not intervened, subsequent generations
would probably have created a reasonably well-rounded worldview. Yet, ever sensitive to the nuances and complexities of an
inherently contradictory cultural process, he makes a necessary
concession to Louis Rubin and others who deny the special slaveholding nature of antebellum southern society and culture. He
acknowledges that the vision of a "plantation on a hill" constantly
ran afoul of the entrepreneurial, acquisitive, and commercial realities of a slaveholding society based upon commodity production
for a world market. For the exigencies of that market threatened
to make a mockery of the vision and to subvert the organic social
relations essential to its material foundations.

8. Ibid., 220.

The southern intellectuals recklessly forged ahead and almost ruined themselves by widening and deepening their commitment to slavery, which Simpson sees suggestively, if problematically, as an assimilation of slavery to Mind. Yet Simpson, having carried the analysis to unprecedented heights, stops short. Many among the ablest of those southern intellectuals strove to overcome the contradiction between their organic vision and the subversive realities of the world market. In so doing, they retreated all the more from the Republic of Letters and its assertion of the primacy of the Third Realm. In effect, they foresaw as social tendency and advocated as social policy the evolution of chattel slavery into one or more forms of labor dependency reminiscent of medieval serfdom but adapted to life in an increasingly industrial world. Henry Hughes of Mississippi, whose ideas were winning attention and respect, called for "progress" in a modern, developing world in which all labor would be assigned to "warrantors" regulated by a corporate state.

The moral and ethical foundations for the emerging vision were being laid by the enormously influential theologians, who, among other advantages, guided the South's educational system. During the 1850s their leading spokesmen—the Presbyterian James Henley Thornwell, the Baptist Thornton Stringfellow, the Methodist William A. Smith, and others—embraced one or another version of a corporatist solution to the "social question" (the relation of capital to labor). Yet, in vigorously defending slavery and pronouncing it ordained of God, they denied that it was destined to last forever in its southern form. God had ordained social stratification and had included slavery among the appropriate forms of the subordination of labor, but, even in the reading of the strictest adherents of the literal interpretation of the Word, God had not required that chattel slavery, in contradistinction to less rigorous systems of servitude, remain forever in a morally progressing Christendom. The militantly proslavery Frederick A. Ross, pastor of the Presbyterian Church (New School) of Huntsville, Alabama, opened his powerful tract *Slavery Ordained of God* by chiding those who unwisely insisted that slavery as then practiced in the South must be rendered perpetual. God might well guide his people toward an emancipation that, on close inspection, would mean not bourgeois freedom but some more humane, socially safe form of the subordination of labor to personal authority.

The theologians thereby instructed the secular intellectuals in the art of having and eating their cake: defending slavery, not merely Afro-American slavery but slavery in the abstract, and yet holding out the promise of progress toward a more recognizably Christian system of social relations that would be free of the undeniable evils of the present system. Those theologians were combating, more or less consciously, extreme racism by suggesting that Afro-Americans could be raised to the level of most white workers, who should, however, also occupy a subordinate position in society.

This vision threatened to play havoc with the realities of the political economy of the world market, which had engendered New World slavery in the first place and which alone could sustain it. Every southern political economist and every economically literate theologian—and many were in fact economically literate—understood that the southern social system rested on commodity production for a world market and that, historically, slave labor, much more readily than serf labor, had proved adaptable to the fierce competition engendered therein. Thus, the projected evolution of southern social relations, which would ostensibly open an alternate road to modernity and "progress," disguised the very reaction and premodern restoration it was designed to avoid. Among the southern intellectuals only George Fitzhugh took the full measure of the contradiction and proposed to resolve it by repudiating much of the modern world and destroying the world market. The originality of his thought lies in that insight, not in his advocacy of slavery in the abstract, something that had been advocated by many others for a long time and that, by the 1850s, had become common fare in the South.

That contradiction assailed the thought of the late antebellum southern intellectuals in ways that bear directly upon Simpson's analysis. In the early 1970s Simpson described the antebellum literary situation as one in which the commitment of the southern men of letters to slavery tended to isolate them from the Republic of Letters and to lead them toward a repudiation of the Third Realm. Alone among the intellectual strata of the transatlantic world they identified with their society in a manner that precluded identification with the Third Realm. The exigencies of a slave society embedded in a hostile bourgeois world compelled denial of moral legitimacy to the autonomy of the Republic of Letters and especially to its claims of preeminence as a Third Realm. The southern men of letters were deprived, as it were, of the right, duty, and even possibility of suffering the alienation that increasingly characterized the intellectuals of Western civilization and that liberated them to assimilate the material and social world to Mind.[9]

Simpson subsequently modified his thesis and especially praised Drew Gilpin Faust's *A Sacred Circle*, which demonstrated a strong sense of alienation among a particularly significant group.[10] Simpson's salutary modification has enriched his analysis, but it has also threatened to lead him into a cul-de-sac. Its strength lies in its much fuller appreciation of the tension in southern thought and, in particular, of the intellectuals' desperate, sometimes pathetic, struggle to feel part of the Republic of Letters and to assume a critical stance toward the slave society they were celebrating. That is, his revised analysis permits an appreciation of the extent to which they, and all modern intellectuals, remained bound by the ideological and moral revolution that inhered in the world conquest of the transatlantic bourgeoisie.

9. Lewis P. Simpson, "The South's Reaction to Modernism: A Problem in the Study of Southern Letters," in Louis D. Rubin, Jr., and C. Hugh Holman, eds., *Southern Literary Study: Problems and Possibilities* (Chapel Hill: University of North Carolina Press, 1975), 48–68.

10. Drew Gilpin Faust, *A Sacred Circle: The Dilemma of the Intellectual in the Old South, 1840–1860* (Baltimore: Johns Hopkins University Press, 1977). But see also her subsequent work, which, we believe, substantially modifies her interpretation: especially her fine introduction to the anthology *The Ideology of Slavery: Proslavery Thought in the Old South, 1830–1860* (Baton Rouge: Louisiana State University Press, 1981).

The weakness of Simpson's modification lies in its tendency to conflate the southern critics of marketplace values with the conservative and even radical critics of the rest of the transatlantic world. Faust herself, in *A Sacred Circle*, but not in her later works, fell into this trap. For alone in the West, the southerners criticized "getting and spending," repudiated the "cash nexus," and protested that "things are in the saddle and ride mankind" from the vantage point of a society based on organic social relations. They shared with others in the Republic of Letters a vocabulary of alienation from the bourgeois marketplace that was absorbing the world, but, unlike the others, including Europe's conservative traditionalists who nostalgically dreamed of restoring the ancien régime, they spoke for a social class that held power in a large, rich region that was increasingly aspiring to become a nation-state. Hence, they felt alienated in precisely the same way the slaveholding class as a whole felt alienated from a modern world it sought to join but only on its own unacceptable and war-provoking terms.

The southern intellectuals' alienation partook directly of the tensions that rent their identities as intellectuals and as southerners. They inescapably worked within the dominant discourse of Western bourgeois culture and used the same words, and especially the same groupings of words, to describe, analyze, justify, and criticize the world around them.[11] They proved especially comfortable in turning to Shakespeare or other Renaissance and early modern forerunners of the dominant tradition of their own day. But the Republic of Letters had not preserved its own history graven in stone. It had modified it with changing experience. The truths that southerners, like northerners and western Europeans, accepted as

11. The intellectual history of the Old South in relation to that of the transatlantic world has made great strides in recent years, thanks in no small part to the pioneering efforts of Michael O'Brien, ed., *All Clever Men, Who Make Their Way: Critical Discourse in the Old South* (Fayetteville: University of Arkansas Press, 1982); and O'Brien and David Moltke-Hansen, eds., *Intellectual Life in Antebellum Charleston* (Knoxville: University of Tennessee Press, 1986).

the grounding of human experience had been applied to changing situations and, accordingly, modified by living cultures. Understandably, the southerners claimed that legacy as their own, but, increasingly during the late eighteenth and early nineteenth centuries, they began to adapt it to their own circumstances and commitments. Their attempts led them ever further from the substance of the prevailing bourgeois interpretation of man in society, but they never forsook the vocabulary that they continued to share with their bourgeois rivals. The results provoked confusion.

Southern intellectuals, like literate southerners in general, could readily embrace the bourgeois critique of industrial society. In "getting and spending," they could concur with Wordsworth, "we lay waste our powers." In the same spirit, they could enthusiastically second the Romantics' celebration of nature. But, in the hands of the bourgeois Romantics that celebration had moved beyond the tradition of the pastoral. In personal nostalgia the bourgeois Romantics turned to nature as a temporary and personal retreat from the hustle and bustle of the capitalist world to which they belonged. Raymond Williams has convincingly argued that by the early nineteenth century bourgeois culture's view of the country constituted a direct extension of its acceptance of the city, understood as proxy for capitalist social relations. Yet southerners could still claim the country as an alternate way of life, as the embodiment of admirable social relations. Whereas in the North and in western Europe, the city was irreversibly conquering the country—in reality and in imagination—in the South the country struggled, with considerable success, to conquer the city. Indeed, the low level of southern urbanization, the slow growth of a free labor force, and the persistent commercial, in contrast to industrial, character of the large southern cities all lent aid and comfort to those who nourished the prospect.

Hence the alienation of southern intellectuals had a distinct cast. For western European and northern intellectuals alienation meant the individual's homelessness in the world. That sense of alienation primarily expressed personal psychological malaise or, as the French symbolists would have it, ennui. The intellectuals did draw upon an older pastoral tradition to forge an apparent opposition between nature and society, but they did not seriously propose a return to older systems of social relations. Even the French Romantics' infatuation with the Middle Ages had more to do with style and with their revolt against a constraining rationalism—with the celebration of personal feeling—than with a projected re-creation of a traditional society. No more than the French did the southerners propose to rebuild medieval society in Virginia's or Carolina's "green and pleasant land." Indeed, they largely borrowed their view of medieval society from Sir Walter Scott and other Romantics. Many nonetheless understood that they were attempting to create a modern defense of a system of values that placed society and its order above the feelings of the individual. Thus, when they turned to the pastoral to express their distinct imagination, they were groping for a way of expressing a system of social relations and values that differed radically from those cherished by bourgeois denizens of the Third Realm.[12] In sum, while bourgeois intellectuals were increasingly reducing alienation to a personal matter, southern intellectuals were, however inconsistently, experiencing alienation as social and ideological estrangement from a dominant transatlantic culture the premises of which they did not accept and against which they had a socially grounded alternative. That they drew so heavily on the language developed by their bourgeois opponents confuses but should not be allowed to obscure the issue.

There was another sense, invoked by Faust and Simpson, in which the southern intellectuals felt alienated: However much they supported the southern social system, as professional men— or as those who wished they could afford to sustain themselves

12. For an elaboration of our interpretation of the southerners' conflicted attitude toward the Middle Ages and feudalism see Eugene D. Genovese, "The Southern Slaveholders' View of the Middle Ages," in Bernard Rosenthal and Paul E. Szarmach, eds., *Medievalism in American Culture: Papers of the Eighteenth Annual Conference of the Center for Medieval and Early Renaissance Studies* (Binghamton: Medieval and Renaissance Texts and Studies, 1989), 31–52.

as professional men—they lived uncomfortably in the South. The intellectuals or men of letters of whom Faust and Simpson speak were primarily literary men. Yet the southern intellectual stratum was dominated by ministers, lawyers, physicians, and others who commanded considerable prestige. Men from these professions published widely on scientific, political, philosophical, economic, and even literary subjects. Those who suffered from neglect were primarily poets, novelists, and literary critics who would have liked to earn a living from their chosen work. They complained bitterly of being unappreciated at home and of having to support themselves from plantations only few knew how to operate or from the practice of law or medicine. Augustus Baldwin Longstreet is best known for his writing, but he was also a planter, a Methodist preacher, a college president, a jurist, and a financially successful lawyer.

There is no evidence that they felt guilty about defending slavery and personally owning slaves, but there is much evidence that they felt uneasy about having to protest against their unfair treatment by a society they deeply believed in—as if their protest constituted an act of moral weakness, if not of treason. They knew that the very nature of their society precluded recognition of an autonomous intelligentsia and, to the contrary, demanded subordination of its intellectuals to social and ideological discipline. The South had abundant room for those who thought freely about politics, religion, art, and science, but only if they stood within the moral consensus that slavery promoted and required. The South had little room for those who stood outside that moral consensus and questioned the social relations upon which the slaveholders' civilization rested.

Thomas Roderick Dew, who ranks with George Frederick Holmes among the most erudite southerners of his generation and with John C. Calhoun and George Tucker among its most acute social theorists, unwittingly exposed the dilemma. He denounced the ancien régime of France for stifling criticism of its social and political relations. Notwithstanding the monarchy's patronage of the arts, he argued, it dared not permit that freedom of thought which alone could engender material and moral progress and which must ossify when not allowed to focus on the social and political relations at the heart of any society. So strongly did he feel on this subject that he pronounced the French Revolution epoch-making and defended it as necessary and good despite the horrors of the Terror and Jacobinism. Yet, while reiterating these views in the 1840s, Dew applauded the suppression of antislavery views in the South as a necessary and proper defense of the social order. He never did explain how the South could progress under such conditions, nor did he explicitly abandon his lifelong commitment to freedom of thought as the mainspring of the progress of civilization.[13]

The constraints upon the intellectual life of the South came not only from the coercion of the state, the civil institutions, and a readily mobilized public opinion. They also came from the irresistible tendency toward self-censorship among intellectuals who had honorable reasons for supporting the regime. More ominously, they came from those intellectuals whose commitment to the regime led them to take for granted both the prevailing social relations and their role as defenders of the faith. The proslavery intellectuals as a group fell prey to that tendency, which manifested itself with varying intensity from person to person. And to the extent that an intellectual fell prey, he or she—for some women also assumed the role—separated himself or herself from the Republic of Letters and surrendered any claims to autonomy.

In seeking to establish a tradition, the southern writers recognized their world as a product of history and, as such, as dynamic, changing, and internally rent. Immersed in the bourgeois culture of their epoch, they also recognized it as a product of Mind. Torn between the internal logic of a culture they admired and the claims of the social order to which they committed themselves, they sought to affirm their world's continuity with a valued and living

---

13. For an elaboration see Eugene D. Genovese, *Western Civilization through Slaveholding Eyes: The Social and Historical Thought of Thomas Roderick Dew* (New Orleans: The Andrew W. Mellon Lecture, Tulane University, 1985).

past and yet to reject and reverse the frightening consequences of modernity's assimilation of God to Self and Mind. Their project, notwithstanding its ultimate futility, drew plausibility from the side of the contradictory southern social relations they viewed as positive—the organic, paternalistic side, which offered a vision of continuity with a premodern world ostensibly unassailed by the separation of Self from society. But their literary imagination crumbled before their inability, not to mention unwillingness, to purge Mind, specifically their own minds, of the historical consciousness that had irreversibly transformed it.

Although as a group they fell short of assuming the primacy of Mind, castigating the abolitionists' willingness to place individual conscience above even the Bible if need be, they also fell short of repudiating its power. They sought a contradictory and unrealizable status: Ideally, they would have enjoyed the inflated status of Artist or Genius that bourgeois culture was conferring on those whom T. S. Eliot would claim should be understood only as craftsmen and whom some twentieth-century Marxists would call specialized producers. Yet beneath the nimbus of glory, those bourgeois custodians of Mind owed their status to the values of a marketplace society, and, notwithstanding frequently anguished cries of neglect, to its material rewards as well. The southerners could not readily see that the status could not be divorced from the bourgeois society and culture that engendered it. And the southerners did not want that society and culture. The contradiction between their personal desires and their social commitments accurately reflects their specific historical condition.

In "The Sexuality of History," Simpson analyzes the novels of Elizabeth Madox Roberts and the condition of the modern writer in general, but he also might well have been thinking particularly about the writers of the Old South:

> *A Buried Treasure* ends with an almost medieval delight in the garden of the world. The more complex *Black Is My True Love's Hair* poses the nostalgic possibility of recovering the balladic world. But even these novels turn on the sense of what intervenes between the self of the modern artist and a sacramental connection with "the simple and uncomplicated earth": the terrible

intimacy with history. In this intimacy both metaphysical and physical reality have disappeared. They are illusions generated by the self-consciousness that is history and the history that is self-consciousness. Having modeled our society—a society of science and history—on mind, we believe in the idea but not in the fact: in the idea of the heart but not in the heart; in the idea of the flesh but not in the flesh; in the ideal of the community but not in community; in the idea of responsibility for one another but not in the responsive, and thus responsible, act of sympathy; in the ideal of love but not in the act of love. We believe in togetherness, or in "interaction"; but are alienated from each other.[14]

Antebellum southerners could fasten upon the genuinely organic aspect of the master–slave relation as the cure for the ills, but they could not escape the negation of that aspect imposed by the realities of the marketplace in which their society was embedded.

The history that engendered southern slave society—the living history that no heroic mythmaking could overcome—was the history of an expanding world market that intruded deep into the southern household itself. It should be enough to recall that those black members of "our family, white and black" could be and often were peddled like so many cattle. Proslavery apologists indignantly argued that no southern gentleman would do such a thing unless, of course, compelled by stern economic necessity. They failed to notice, as Mrs. Stowe did notice, that stern economic necessity was an ever present threat in their daily lives and that it betrayed all visions of a garden, of a plantation on a hill, when it did not expose them as palpable fraud. Southerners often wrote as if they could only espouse the master–slave relation as superior to its bourgeois alternative by demonstrating that it had all the features of the lord–peasant relation in a medieval village world that probably never had existed.

14. Lewis P. Simpson, "The Sexuality of History," *Southern Review*, n.s. 20 (1984): 802.

Simpson here expresses more clearly than any other scholar the sound reasons for rejecting as misleading the attribution of a prebourgeois traditionalism to the Old South, but he does so too starkly and invites an alternate misunderstanding:

> The struggle of the Old South was not between a traditionalism rooted in European forms of feeling and emotion and an outside (or inside) insurgent modernism. Under the historical circumstances that it faced—under the historical nature of its existence—the South's struggle was between the rise of a unique slave society and the forces of modernism.[15]

Those antebellum southern writers, while self-consciously modern men, had a noticeably conflicted attitude toward the Middle Ages. They deplored the material and intellectual backwardness of the Middle Ages and, in any case, knew that plantation slavery departed from the ideal as well as the practice of medieval seigneurialism. But they also knew that slavery shared with seigneurialism a firm repudiation of marketplace values, and they aspired to a resurrection of the spirit of premodern social relations. It is no argument that the organic relations of the slave plantations were often brutal and subverted to greed. So were the organic relations of the medieval villages and manors. They were each, albeit in radically different ways, based on a political economy in which men faced men unmediated by the market and the consequent ravages of what Marx called the fetishism of commodities.

On this matter Simpson writes: "The Old South sought not to root the rationale of its difference from the modern world in the deep places of the mind; but, to the contrary, to found its existence and establish its differences from modernity on a new mind."[16] We agree, but we do not accept the implication that the southern struggle for a new mind precluded a legitimate quest for continuity with European civilization. The deepening

---

15. Simpson, *Brazen Face of History*, 265.

16. Simpson, "The South's Reaction to Modernism," in Rubin and Holman, eds., *Southern Literary Study*, 55.

religious consciousness in evidence during the nineteenth century deserves more attention than Simpson has so far given it. That consciousness encouraged a sense of continuity with premodern Europe as necessary to its sense of a southern slave society that could claim to be the rightful heir of the Christian tradition. And the theologians of the 1840s and 1850s left no doubt that they regarded the subjugation of labor in a stratified society as God-ordained. Simpson is right to insist that the southerners knew that slavery was not seigneurialism or feudalism and that they, as slaveholders, were very different people from medieval lords. But he is in danger of obscuring their sense of a strong link to medieval feudalism in the organic—that is, noncommodity—relation between the classes and thereby of obscuring what they themselves recognized as a measure of shared sensibility.

Simpson may also be too rough on William Gilmore Simms and Henry Timrod in his generally illuminating discussion of their tortured relation to modernity. Their commitment to the politics of slavery, he argues, made them unable to conceptualize "the ironic drama of their careers or to grasp the ironic meaning of the South as a modern slave society."[17] Simpson assumes that if they had glimpsed the irony they would have been plunged into a crisis of conscience, rent by their loyalty to the regime and their dedication to the world of letters. We would suggest, as an alternative, that they may well have glimpsed, and more than glimpsed, the dilemma of trying to reconcile the irreconcilable and, in the end, bravely made their choice.

Simpson's treatment of the southern alienation of Self from Self and therefore from society—of the extent to which they too succumbed to the lure of the Third Realm—displays some disquieting ambiguity as well as considerable strength. Step-by-step in his essay "The Ferocity of Self: History and Consciousness in Southern Literature" he modifies his earlier formulation by moving toward a judgment of southern society as psychically rent. We have no

17. Simpson, *Brazen Face of History*, 265.

quarrel with the judgment but confess to being uneasy at the extent to which it appears to fold the southern experience into the broadly American. Gently parting company with Allen Tate, he writes that the Old South "in its inmost nature was centered less in family than in self." Simpson is no longer at home with Tate's insistence that the Old South was "a society of manners and custom" with the family at its heart.[18]

In this essay Simpson effectively challenges the southern Agrarians' notion that a modern writer could, as an act of will, reject the world of isolated and fragmented selves and identify, in Simpson's words, "with the old corporate, hierarchical society of manners and customs, in which the problem of being a self never arose."[19] As a critique of the Agrarians' utopianism and of Tate's curious interpretation of the Old South as a feudal or seigneurial society— and he might have added, those of the no less formidable Richard Weaver and the learned historian Raimondo Luraghi—the essay scores heavily. Here and elsewhere Simpson demonstrates that the genie of self-consciousness and its assimilation of history to Mind cannot be put back into the bottle and could not have been in the Old South. Put another way, antebellum southerners, whatever their protests and aspirations, were products of the cultural revolution unleashed by the Renaissance and Enlightenment and could not escape knowledge of the fundamental antagonism between Self and society.

Simpson here invokes Hegel, who introduced the concept of alienation into Western thought, and he might profitably have invoked the fate of that concept at the hands of Karl Marx, who set about to abolish the alienation of Self from society by treating it as a historically specific attribute of capitalism. The great social and political movement that he founded made enormous conquests and had historic accomplishments to its credit, but it signally failed even to approximate Marx's dream and now lies in ashes.

18. Lewis P. Simpson, "The Ferocity of Self: History and Consciousness in Southern Literature," *South-Central Review*, nos. 1–2 (1984): 67.
    19. Ibid., 69.

Despite pretenses and ritual bows, the feeble remains of that movement no longer even believe in the dream. That much has been widely noticed. What has largely gone unnoticed is Marx's own failure to assimilate his dream of a liberated Communist New Man and New Woman to the profound interpretation of history that marked the height of his genius.[20]

The experience of Marx, of Marxism as theory and practice, and of the socialist world, like the experience of the slave society of the Old South, suggests that the liberation of Mind effected since Petrarch has been irreversible. Marx and Engels opened the *Communist Manifesto* by praising the bourgeoisie as the most revolutionary class in world history. They did not expect it to remain so, but it has, bequeathing to the classes it has overthrown and to those which have overthrown it an inescapable cultural legacy.

Slave and socialist societies are not thereby reduced to variations on bourgeois society, much less to variations on each other. It may be useful, even necessary, to elaborate the ways in which all modern societies correspond, but not at the expense of careful attention to essential differences. And as with societies in their political-economic aspect, so in their cultural. Simpson, we fear, is once more in danger of conceding too much to that "middle-class" interpretation of the Old South which he has so long and effectively contributed to demolishing.

Skillfully invoking two celebrated essays on the phenomenology of slavery—Jefferson's Eighteenth Query in *Notes on the State of Virginia* and Hegel's "Lordship and Bondage" in *The Phenomenology of Mind*—Simpson makes slavery the expression of the dark side of the Self on which southern society presumably centered. But

---

20. For an elaboration see Elizabeth Fox-Genovese and Eugene D. Genovese, "Illusions of Liberation: The Psychology of Colonialism in the Work of Octave Mannoni and Frantz Fanon," in Stephen Reznick and Richard Wolff, eds., *Rethinking Marxism: Struggles in Marxist Theory. Essays for Harry Magdoff and Paul Sweezy* (Brooklyn: Autonomedia, 1985), 127–50; and Genovese, introduction to *In Red and Black: Marxian Explorations in Southern and Afro-American History*, rev. ed. (Knoxville: University of Tennessee Press, 1984), esp. xxvii–xliii.

the burden of his decades-long interpretation of the Old South as a slave society compels stern modification of his own modification. Tate was not entirely wrong in seeing that society as family-centered, in contrast to the bourgeois society of the North and the transatlantic world generally. Nor was he entirely wrong in seeing that society as heir to Europe's prerevolutionary Christian civilization. As first approximations of a complex and internally rent reality, Tate's judgments serve well. But Tate was wrong to pretend, in his more flamboyant passages, that the Old South could be understood wholly in such terms and that its spiritual life and ethos largely escaped contamination. He knew better, as his private correspondence makes clear, but he was interested in remaking the modern world, not in historical precision. The price he paid for his liberties with history, the price paid by the Agrarians and by Richard Weaver and M. E. Bradford, was to reduce slavery to a blemish on southern society—a problem, an unfortunate accident—and thereby to obscure slaveholding as the essence of the society they revered.

Simpson's determination to unearth the ideological and psychic contradictions in what he clearly affirms as a novel slave society leads him to the brink of uncharacteristic polemical excess. The southern assertion of Self, with its attempt to establish slavery as a possible foundation for Mind, had a special character that marked it off from its bourgeois rivals in ways that Simpson reveals throughout his work. But those ways were not disembodied creations of Mind nor even solely direct projections of an attempted assimilation of slavery to Mind. They were also products of a political economy based on the master–slave relation that created a world of material reality as well as of social ideal. Tate, Weaver, and the remarkable southern conservatives whose thought has been a jewel of twentieth-century American letters—even if not yet recognized as such in New York and its colonies—paid dearly for their contempt for the materialist interpretation of history, and their historical judgment has remained suspended among ideal constructs. Simpson has transcended their performance as historians and has established himself as our greatest cultural historian of the South by focusing his clear eye on the social relations that shaped political, economic, and cultural life. But he will, we trust, not cavil at our saying that he remains heir to the thought of those whose historical performance he has transcended. If he has built on their impressive accomplishments, he has also clung to their essential idealism. He notes that the intellectuals assimilated slavery to Mind, with fateful consequences. No doubt. But only after their own assimilation to a master class for which slavery was, above all, the decisive form of its power.

The temptation of idealism haunts Simpson much as the temptation of Mind haunted the antebellum southerners. For Simpson's subject is Mind and its products. The bourgeois culture that shapes us all has ensconced Mind as its centerpiece and standard. Under such conditions, how can mere mind resist that lure? Under such conditions, how do we resist the compelling insight that history itself reduces to Mind's fabrication. The problem lies less in that recognition of the fundamental subjectivity and, hence, the ultimate isolation of the individual mind than in its own kind of totalitarian pretensions. Systematic idealism has built prisons that rival those of mere material life. For Mind, in assimilating history and the world to itself, denies not merely the countervailing force of material reality, but the consciousness of other minds. Simpson at his customary best grasps that danger and the tensions it pretends to obliterate or transcend. History, whether of social relations, which are the historical form of material conditions, or of intellectual relations, which are the historical form of the relations among minds, will not down. The illusion of history as the mere product of Mind constitutes the great deception of taking Mind at its false word that it has subsumed all minds to itself. In the end, the deception lies in labeling interpretation as Truth. As the most skilled of interpreters, Simpson in particular should recognize the temptation of Mind as precisely temptation. Only on condition that we find the language with which to restore history to its proper role as the whetstone of Mind—or perhaps as its opposing magnetic pole—can we harness the revolutionary implications of the bourgeois dream of Mind to the service of a society capable of anchoring it.

Antebellum southern culture, as a distinct strand in bourgeois culture, has wrestled with the angel—or demon—of Mind. Yet its sense of its own history survived Mind's reductionism through its explicit and extreme subordination of some to others. Confusion persists among those who fear that to justify this history's role in the life of the culture means to justify slavery. Simpson unambiguously says "no." Perhaps that "no" has strained his empathy for those who in pressing the claims of history have also implicitly defended oppression or, perhaps worse, abstracted from it completely. Yet again, his understandable admiration for the heights of Western culture may have led him to accept somewhat uncritically its own terms. Simpson, more than any other critic, has penetrated the nature of southern society. The clarity of his gaze, even more than any of his discrete judgments, testifies to the unique power of a mind in contest with other minds—with the history that never totally succumbs to its particular vision.

7

Proslavery in Transatlantic
Conservative Thought

Larry Tise's doctoral dissertation on proslavery thought has ranked as a succès d'estime since its completion in 1974, and both Tise and the University of Georgia Press are to be congratulated on the long awaited publication of this handsomely printed revised version. Learned, thoughtful, imaginative, iconoclastic—and infuriating—*Proslavery* should provoke valuable debates and fresh thinking and research for years to come. Even those annoyed by its wrongheadedness ought to appreciate its valuable scholarship and insights. Critics and adversaries, who are likely to be legion and to encompass diverse viewpoints, will, one hopes, recognize that he has put us all on our mettle.

Tise makes large claims, few of which he can sustain despite much of value in the attempt. In his preface he declares that from the Civil War to the present previous writers on proslavery have been flatly wrong on just about everything of importance. No few of those writers may be expected to gasp when told that they have "fallen into the unfortunate trap of treating proslavery morally rather than historically" and "have thereby almost totally misunderstood the rich flow of American experience and social impulse between the American Revolution and the Civil War." Tise declares proslavery more a national and international than a sectional ideology and identifies it with a conservative "counter-revolution" against the democratic ideologies of the American and French revolutions. Yet in exposition, Tise himself takes largely sectional ground, with New England, rather than the South, as the culprit.

A caveat: I have not followed Tise in limiting the discussion to the period before 1840, for even he brings two full chapters and parts of other discussions down to the 1860s. By discussing some events that occurred between 1840 and 1861, I may have done Tise some injustice. I assume that a discerning reader will be able to file the proper discounts.

Tise decries as prejudgment the common practice of relating proslavery ideology to "racism, class consciousness, sectionalism, or some other factor" and insists upon viewing it as "merely one strand of social thought" in an America that was backing away from the radicalism of the American and French revolutions. Along the way he offers a wide variety of expositions and interpretations of the evolution of conservative thought and action, to which this review cannot begin to do justice but which render this book required reading.

Required reading does not imply sound interpretation of essentials. This is hardly the first case of a dangerously misleading book's having more to offer than a shelf of its sound but unimaginative and heuristically uninteresting competitors. Where Tise is sound and especially creative is in his demonstration that virtually all of the leading themes of the proslavery argument of the 1850s had been current in Britain and North America during the seventeenth and eighteenth centuries. And on the strength of that demonstration he preaches a powerful sermon on the terrible dangers inherent in central strains of our national development. The more serious attention his sermon receives, the better and safer a country the United States will be.

Critics might easily begin with Tise's sometimes contradictory evaluation of the ideological effects of the American Revolution and the fate of natural-rights theory. Limitations of space forbid the critique his evaluation deserves, but much of it may be deduced from a consideration of his discussion of Federalism. By establishing the ideological and personal links between Federalism and proslavery, Tise provides a strong and welcome corrective to the received wisdom of a Federalism that carried a firm rejection of slavery in its womb. His extended discussion of the proslavery views of the New England Federalists, especially the divines, refutes widely held views.

He nonetheless risks distortion by making no distinction between the northern Federalists' acceptance of slavery as a social institution, divinely sanctioned and useful for the maintenance of social order, and the southern Federalists' growing awareness that slavery provided the rock upon which they were building a social system and, indeed, a civilization. He might have noticed, in his attempt to puff up the political influence of the northern proslavery Federalists, that they quickly and decisively lost the battle to save slavery in their own states—to the extent that they waged it at all—whereas the southern Federalists, in lockstep with their Democratic-Republican adversaries, had no substantial battle to fight in defense of a slavery that had already become the practical, not merely the theoretical, basis of their social system.

The disappearance of the Federalist Party causes Tise no pain, but it should. He argues ingeniously that the proslavery divines helped to seal the party's fate by rejecting its accommodation to rough-and-tumble democratic politics and eschewing party politics for moral reform. But then, what greater proof do we need of their having been beaten in the North? What clearer evidence do we need that the northern proslavery vanguard was in retreat at the very moment its southern counterpart was gaining momentum? Tise argues that the divines' control of the northern schools gave them tremendous influence and power. In general it did, but step-by-step the divines were splitting ideologically between conservatives, not all of whom were proslavery, and theological and political liberals. He provides no evidence that the proslavery conservatives were able to use their influence and power to impose a proslavery ideology on the North, although there can be no question that they fought long, hard, and with some success against the rise of abolitionism and free-soilism.

Tise makes no attempt to demonstrate firm links between the thought of his favorites at Yale, Princeton, and Andover and the *mentalité* of the mass of the northern people. As generally acknowledged, the northern intellectuals in general and these conservatives in particular were increasingly alienated from their society, but the same cannot be said for the southern intellectuals, except in a special and limited sense that has no bearing on the issue at hand. Regrettably, Tise conflates the ideas, the very words, not to mention the blather, of declining northern sectarians who were increasingly out of touch with the people of their heartland with the unfolding ideology of a rising southern intelligentsia deeply rooted among its own people. In discussing southern intellectual life, Tise falls prey to the received wisdom he so often excoriates, gravely underestimating its quality and resonance. He thereby misses the extent to which the high culture of the intellectuals was in tune with the *mentalité* of the people of the towns, villages, and countryside.

The difficulties with Tise's interpretation of Federalism do not end there. He lashes out at those who have long viewed Federalism as the seedbed of antislavery, and he shows that they have neglected a powerful proslavery tendency within Federalist thought. But he never does treat the antislavery aspects of Federalism with the care he devotes to the proslavery. He bypasses them, as if by establishing the existence of a counter-tendency he has exorcised the tendency. In fact, what he has done is to demonstrate high tension between warring tendencies—an important contribution prefigured, as he graciously acknowledges, in the work of Linda Kerber. Yet he seems to believe that he has refuted the basically sound thesis that Federalism nurtured antislavery. Empirically and logically, he has done no such thing.

Tise's vast claims to originality are bound to irritate his colleagues, whose work he seems—I am sure inadvertently—to hold in low esteem. If I may speak personally: He can be fair and even generous to a few opponents like Genovese, but he is cavalier to too many others. He does not begin to do justice to the exemplary work of Lewis Simpson and Drew Faust, and his treatment of William Sumner Jenkins, whose *Pro-Slavery Thought in the Old South* deserves to be regarded as seminal and remains indispensable, is unworthy of him. Worse, his impatience with the work of predecessors and colleagues exposes a critical flaw in his own thinking that vitiates much of his interpretation of Federalism and much else.

The negative side of his performance flows from a deeper source than his impatience, although, paradoxically, the same might be said for much of the positive and intellectually powerful side as well: It flows from his philosophically idealist method and, within it, his idée fixe on the nonsouthern origins of a proslavery worldview. At the outset he wrecks his case by identifying the defense of slavery per se with the concept of a worldview based upon the master–slave relation—a worldview that, contrary to his repeated and unsubstantiated denials, arose only in the Old South, however incomplete and fragmented it may have remained.

Tise assimilates a conservative ideology that has room for slavery to the worldview of a slaveholding society. And no wonder. For by "slave society" he means no more than a society that tolerates slavery. Consequently, some of his most vigorous polemics fall well wide of the mark. For some of the scholars he criticizes (Simpson, Faust, Genovese) have something vastly different in mind. Following Sir Moses Finley, they mean by "slave society" a society based upon the master–slave relation. They therefore view the Old South as a society in the process of developing a culture and worldview appropriate to that fundamental social relation.

Tise repeatedly confuses realms, as when he writes of the United States as a whole, "The Revolution was the first major crisis that challenged the social and moral values of a slave society." The Revolution challenged the social and moral values of a northern bourgeois society that tolerated slavery. On his own account no serious challenge arose in the slave society of the Lower South and only a feeble challenge arose in the slave society of Virginia. His evidence and best discussions of the South contradict his assertion that "Americans"—he ought to have written "northerners"— were committed to building a nation on freedom. In South Carolina, Georgia, and Virginia that meant—whatever else it meant— freedom to own slaves, and, for the great mass of the people at least, the contradiction that wracked the North did not exist.

More clearly than any other writer, with the exception of David Brion Davis, Tise has taken the measure of the reactionary and

sinister aspects of the conservatism of nineteenth-century bourgeois thought, and his explication and critique of those aspects
show him at his formidable best. The trouble arises from his
assumption, into which his philosophical idealism betrays him,
that the same ideas had roughly the same historical meaning and
significance in radically different social contexts.

Proslavery thought in the West Indies provides a case in point.
Because Tise sees that the West Indian slaveholders defended slavery within a broad stream of counter-revolutionary conservative
thought, he thinks that he has refuted the argument for the
uniqueness of the proslavery worldview of the Old South. Richard
Dunn, in the *Times Literary Supplement,* has already taken him to
task for misreading the sources, and Tise may expect to hear growls
from other authorities. For Tise simply does not analyze the arguments in social context. Thus he dismisses the thesis that contrasts
a unique slave society in the Old South with a colonial-capitalist
society in the British West Indies without the slightest effort to
examine the political economy and fundamental social relations
of either. It has been a long time since an intellectual historian of
Tise's high quality carried the methods of philosophical idealism
to such lengths in historical interpretation.

The consequences reappear forcefully in his discussion of southern unionism. Southern historians have long understood that the
vast majority of southern unionists in the Lower South, and probably a good majority in the Upper as well, were ardently proslavery,
and Tise advances our understanding of the extent and depth of
their commitment. Unfortunately, he mars his contribution by
two extraordinary assertions, the more bizarre of which holds the
nullifiers and subsequent secessionists to have been less committed to slavery than the unionists.

In Tise's reading, even the unionists could not arrive at the "logical conclusion" of their proslavery until they had fully absorbed an
imported Yankee conservatism. The nature of that "logical conclusion" remains hazy but appears to be a commitment to southern
nationalism—a formulation that renders the whole argument curiouser and curiouser. Among other difficulties, it does not seem to
have occurred to Tise that the unionists, unlike the radicals, had to

harp on proslavery during and after the nullification crisis because their very unionism opened them to the charge of disloyalty to the South. In contrast, the radicals could safely assume that everyone knew they were sound on the goose.

Tise's refusal to credit the rise of a new southern worldview and his excessive concern with the ministers have led him astray. His concern is excessive, notwithstanding his sound insistence upon a major role for the ministers, northern and southern, in the development of proslavery. Thus he ignores the thought of such men as Andrew Johnson, Albert Gallatin Brown, and Alexander Stephens, who spoke for the yeomen and small and middling slaveholders and yet embraced the doctrine of "slavery in the abstract." In particular, he ignores the widespread argument, prefigured by Thomas Roderick Dew and embraced by Francis W. Pickens among many others, that free-labor societies were sailing into a crisis from which they would not be able to extricate themselves without the reintroduction of some form of personal servitude. They concluded, as did the unionist Fitzhugh himself, that the South would be mad to secede and risk a devastating war or international isolation and hostility when all it had to do was to bide its time and wait for its assailants to confront the dissolution of their own societies. Proslavery northerners, in contrast, defended slavery as a useful, geographically restricted appendage to a free-labor system they supported.

To be sure, Tise's idealist method has its uses and its charm. It offers a breath of fresh air in its cool disposal of the increasingly trivial—or rather, trivialized—social history with which we are being inundated. There is a special pleasure these days in being able to read a book that takes ideas and intellectual history seriously and eschews the reductionist and pseudo-anthropological cant that "political correctness" has transformed into the new orthodoxy of a historical profession in disarray. But it is one thing to eschew the reduction of ideas and ideology to the status of a reflex of economic and social interests; it is another to write as if ideas—indeed, words—embrace the same content in essentially different social settings.

Up to a point there is something useful in Tise's analysis of ideas as, as it were, things in themselves. Regrettably, he pushes his argument well beyond that point. For he equates two distinct movements: the theoretical defense of slavery by northern conservatives who lived in and supported a society based upon bourgeois social relations and who, on his own showing, had little political power and were in steady decline as an elite; and the theoretical but also practical defense of slavery by southern conservatives who lived in and supported a society based upon slave labor and who functioned within the marrow of a vigorous and politically powerful elite, not to say dominant social class.

In bringing the ministers to center stage, Tise does not notice that a growing legion of proslavery southern—but not northern—ministers were proclaiming slavery as the wave of the future and as the Christian solution to the conflict of labor and capital in the capitalist countries. South Carolina's great and enormously influential James Henley Thornwell ("the Calhoun of the Church") took unambiguously Fitzhughian ground. In Virginia, Thornwell's fellow Presbyterian, George Armstrong, did the same with only slightly less force when he declared that the southern social system "may well be" the Christian solution to the social question—to that great problem of the responsibility of capital to labor about which the wisest heads in Europe were confessing themselves "at fault."

To these voices could be added those of such outstanding Old School Presbyterian divines as R. L. Dabney and Benjamin Morgan Palmer, as well as the New School Frederick Ross, whose proslavery extremism provoked a tirade from Abraham Lincoln. The Presbyterian divines guided the educational system of the South and trained much of its political and social elite. They also led the way for their denominational rivals on matters of social, economic, and political policy. In their contributions to an emerging proslavery worldview in which the southern social system would be the model for a new world order they were joined by Baptists like Thornton Stringfellow and E. W. Warren, Methodists like William A. Smith and Parson Brownlow, and a host of others.

What prominent northern divine took such ground? Not Charles Hodge, Princeton's outstanding theologian who staunchly defended slavery as biblically sanctioned and who upheld southern rights in both northern and southern publications, but who had little use for slavery as social policy. In fact, Hodge voted Republican and stood by the Union in the secession crisis and after. Between Hodge and Thornwell there yawned an ever widening gulf in worldview, notwithstanding their common denial that slavery was sinful. Thus Hodge and Thornwell fought side by side for Old School Calvinist orthodoxy during the Presbyterian schism of 1837 but before long found themselves at loggerheads within the Old School itself. The issues, which began with ecclesiology, quickly passed into theology and sociopolitical doctrine. Hodge and his compatriots looked like ultra-conservatives in Princeton and the North but looked increasingly like liberal temporizers in Columbia, South Carolina, and the South. They were, if Thornwell, Palmer, and their southern associates may be credited, infected with the virus of modernism despite their best efforts at resistance. Only in the South did the social conditions exist to sustain a genuinely conservative—a genuinely proslavery—worldview.

Tise offers an instructive discussion of the proslavery tendency as part of the conservatism of modern northern Calvinism, but, failing to recognize the limits of his argument, he misses the steadily widening schism between it and its southern counterpart. In order to strengthen his exaggerated claims for the power of the conservative northern divines and for the northern origins of proslavery, he makes much of the Congregational-Presbyterian Plan of Union of 1801, but, incredibly, he does not note, much less analyze, the war that the southern divines were waging against it by the 1830s. Nor does he note the disproportionate strength of the Old School in the South. Perhaps more important, he does not note that the New School churches in the North retreated, despite fierce rearguard actions, from theological orthodoxy and accommodation to slavery, while the few New School churches in the South hewed much closer to theological orthodoxy and were as firmly proslavery as the Old School churches. There were few theological liberals among the New School divines of the South, and even the generally outspoken Frederick Ross seems to have muted his theological heterodoxy until after the War.

The consequences of Tise's method are calamitous even when they accompany illuminating discussions of discrete problems. For example, he tells an important and heretofore largely submerged story of the proslavery tendencies of the great northern educators at Yale, Princeton, and Andover. The many set pieces of this kind prove richly rewarding, but the sociopolitical implications of the Unitarian triumph at Harvard and the subsequent radicalization within the Unitarian movement go unnoticed, as do the ramifications of the questionably orthodox New Haven theology. Certainly, no simple correlation can be made between those momentous theological shifts and the emergence of immediatist abolitionism, but the southerners plausibly read the shamefaced retreat from orthodoxy as supreme evidence that the bourgeois society of the North was fundamentally corrupt. They concluded that even its most dedicated conservatives lacked the social ground on which to stand. From the vantage point of Columbia, as well as Richmond and elsewhere in the South, northern society, not just Hodge's ecclesiastical backsliding, was "utterly rotten."

Continuing to berate previous scholars, Tise rejects a "final formulation held in common with others" that the threat of abolitionism provided the occasion for the full revelation of an already well developed southern proslavery ideology. It is not clear just who has held so mechanistic a view. In any case, Tise bypasses a much more formidable argument, which Jenkins suggested and more recent writers, notably Lewis Simpson, Drew Faust, and Elizabeth Fox-Genovese, have developed—an argument that Calhoun, Dew, and a host of antebellum southerners made on their own behalf. According to that argument, a defense of slavery had been implicit in the specific type of republicanism that had long since taken root in the South but could not emerge explicitly until external challenge compelled a confrontation with the contrary ideological tendencies inherited from Enlightenment liberalism and crystallized in the defense of the American Revolution.

Tise himself sometimes argues this way, with the vital difference that he sees not a process of self-recognition but a migration of ideas from North to South and a response to specific political crises. He does demonstrate that proslavery had a long history in the North and across the Atlantic, and his exploration of that history constitutes one of the most impressive features of his book. In particular, he scores well in demonstrating that the quest for social order in an ideologically explosive era led many conservatives to insist upon the divine sanction for and social utility of slavery in all societies, including those based primarily upon free labor. But his notion that southerners had to learn this lesson from northern conservatives falls well short of being convincing.

Tise underestimates the indigenous roots of southern proslavery, but nothing short of a full review of southern thought from 1790 to 1830 would constitute an adequate reply to his own reading. For the present it will have to suffice that he goes astray by homogenizing northern and southern viewpoints in his attempt to recast the periodization of proslavery thought. He regards the mature southern proslavery argument, which was discernible by the 1830s and came on in a rush in the 1840s, as an echo of the northern argument. The difference, however, proved decisive. In the North, as in Britain and on the continent, some conservatives longed for—or pretended to long for—the good old days of organic social relations, and they railed against the cash nexus and the market's conquest of society and morals. But notwithstanding politically isolated, idiosyncratic individuals and plain cranks, British and northern conservatives steadily surrendered to the power of the market, to a triumphant and allegedly received scientific political economy, and to the free-labor system, however much they continued to defend black slavery in the colonies or even wish for a small dose of white slavery at home to keep the working class in line.

Where did any substantial and politically influential conservative ideological movement assert that a return to slavery was the only solution to the social question posed by the gloomy forecasts of Ricardo's law of the falling rate of profit and Malthus's law of population? British and northern conservatives concluded, to the contrary, that since capitalism must inexorably immiser-ate the laboring classes, slavery would disappear everywhere ex-cept perhaps on the colonial and tropical periphery of the world market. Southerners also invoked these arguments from political economy, but they drew opposite conclusions, most forcefully in the extraordinary work of Thomas Roderick Dew, who wrote a good deal that remains intellectually more powerful than the *Review of Debates,* which appears to be all that even most southern historians read these days. They concluded that the outcome of immiseration would be politically untenable and morally beyond the pale. In consequence, even those who were by no means hostile to material progress, as many others were, saw the future world as based upon slave, not bourgeois, social relations. They held the social relations of their own society up as a model for a Christian world and sought, however vainly, to create a new kind of civilization.

The most puzzling part of Tise's interpretation is its failure to confront the southern critique of northern conservatism. From the hints in John Randolph and John Taylor to the probes of Dew and Chancellor Harper to the polemics of James Hammond and George McDuffie, the groundwork was being laid for the ultimate assertion that modern civilization could only survive through the reintroduction of some form of personal servitude. Hence the southern ideologues, including an array of intellec-tually impressive divines, savaged the northern conservatives on precisely this point. Our well-meaning northern brethren, they tirelessly exclaimed, do not understand that the great social and moral evils against which they inveigh cannot be contained in a society based upon free labor. They can be contained only in a society in which a privileged class assumes personal responsibility for the laborers through direct ownership—a society that does not merely tolerate slave labor, but is based upon it. This challenge revealed, as nothing else, the extent to which a uniquely proslavery worldview had emerged in the South. That worldview had been building for more than half a century, although it did not come to full expression until after 1840, the date at which Tise chooses to close much of his discussion. Its formulation represented a slow but portentous separation from the British and northern proslavery conservatism that never could repudiate its bourgeois moorings.

I fear that I have not done justice to the merits of this rich and rewarding book, but I do hope that, in criticizing it as sharply as possible in so few pages, I have paid tribute to its accomplishments. It is a book to be argued with at length, and justice to it would require a book at least as long. One such is hereby promised; let us hope more will be forthcoming at other hands. With all the faults that might be charged to *Proslavery*, would that we were getting more books like it.

8

Higher Education in the Defense of Slave Society

As is well known, the slave states sent a higher proportion of their white youth to college than did the free states. Although most southern college students undoubtedly came from well-to-do families, an important minority did not. Throughout the South schoolteachers kept their eyes open for especially talented students, whose education in classical academies and colleges was then paid for by wealthy patrons. No one has yet counted, but there can be no doubt that a significant portion of the political, religious, and intellectual leaders of the Old South had modest origins and rose under the patronage of wealthy planters.

Since a substantial portion of the southern elite did go to college, the moral and philosophical instruction they received became a source of concern to political and social leaders. Only an occasional zealot sought to impose a narrow ideological or political agenda upon a southern people quick to assert their right of private judgment in matters both divine and secular. There is, in fact, no reason to believe that southern colleges restricted academic freedom more than northern colleges did. But the first and greatest problem for southern educators was to counteract the growing transatlantic revulsion against slavery as a moral as well as social evil.

The classical academies and the colleges self-consciously prepared southern youth to serve as citizens of a slaveholding republic, much as those of the free states prepared northern youth to serve as citizens of a bourgeois republic. But northern schools steadily moved toward training in those "practical" subjects necessary for business, professions, and trades, for that very training was considered necessary for citizenship in a democratic, progressive society. Hence, despite fierce resistance from conservatives, northern educators slowly de-emphasized the Greek and Roman classics. The South, in contrast, although also subject to assaults from educational progressives, held fast to the eighteenth-century view of education as the pursuit of gentlemen and of those who aspired to be gentlemen. Southern educators espoused a broadly conservative worldview that stressed the necessity for social stratification, the authority of the male head of household, and the basic tenets of Christian orthodoxy. Northern conservatives shared much of this vision, but they remained wedded to the free-labor system, the socially destructive tendencies of which they sought to rein in. Their southern critics pitied them, arguing that the irresistible tendencies of the free-labor system meant the transformation of everything, including morals and spiritual values, into commodities. That was the meaning of their insistence that abolitionism spelled religious heresy, social anarchy, and the collapse of republican polity.

The South pioneered in religious liberty and did not disgrace itself, as the Northeast did, with the burning of Catholic convents and the nastier forms of anti-Semitism. But the southern churches upheld such tenets of Christian orthodoxy as original sin and human depravity while the northern churches were steadily plunging into theological liberalism and a rosy view of human nature. Here I must restrict myself to a few assertions and one critical point. The southern colleges had dedicated, well-qualified, if underpaid and overworked, professors who labored under difficult conditions to civilize a frontier society and raise it to the highest possible standards of Christian faith and behavior—as they understood those concepts. In so doing, they defended slavery, and they did so at an immeasurably higher intellectual level than we now care to acknowledge. They succeeded in inculcating proslavery views in southern youth less by efforts at narrow indoctrination than through the communication of a worldview that linked Christian orthodoxy to republican political standards and time-honored social values.

The educational work of the divines proved decisive, for their influence in secular as well as denominational colleges remained paramount. Having demonstrated, to the satisfaction of their communicants and of southerners at large, that the Bible sanctioned slavery, they positioned themselves and their secular allies to construct a worldview appropriate to a slaveholding society without slipping into potentially divisive ideological and political specifics. Their task was made easier by the preparation students received in the academies and, on a larger scale, in the old field schools and the Sabbath schools. At all levels teachers, many of them ministers, eschewed specifically theological indoctrination but promulgated broadly accepted Christian doctrines.

Slavery was a common topic of discussion and debate in the student societies and publications, although it rarely if ever became an obsession and only occasionally qualified as the principal object of attention. In the late eighteenth century and immediately thereafter students debated slavery vigorously. At the University of North Carolina, for example, they seem to have accepted slavery as a fact of life—but only grudgingly. They thought it a social and political evil but feared the consequences of emancipation. Significantly, for a state university, the professors censored student criticism of religion much more readily than they censored criticism of slavery.

The reputation of southern colleges for religious and political radicalism spread during the eighteenth century and carried well into the nineteenth. Even after the turn of the century students at the College of William and Mary were debating the existence of God and whether Christianity has been beneficial or injurious to mankind. William J. Grayson recalled, to his disgust, that students at the College of South Carolina, who knew nothing of Shakespeare or Milton, were deep into Paine's *Rights of Man* and *Age of Reason*. For many years Paine remained a hero to many students across the South. At the notoriously liberal University of North Carolina, Professor Samuel Allen Holmes, an anarchist, denounced virtue and integrity as "deceptions and injurious pretenses" and called upon students to resist authority. The students paid heed, indulging themselves in one of those ubiquitous campus riots and beating up some instructors.

In rebellion against parents and the older generation, many of the brightest and most articulate students espoused radical notions of all kinds and perceived the reigning mores as old-fashioned and repressive. In this respect the rebels resembled college students in other climes and times. Few of their elders over-reacted, for they remembered their own youthful passions and follies. Parents reminded themselves that boys will be boys, and, in the event, precious few students carried their radicalism beyond their college years. Nevertheless, with slavery's coming under increasing attack throughout the transatlantic world, southern political, social, and religious leaders knew they had to take measures.

As late as the 1840s, when professors were coming under ever closer scrutiny, students across the South retained some freedom to criticize and even condemn slavery and had some exposure to antislavery views. During the Missouri controversy, the Raleigh, North Carolina, *Minerva* published several antislavery articles, some written by college students. Judge William A. Gaston denounced slavery as a social evil in a well-received address to the students at the University of North Carolina in 1832, and as late as 1841, Edward Pringle, scion of an elite low-country family, called for the abolition of religion as well as slavery. At the same time, his brilliant classmate, William Henry Trescot, ridiculed Calhoun and assorted southern political pieties. Soon thereafter Trescot emerged as America's first great diplomatic historian and a champion not only of slavery but also of secession.

On campuses, as in the larger society, a repressive atmosphere slowly descended in the wake of an evangelical fervor that found criticism of Christianity offensive, and it gained momentum in the wake of a series of political shocks (Missouri, Denmark Vesey, nullification, Nat Turner, Garrison) that encouraged an identification of slavery with social order in general and southern values in particular. But repression by itself could never have been enough, for hot-blooded southern youth often proved bolder than their professors in insisting upon the right to think for themselves.

Yet one of the more significant events in the dreary Hedrick affair—Professor Hedrick was fired by the University of North Carolina for supporting Frémont in 1856—came from the students, who burned Hedrick in effigy at a mass meeting on campus. In fact, students were burning books as well as effigies. The extent of the book burning remains unclear and may well have been much exaggerated by those unfriendly to the South. But undoubtedly, it was spreading. The works of Voltaire, Rousseau, and Paine, to say nothing of Boccaccio, went up in flames. At Oakland College in Mississippi, considered a unionist stronghold, P. K. Whitney, a member of the editorial committee of the student magazine, vigorously defended slavery and justified the book burning. He acknowledged that the South was becoming prudent in the purchase and circulation of books and was "committing to the flames or excluding from the sight of its youth, such books as breathe an abolition spirit, advocate abolition doctrines, or are in any manner obnoxious to the health, growth, and prosperity of pure Southern principles."

A cautionary note: At about the same time, Western Reserve College in Ohio was firing three professors for their proslavery views.

Proslavery should not be confused with secessionism or any particular political tendency, for unionist professors and students generally defended slavery as vigorously as did their secessionist colleagues. Students, like other southerners, divided on politics between Whigs and Democrats, moderates and extremists, unionists and secessionists, but, like other southerners, they divided less and less over time on slavery itself, moving steadily toward a defense that carried them beyond the race question.

The campuses always had their share of political extremists, more so among students than among professors. The rebellious impulse that drew the youth of the early nineteenth century to Tom Paine drew them to proslavery and secessionist extremists in later years, often in continued rebellion against more cautious parents. Charles Plummer Green of Virginia crowed in 1836 that the rising student generation supported Calhoun and nullification. Doubtless, he exaggerated but probably not by much. In Lexington, Virginia, for example, residents regarded the students at Washington College and the Virginia Military Institute as secessionist hotheads. In 1861 the students forced the unionist president of Washington College to resign.

At some colleges students got heavier and less subtle doses of proslavery doctrine than at others. Emory College at Oxford, Georgia, the most important Methodist college in the Lower South, became a bastion of militancy, contributing significantly to the schism in the national church in 1844. The Rev. William J. Sasnett, who taught political economy, held forth with particular fervor in defense of slavery as a God-ordained social order based on a frank recognition of inequality among men.

The campuses nonetheless remained politically divided until Lincoln's election and even for a short while thereafter. At the University of Virginia, which would contribute the corpses of five hundred former students to the Confederate war effort, professors and students alike retained high hopes for the Union in 1860, supporting the candidacy of John Bell. It had been the fearful, politically moderate professors who refused to allow Henry Winter Davis of Maryland, an alumnus critical of slavery, to speak on campus in 1857; the students had wanted to hear him. There is no reason to believe that many, if any, shared Davis's views, but every reason to know that, unlike their professors, the students welcomed political excitement.

Notwithstanding continuing differences over partisan politics, the defense of slavery passed from apologetics to an indictment of the free-labor system and the celebration of the superiority of slavery as a social system. In campus publications and class papers and addresses, students echoed Calhoun in defending slavery and states' rights primarily as bastions against the pernicious doctrines of equality and majority rule. Universal manhood suffrage came under heavy fire. According to T. M. Garrett, a student at North Carolina, our forefathers erred badly in not providing "a sufficient safe-guard against the tyranny of the majority." A student in Mississippi declared, "Men are not born on an equality, and the course of nature cannot be changed with impunity. . . . In no democracy do men govern themselves." Thomas Burke Burton of North Carolina saw universal manhood suffrage as the culmination of assorted radical doctrines and as a threat to slavery: "So soon as property ceases to be represented, its great constituent, slavery, will be exposed and there are many in our midst inimical to the institution who only await an opportunity to act out their sentiments."

With mounting stridency, students hailed slavery as a blessing and, in the words of a young Mississippian, a "most cherished institution . . . [that] gives vitality and support to the South, and wealth and employment to many other peoples of the world." To a growing number of students, slavery also offered a solution to the dangerous problem of the relation of labor to capital in modern society. The alarms had sounded well before the crisis of the 1850s, as students responded to the warnings of Thomas Roderick Dew and James H. Hammond, William Harper and Calhoun, and saw Western civilization in danger of collapse.

The revolutions of 1848 shook the campuses and occasioned widespread discussion of socialism. Jesse Harper Lindsay, Jr., in his graduation speech at the University of North Carolina in 1851, presented the commonly held view:

> The late revolutions of Europe have not been of a political but of a social nature. The tendency toward equality and universal suffrage, as a political right, is not the only characteristic of the changes of the nineteenth century. *Social reform* and *perfectibility* must also be attempted. Socialism, however, is no new doctrine. From the earliest time men have been shocked and grieved at the evils which have prevailed in almost every form that society has yet assumed. Subtle and ingenious thinkers have devised model Republics in which no misery should exist—earnest and zealous philanthropists have endeavored to realize their highest imaginations and put them in operation.

Lindsay wanted no part of socialist solutions to the problems at hand, for they would plunge "the whole fabric of government in one universal and overwhelming ruin."

At the same commencement, James A. Washington elaborated on the social conditions that socialists were vainly trying to correct. He spoke of the terrible struggle for survival of hundreds of thousands of poor people in London and other great cities: the pleas for bread, the rampant crime, the widespread prostitution, the frequent suicides of hapless workingmen. Nor did he restrict himself to the industrial and urban parts of the world. Misery, he noted, was plaguing Russia and Prussia, Austria and Poland, Ireland and India. Ireland especially caught the attention of southern youth. "Ireland's misery," exclaimed Junius Irving Scales in 1853, "has ever been England's shame." Scales recounted the early conquest and the ruthlessness of Cromwell and concluded that, notwithstanding some reforms, the Irish peasants were still starving.

Another student, William Watts Glover, elaborated an argument that was becoming increasingly popular on the campuses. "The great mass of mankind," he said, "are naturally disposed to avoid labor and toil." Comparing free labor with slave, he added, "If we look to the laboring class of any community or to the poor of any country, we find there many poverty stricken wretches in a more deplorable and abject condition." Glover scouted emancipation as a snare: "It is under the free system of labor where we find extensive poverty and suffering."

The victory of proslavery on the college campuses owed much to the teaching of moral philosophy. Indeed, the one course required of all students almost everywhere was in moral philosophy, which related the teachings of Christianity, as filtered through the Scottish Enlightenment, to history, political science, and political economy. In all but a few cases the president of the college taught that course, and usually he was a minister.

Of special importance were courses in law, for the law offered young southerners who preferred a profession to planting their safest course to power, prosperity, and fame. Only small numbers went to law school, but large numbers took law courses in college. The line between courses in law and those in political science and constitutional theory proved hard to draw, for the substance was intertwined. In consequence, the history of legal education, broadly defined, becomes the history of political education.

Thomas Jefferson took special pains to shape the teaching of law and therefore of political science at the University of Virginia, and as the prestige of "Mr. Jefferson's University" rose, his views had a widespread influence on colleges across the South. Those views did not include his early denunciations of slavery, which were generally ignored, but did include support for states' rights, limited government, and strict interpretation of the Constitution. Jefferson, in endorsing academic freedom, demanded that professors be allowed to choose their own textbooks. But he made one exception: The professor of law must assign textbooks approved by the Rector and the Board, for Jefferson insisted upon proper "republican," that is, Anti-Federalist, instruction. Thus he wrote Joseph Cabell in February 1825:

> There is one branch in which we are the best judges, in which heresies may be taught of so interesting a character to our State and to the United States, as to make it a duty in us to lay down the principles which are to be taught. . . . It is our duty to guard against any such [Federalist] principles being disseminated among our youth, and the diffusion of that poison by a previous prescription of the texts to be followed in their discourses.

Jefferson would tolerate Federalist professors in subjects considered politically safe, provided—let it be noted—that they would not prove obnoxious to Virginians on the slavery question. Jefferson knew what he was about, for in the decades ahead law courses at southern colleges became a prime vehicle for the dissemination of political theory, although not always of a kind he would have approved of. These courses attracted all kinds of students, not merely those who intended to become lawyers. Leading educators insisted that proper preparation for the law required a sound general and especially classical education and that preparation for civil and political life required an introduction to legal history and theory.

The careers of the Tuckers, a distinguished succession of legal scholars associated with the College of William and Mary and the University of Virginia, nicely chart the political and ideological drift in the teaching of law and political science in the South. St. George Tucker, the family patriarch, boldly wrote and spoke against slavery and made a futile effort to convince Virginia's legislators to adopt his plan of gradual emancipation. He edited and annotated an edition of Blackstone's *Commentaries*, which long proved immensely influential throughout the United States. For decades his edition of Blackstone, with its ringing editorial advocacy of strict construction and states' rights, provided a focus for discussion in colleges in the Southwest as well as in Virginia and the Carolinas. His proslavery and politically militant son, Nathaniel Beverley Tucker, who occupied his father's old professorial chair at William and Mary from 1834 to 1851, justly claimed that he was carrying on where his father had left off.

St. George Tucker opposed the consolidationism advocated in Virginia by John Marshall and other Federalists, and he helped lay the foundation for the political and constitutional doctrines the South came to champion. While implicitly rejecting nullification, he insisted upon the right of a state to secede from the Union. At the beginning of the nineteenth century he foreshadowed Calhoun's doctrine of concurrent majority by suggesting that, to preserve representative democracy under the Constitution, a federal council should replace the American presidency.

St. George Tucker continued to criticize slavery in his prestigious courses at William and Mary, but his antislavery views did not remotely have the impact in the South that his political and constitutional views had. A strong supporter of the Union, he nevertheless insisted that oppression by sister states would justify secession, much as Britain's oppression of the colonies had justified secession from the Empire. Beverley Tucker never said it better.

St. George Tucker's aversion to slavery did not die with him. His other son, Henry St. George Tucker, earned the respect and admiration of his fellow Virginians for his work as a jurist and legal scholar. They even put up with his well-known antipathy toward slavery. The content of Henry Tucker's views on slavery and the restraint with which he presented them rendered him less than dangerous even in the eyes of most fire-eaters. The moderately antislavery and decidedly unionist Henry Tucker had more in common with his radical brother than either might have wished to admit. For Henry's criticisms of slavery as an evil had little discernible influence on his students. He assuredly did influence many students, but primarily through his constitutional doctrines.

In the early 1840s, Henry Tucker drew large numbers of students to his courses at the University of Virginia, at a time when law students constituted a quarter of the student body. He laid out his views with special clarity in his book, *Lectures on Constitutional Law* (1841), which became a favorite constitutional text among educated Southerners. Although personally opposed to secession, he acknowledged the revolutionary right of secession by a state that had reached the end of its patience with federal oppression. The lectures, in fact, dealt much less with constitutional law than with the states' rights principles he regarded as its basis. He remained a lifelong friend of John C. Calhoun, whose young son he took under his wing at the University of Virginia.

Henry Tucker did not stand alone as a critic of slavery whose students might be excused for having experienced him primarily as a southern-rights man and, in effect, an apologist for slavery. Alexander Peter Stewart of the University of Nashville, Francis Lieber at the College of South Carolina, and George Tucker and John Barbee Minor of the University of Virginia may serve as examples. But Lieber, like others, especially in the Lower South, taught, spoke, and acted so cautiously that neither his students nor anyone else knew his real views. His students did, however, remember his historical justification for the rise of slavery in world history and, especially, his endorsement of Calhoun's political theory and criticism of radical democracy.

Legal education had a much more direct political impact in the South than in the North, in part because of sectionally diverging attitudes toward professionalism. The South resisted, on the whole successfully, the tide of professionalism in legal education that was proving irresistible in the North. College-educated southerners who were headed for the legal profession continued to receive an education designed to produce citizens and gentlemen in accord with older values.

As time went on, a decreasing number of lawyers were being trained in law schools, but more and more ordinary college students were taking courses in law or courses in which legal studies constituted an important component. Here too, Thomas Jefferson cast a long—and conservative—shadow. His prescribed program of study for law students virtually called for mastery of all human knowledge. The performance fell well short of the ideal, but the ideal provided the principal instructional thrust in southern colleges, whereas, despite occasional pretenses, it was being abandoned in the North. Ironically, southern colleges were able to remain closer to Jefferson's ideal because they rejected that part of his program which would have significantly curtailed the Greek and Roman classics in order to make way for ostensibly more practical and modern subjects.

By the 1820s the accumulation of case law was propelling a retreat in the North from a more philosophical and humanistic curriculum. Only three appeals in corporate law reached the Supreme Court before 1815, but by 1822 the accumulation of cases before the courts made a casebook necessary. In consequence, and with far-reaching implications for sectional cultural divergence, an increased emphasis on positive law displaced a concern for natural law, which nonetheless remained strong in the South.

In the North, the law schools at Litchfield and Harvard set the pace in the narrowing of legal education to technical pursuits. Harvard did not assume pride of place in legal education until the 1830s, when Mr. Justice Story assumed the professorship of law and transformed the course of study. But even in the eighteenth century Harvard had begun to move toward professionalization, slowly severing legal and political studies from ethics and moral philosophy.

Story's widely praised Inaugural Address said all the right things about the indissoluble link between the study of law and the study of philosophy, history, rhetoric, and oratory, but his sermon bore little resemblance to his subsequent practice. Story had little patience with the idea that he ought to teach "government" in order to prepare students for leadership in the republic. He insisted that law students should have already had a proper college education and require no further formal instruction. As Harvard went, so did its northern imitators.

The College of William and Mary preceded Harvard and all other American colleges in teaching law, first under George Wythe and then under St. George Tucker. Its program in legal studies set the tone for the South. The University of Virginia followed suit, and by the 1840s North Carolina, Mississippi, and other southern colleges were establishing law departments, which unlike their northern counterparts, maintained the old ways.

Everywhere in the South the colleges introduced the teaching of law as a separate course or strengthened the legal-studies component of courses in political science and moral philosophy. Everywhere the colleges rendered professionalism subservient to the training of a broadly educated political and social elite. Robert Ferguson, with his eye primarily on the North, has suggested that the legal community wavered badly after the 1830s, as its time-honored republican principles began to founder. The slavery controversy and the increasingly intense sectional conflict called national unity into question, and men like Clay, Webster, and Rufus Choate felt compelled to speak less of great principles and more of the Union as a virtue in itself that required compromise between competing principles.

Some such tendency left its mark in the South, especially among the more fervent unionists, but even they, faced with the necessity for elaborating a broad defense of slavery, continued to stress the basic principles of social order. Those less wedded to the Union had no problem at all. And the defense of the basic principles of social order led the defenders of slavery, including most of the unionist professors of law, to stress the historical, philosophical, and theological grounding of legal thought.

The southern students' deep interest in politics led even those with no interest in a legal career to flock to courses in which the law was being taught in relation to history and, specifically, the place of slave societies in history. Legal scholars were providing some of the most learned and challenging treatises on the significance of slavery in world history. George Sawyer opened his *Southern Institutes* with an explanation that had parallels in the even more influential treatises of John Fletcher and Thomas R. R. Cobb. Aristotle and other early authorities, Sawyer began, demonstrated that the master–slave relation, in some form, contributed to the bedrock of social order. Thus the material and moral progress of civilization required the formal elaboration of the legal systems appropriate to this relation.

In a similar vein, Cobb wrote, "Philosophy is the handmaid, and frequently the most successful expounder of the law. History is the groundwork and only sure basis of philosophy. Therefore, to understand aright the law of slavery, we must not be ignorant of its history. . . . [Slavery] has been more universal than marriage and more permanent than liberty." In stressing the ubiquity of slavery in world history, Sawyer and Cobb were speaking for just about every legally trained defender of slavery: Calhoun, Harper, Hammond, George Frederick Holmes, George Fitzhugh, Beverley Tucker, James P. Holcombe, Henry Hughes, Albert Bledsoe. In their view all societies had recognized slaves as lawful articles of commerce and recognized the property rights of masters to the labor services of their slaves. The existence of slavery from the earliest times resulted in a virtual common law that could be set aside only by the positive action of the state. In essence, they declared that there was nothing "peculiar" about slave society. Rather, it was free society that constituted, in Fitzhugh's words, "a small and recent experiment."

The appeal to history, including legal history, proceeded in intimate association with the appeal to Scripture and biblical history and prepared the way for the doctrine of slavery in the abstract. At a time in which Justice Lemuel Shaw of Massachusetts, along with lesser jurists, was abandoning natural for positive law in the elaboration of legal doctrine especially in economic cases, southern jurists and legal scholars were insisting upon the sanctity of the law as God-inspired. "Moral philosophy," wrote Jasper Adams, "has important relations to, and connections with law." Scripture recognizes civil government as binding on conscience, and Christianity provides the ultimate standard to which international as well as national duties must be referred. The Rev.

Mr. Adams published those views in 1837 out of his lectures at the College of Charleston, which he served as president. A transplanted Yankee, his views had national, indeed transatlantic, roots, but they captured the prevalent ideal of legal education in the South at the moment it was in retreat in the North.

The hegemony of the slaveholding class thus arose less from crude methods of proslavery indoctrination than from the projection of an authentic worldview—authentic in the sense that it embodied a coherent and integrated philosophy of life and far transcended mere apologetics for economic exploitation and racial oppression. And note: hegemony implies no uniformity in thought or action. To the contrary, it implies a great diversity that must be kept from tearing society apart. It assumes conflict and requires that a consensus be enforced only on the central questions of the moment—in this case, the defense of slavery and racial stratification.

Southern educators made an important contribution to that hegemony by advancing a religiously grounded, socially conservative philosophy in which the defense of slavery emerged as only a strain in a much broader defense of Christendom against modernist heresies, religious and political. Educators exposed southern youth to a worldview that integrated Christian morals, political principles, and cultural standards. That worldview contained much that remains defensible, including an acute critique of the social atomization of modern society and of the destructive consequences of political and economic centralization. And many of those who taught it ranked as selfless, admirable, dedicated Christians. That, I suggest, constituted no small part of the regime's staying power and ability to evoke passionate loyalty.

What may be said in rebuttal was summed up by an old black woman who had lived through slavery: "What white folks did to black folks in slavery times, they won't never be able to pray it away." The juxtaposition of the slaveholders' remarkable achievements and that black woman's unanswerable indictment lays bare the genuine tragedy of the Old South—the tragedy of a strong, honorable, gifted people who ended by placing their formidable talents in the service of an enormity.

9

The Poet as Social Critic

Long before the War for Southern Independence the world, or at least New York and New England—the part of the world that counts—was being told what has since become Yankee gospel: The men of the Old South had no minds, only temperaments. Such stupidity, reiterated by bigots, ignoramuses, and damned fools, could not today be uttered about, say, blacks or women without provoking outrage. It nonetheless continues to plague American letters. The Old South had no intellectual life worthy of note, at least according to a great majority of our intellectual historians, who do not so much condemn as ignore it. In recent years, thanks largely to a small band of determined warriors led by Michael O'Brien, that allegedly nonexistent intellectual life has miraculously been intruding itself into academic circles. Better late than never, even well over a century late. For those who have been smarting under the ideological claptrap that has long passed for history, the publication of William J. Grayson's autobiography comes as a powerful salvo in what promises to be a protracted war. That the salvo comes buttressed by Richard Calhoun's illuminating introduction and judicious editing makes it all the more noteworthy.

The kernel of truth in the long record of politically motivated historical lying may be found in the backwardness of southern fiction relative to northern. William Gilmore Simms was no Nathaniel Hawthorne. For poetry the record is less clear, except for those who transform Poe into an honorary Yankee and choose to forget Henry Timrod and Thomas Holly Chivers. I do not wish to argue. With due respect for Timrod and Chivers, whose best work remains impressive, the Old South did not produce an Emily Dickinson. But then, apart from Miss Dickinson herself, neither did the North. (Admittedly, I am not a Whitman fan.) Still, it is a strange bias that makes the novel and poetry the sole measure of intellectual accomplishment.

Grayson's warmest admirers would not, I suspect, consider him more than an interesting minor poet, but even his detractors ought to be able to appreciate his general intellectual quality and to recognize, if only from reading his autobiography, that he was participating in a transatlantic community with a rich intellectual life. Suffice it to note that, whatever the extent of and reasons for the Old South's backwardness in the output of literature, narrowly defined, it produced intellectuals whose work ranked with the best the North had to offer and in some cases overmatched it: George Tucker and Jacob N. Cardozo in political economy; John Randolph of Roanoke, John C. Calhoun, and Albert T. Bledsoe in political theory; James Henley Thornwell, Robert Breckenridge, and Robert L. Dabney in theology and ecclesiology; Thomas Roderick Dew and William H. Trescot in the interpretation of history; George Frederick Holmes and Hugh S. Legare in social and cultural criticism. To the list we might well add William Harper, James H. Hammond, N. Beverley Tucker, Thomas R. R. Cobb, George Fitzhugh, Henry Hughes, Henry A. Washington, Edmund Ruffin, Joseph LeConte, and others.

With the exception of Randolph and George Tucker they all defended slavery, and even Randolph and Tucker joined the others in a spirited defense of traditional southern values. Their work, for the most part, went onto the garbage heap of history on "the night they drove Ol' Dixie down." Yet they did a good deal more than defend slavery, and much of their thought has passed into some of twentieth-century America's most penetrating social and literary criticism at the hands of southerners who, alas, are largely ignored in Academia: Allen Tate, John Crowe Ransom, Donald Davidson, John Gould Fletcher, Richard Weaver, and, more recently, M. E. Bradford, John Shelton Reed, Thomas Fleming, and Clyde Wilson.

Influence aside, the best of the work written in the Old South would repay careful reading today. Let me settle for two personal favorites: Thomas Roderick Dew's astonishing study of the history of Western civilization, *A Digest of the Laws, Manners, Customs, and Institutions of the Ancient and Modern Nations*, and Thornwell's four volumes of sermons and discourses on theology, ecclesiology, and society and politics.

The place of poetry in the Old South has yet to be studied thoroughly. The few books of poetry published in the South or by southerners do not appear to have sold well—a circumstance that underscores the modest success of Grayson's *The Hireling and the Slave*—and too often historians, literary and other, have erroneously concluded that the southern people, the planters in particular, had little interest in poetry of any kind. Yet Shakespeare's work may well have been, after the Bible, the most widely read and discussed in planter circles, where it was readily quoted with ease. The religious and agricultural journals regularly published the work of known, fledgling, and perfectly dreadful poets. Slaveholders, male and female, wrote poetry, or what they hoped would be received as poetry, all the time. Southern college students read major poets and filled notebooks with their own poems. Swains sent their young ladies love poems, mostly their own creations, as a matter of course. Battle-hardened politicians like S. S. Prentiss of Mississippi and Zebulon Vance of North Carolina wrote poetry that won the admiration of some contemporaries. Planters and their ladies filled diaries, correspondence, journals, and even plantation account books with their favorite printed poems as well as their own efforts. In short, Jefferson found little support for his opinion that poetry should be eschewed almost as readily as novels.

What it all means remains debatable, but the widespread passion for poetry may help account for the respect accorded well-known poets, at least in elite circles, when they spoke up on social and political questions. And a number of poets did yeoman service for the proslavery cause. Chivers entered the lists with newspaper articles that blistered the free-labor system of the North, where he spent much of his time. Timrod, the poet laureate of the

Confederacy, celebrated the slaveholding South as the beacon for a new world order. Father Abram Joseph Ryan, the politically militant Catholic priest, became the Poet of the Lost Cause. But no single effort had the circulation and impact of Grayson's *The Hireling and the Slave.*

Richard Calhoun, in his searching and wide-ranging introduction, suggestively points to a correlation between literary and political styles, most notably with respect to the quarrels between the politically conservative and poetically neoclassical Grayson and the politically visionary and poetically romantic Timrod. He would, I am sure, agree that such correlations should be pushed only so far and that it would be an injustice to both men and a sin against the canons of literary criticism to reduce their poetical styles to political bedrock. Yet, as Calhoun notes, Grayson's cultural and political conservatism does provide an intriguing contrast with the romantic Timrod's politically radical flights of fancy.

Calhoun draws our attention to Grayson's brave defense of the Union, which has largely been forgotten, much as his defense of slavery has not been forgiven. Calhoun recognizes that proslavery and unionism coexisted comfortably in the minds of such unionists as South Carolina's Benjamin F. Perry and James L. Petigru. Grayson's thinking brought him close to the position taken by a wavering James H. Hammond in the 1850s and much closer than is usually recognized to the worldview of Timrod and the extreme proslavery theorists. Calhoun suggests that, unlike Timrod, Grayson did not recommend the social system of the South as a model for a new world order—that, in effect, he did not take the high ground of Timrod's "Ethnogenesis," which, in some respects, reads like a poetical version of Fitzhugh's *Sociology for the South.*

Calhoun is certainly right so far as Grayson's explicit ideological stance is concerned. But we would do well to pay careful attention to Calhoun's caveat: Grayson did not reflect much on the logic of his own position. Had he done so—had he sought the ideological consistency expected of a social theorist rather than a poet—he would have ended with Fitzhugh, much as Timrod did, in seeing some form of slavery as the only solution to the struggle between labor and capital that was wracking Europe, troubling the North, and threatening to destroy Western civilization. To appreciate the course of Grayson's thought we must take full account of the extent to which the defense of "slavery in the abstract" (slavery as the natural and proper condition of labor regardless of race) was sweeping the educated circles of South Carolina in the 1840s and 1850s.

The proponents of "slavery in the abstract" included fire-eaters as well as unionists, but here we are concerned with the unionists with whom Grayson identified and whose particular version of the ideologically extreme proslavery view paradoxically led to political moderation. Indeed, Fitzhugh himself opposed secession until the final hour. In South Carolina the great and influential Presbyterian divine James Henley Thornwell also held out against secession as long as he could and proclaimed that the capitalist countries were inexorably being driven to restore some form of slavery. Thornwell did not have to read Fitzhugh to arrive at that conclusion, which in fact had been drawn by a good many southern theorists before Fitzhugh came on the scene. (Fitzhugh did make original contributions to the discussion, but they need not concern us here.) Thornwell deduced his conclusions from a study of the reigning laws of Ricardian and Malthusian political economy, which like other well-educated southerners he knew well but reinterpreted in the light of Christian ethics. As for Grayson, it was enough that he followed the practical workings of those so-called laws in the parliamentary reports on the ghastly conditions of British working-class life.

If we grant that Grayson deplored the fate of the working classes under the wages system and that he held up slavery as a humane alternative, does it follow that he, like Fitzhugh loudly or Thornwell gingerly, advocated the enslavement of all labor? Grayson himself denied it. He wrote, in his notes to *The Hireling and the Slave*, that he sought only to defend black slavery and that he believed the racially superior whites of Europe might find their own solution to the social question. Yet he admitted that he saw no solution in sight and that conditions were growing worse. More to the point: the poem itself is not merely a defense of black slavery; it is a damning attack on the free-labor system. Even in the notes, where he recited the slaveholders' litany of capitalist crimes—no work, no food, no home, no human fellowship, no social responsibility for the working classes—he added, with emphasis: *"This is seen among hirelings only."* The schemes of reformers he dismissed as "vain," for the misery was inherent in the system.

In *The Letters of Curtius,* Grayson was blunter:

> Slave labor is the only organized labor ever known. It is the only condition of society in which labor and capital are associated on a large scale in which their interests are combined and not in conflict. Every plantation is an organized community, a phalanstry, as Fourier would call it—where all work, where each member gets subsistence and a home and the more industrious larger pay and profits to their own superior industry.

Could Fitzhugh or Henry Hughes have said it more forcefully?

The unionists who took that extreme ideological ground denounced secession as madness. They agreed with James H. Hammond, whose heart but not head lay with secession, that the South lacked the requisite human and material resources to win a war of national independence and that slavery could only be secured within the Union. They took the measure, as most secessionists did not, of the moral and political isolation of the South and pleaded with their southern adversaries not to play *va banque* with the very existence of the South and its social system. After all, if they were right in arguing that "free society" was sailing into a catastrophe, that its social system was doomed, and that some form of slavery was the wave of the future, then their politics made sense. As Francis W. Pickens wrote Benjamin F. Perry from Europe during the 1850s, all the South had to do was to restrain its hotheads and wait for European society to unravel. The hostility of the bourgeoisie to slavery would abate as it found itself pushed by the threat of revolution to abandon its system of class relations. Grayson spoke in such accents, no doubt with less dialectical rigor than some but with considerably more rhetorical power than most.

In other respects, too, Grayson should be read in the context of the debates within an intellectually vigorous slaveholding class in South Carolina and, more broadly, the South. I do not wish to be understood as suggesting that he should be viewed primarily as a social critic, much less as an ideologue. Respect for the man and his life's work require that we begin and end with his own primary concern—poetry—as Calhoun has done. But, however we assess the relation of his poetry to his social and political thought, Grayson clearly took that relation seriously. In so doing, despite his overt political stance he contributed more than he knew to the struggle for a southern nationality and slaveholders' worldview. That he so clearly foresaw the terrible outcome measures the extent to which the tragic history of his beloved South and his social class was also his own.

10

The Slaveholders' Contribution to the American Constitution

The word *equality* does not appear in the Constitution of the United States—except for a reference to equality among the states. And neither does the concept. Nor does the Constitution, including the Bill of Rights, say or imply anything about individual rights beyond those sanctioned by the Common Law, to which our country became heir, albeit with some reluctance. The authors of the Constitution and those who vigorously debated ratification in the states were by no means egalitarians in the sense made famous by Rousseau or Paine, Robespierre or Bakunin. And they certainly were not libertarians.

We are now told that we cannot know the intentions of the Founders, and that we have a "living Constitution"—that is, a document which means no more than the Supreme Court says it means at any given moment. It is difficult to see how anyone could credit these assertions after reading the appropriate documents. The Founders obviously could not anticipate the problems of later generations, especially those of our revolutionary high-tech society, but they did lay down firm principles to be applied to subsequent problems.

We may, if we wish, repudiate those principles and establish new ones by amending the Constitution in accordance with established procedures. We may not, if honest, pretend that the principles were not made clear and then proceed to exclude the public from rendering judgment through their elected representatives in the amendment process. As for the concept of a "living Constitution," it may fairly be asked: Why pretend to have a Constitution at all, if a majority of an appointed Supreme Court—the organ of state least accountable to public opinion—can make the Constitution say whatever it wishes?

The egalitarian ideology of the French Revolution cannot legitimately be read back into the founding of the American Republic. The southern slaveholders signed and ratified the Constitution without blushing because it did not remotely imply egalitarian doctrine. Nor did the Bill of Rights give individuals a blank check on freedom of speech, press, religion, or anything else. The slaveholders, however great their crimes against black people, mounted the first and only serious native-born critique of the totalitarian tendencies that have run wild in our century. And if I am asked how slaveholders could have laid the foundation for a constitutional and democratic republic, I must answer with the dictum of the medieval scholastics: "Existence proves possibility."

Among the shameless pretensions that now inundate us, my personal favorite is the so-called deferred commitment to equality. A product of the imagination of ideologues, it rests on the extraordinary claim that the Declaration of Independence should be considered part of the Constitution—a claim made popular by the abolitionists, sanctified by Abraham Lincoln, and now happily promoted by the media. If the Founders had intended any such thing, they would have said so. At the least, they would surely have alluded to such presumed egalitarianism somewhere in the text of the Constitution. And the American people, who ratified it only after searching debate, surely would have noticed and had something to say about it.

To make matters worse, these egalitarian claims rest on a gross misrepresentation of the Declaration itself. For, demonstrably, the signers did not understand the Declaration to mean what modern egalitarians claim it means. It should be enough to recall that a slaveholder wrote it and that slaveholders signed it. Some Americans, like Hamilton, Jay, and Madison, abhorred slavery, but even they accepted it as a fact of life and specifically sanctioned it in the Constitution they helped to write and forcefully defended. As Madison and others admitted, if the Constitution had not guaranteed the right to own slaves, it could never have been ratified. Now, whatever the Founders may have been, they were neither cowards nor hypocrites. They bravely staked their heads in defense of principle during the Revolution, and, subsequently, they fought to create and sustain a remarkable experiment in popular government that few beyond our shores thought other than wildly utopian and unrealizable.

The commitment to national self-determination that informed the Declaration and the commitment to the kind of freedom that Burke liked to call "a manly and well-ordered liberty" inspired stern resistance to those features of the Constitution that concentrated power in the hands of the national state. The Anti-Federalists who opposed the Constitution came within a whisker of prevailing, and, subsequently, a substantial number of those who supported ratification denied that the Constitution could legitimately be turned into an instrument of national consolidation.

That resistance eventually took the form of what came to be known as "strict construction" and the doctrine of states' rights, both of which have had a terrible press in this century. Twice in our history the doctrine of states' rights became the banner of those who were sustaining reprehensible causes—first slavery, and then racial segregation. No wonder, then, that most Americans reasonably assume that states' rights doctrine was never anything more than a rationalization to protect the material interests of predatory slaveholders and their spiritual descendants. And since, historically, the South has been the primary base for the doctrine of states' rights, the condemnation of the South and all its works has provided good sport for those who deconstruct the historical record to make it say whatever they want it to say. Yet states' rights was also the banner of those who had another cause altogether— the banner of fierce resistance to the centralization of power in the hands of those who served the interests of big capital.

During the eighteenth century and the early years of the nineteenth, outstanding Virginians espoused strict construction and opposed the concentration of power in the national government:

George Mason, Thomas Jefferson, John Randolph of Roanoke, St. George Tucker, and John Taylor of Caroline, among others. If strict construction and states' rights were merely or essentially a facade for the defense of slavery, we need to account for a disturbing and incontrovertible fact. Of the five, only Taylor was proslavery, and even he regarded slavery as an inherited misfortune to be tolerated rather than celebrated. The others spoke out boldly against it. In their minds and to a considerable extent in their political practice strict construction and states' rights had nothing to do with slavery.

On the other side of the struggle over the Constitution, its supporters, including the firmest nationalists, were as strong in the South as in the North. How else could we account for ratification in Virginia, the Carolinas, and Georgia? Subsequently, the nationalistic Federalist Party gave a good account of itself in the South until the War of 1812, after which it waned in the South as well as in the North. And afterward, many of the wealthiest and most powerful planters supported Whig nationalists like Henry Clay and even John Quincy Adams. No few conservative planters looked to the national government for protection against slave revolts and the leveling tendencies of nonslaveholders. They supported ratification and subsequent nationalist policies, arguing that slavery would be better protected under a property-conscious Federalist government than under a Jeffersonian government based on a majoritarian democracy.

In the next generation, even John C. Calhoun, who would emerge as the high priest of strict construction, long took nationalist ground. Not until the struggle over Missouri did southern opinion conclude that the national government represented a threat to property and local power, rather than a protective umbrella. Southern Federalists and Anti-Federalists were both generally proslavery and were quarreling over the best way to protect slavery and southern rights. Mason, Tucker, Randolph, and Jefferson defended strict construction not because they wished to strengthen slavery, but because they felt threatened by the political dictation of northeastern capital.

Southerners were not alone in advocating strict construction and states' rights. That constitutional interpretation commanded a substantial following in the North. Secessionist doctrine had in fact arisen in New England long before it made a ripple in the South. During the 1820s and 1830s, well after the Hartford Convention, two of the earliest and most powerful constitutional defenses of states' rights came from United States Supreme Court justices who hailed from Pennsylvania: William Rawle and Henry Baldwin. Rawle, although a strong nationalist, agreed with Baldwin that the Constitution did reserve enormous power to the states and that a state could lawfully secede from the Union. And notoriously, the antislavery radicals invoked states' rights to justify their refusal to enforce the Fugitive Slave Law.

Thomas Jefferson, perhaps more than any other man, stood astride the paradoxes. He wrote the draft of the Declaration, which announced that all men were created equal and entitled to life, liberty, and the pursuit of happiness, and for good measure, he pronounced that extraordinary assertion "self-evident." Jefferson denounced slavery as an abomination in memorable passages in his *Notes on Virginia*, but he refused to participate in the fight against it. And he believed in the inferiority of the black race. Indeed, he flirted with a scientific racism that was significantly more extreme than the cultural racism espoused by the great majority of his fellow Virginians. We confront here an apparent rather than a substantial contradiction.

The juxtaposition of Jefferson's views makes no sense if read through the eyes of Lincoln's Gettysburg Address, as it is now fashionable to do. His simultaneous belief in the inferiority of blacks and his opposition to slavery present no difficulty. With Mason, Tucker, Randolph, and many others, he sensibly denied that a republic, with its requisite of an active citizenry, could survive if an inferior race had access to political power. Were we to accept his notion of racial difference, we could not escape his conclusion that the blacks had to be denied civil rights. And we would have to accede to his—and Lincoln's—grand scheme to exile the blacks to Africa, the Caribbean, or wherever. But, as Jefferson saw, the presumed superiority of a race provides it with no license to exploit, much less enslave, another. Nor does such alleged racial superiority deny that slavery, with its extraordinary concentration of power in the hands of some people over others, encourages the moral and material decadence of a self-appointed superior race.

The serious difficulty arises from the allegedly self-evident truth that all men are created equal—all individuals, mind you, not just races or sexes. For if they are, how could one possibly sustain a doctrine of racial stratification or, indeed, of any kind of social stratification? Jefferson had the wit to recognize that difficulty. Yet he never retreated from either of his apparently contradictory formulations. The difficulty disappears once we lift the hymn to equality out of the context of the French Revolution's radical ideology and out of our twentieth-century romance with radical egalitarianism. For the Declaration had nothing to do with either. Nor did those who signed it, or rallied to it, believe for a moment in a literal reading of its proclamation of equality—and for the good reason that one has to be mad to think that any human being who ever walked the earth has, literally, been equal to any other in intellectual or physical endowments or in talent. Rousseau himself knew better, even if many who invoke his authority do not. Our forebears must, therefore, have had something else in mind—and they did.

For one thing, they declared that men had been "created" equal—a formulation that rests on a belief in God. There were only a handful of Deists and skeptics among them, as M. E. Bradford has demonstrated, and even they accepted the idea that a republic based on the consent of an enlightened people must have a moral consensus. All agreed that that consensus, at least for our own people, must be based on the teachings of Christianity. When they declared "truths" to be self-evident, they assumed the existence of objective truth and were thereby appealing to the judgment of a transcendent Creator.

It is true that Jefferson went to great lengths to try to separate Christian morals from Christian theology. Twice he performed the quixotic exercise of trying to rewrite the Gospels without the Trinity; without the doctrines of original sin and human depravity;

without the miracles ascribed to Jesus and the Apostles; and without everything else not to his taste. For Jefferson, Jesus was not the Christ (the savior) but a great moral teacher. Jefferson also committed the indiscretion of trying to prove that Christianity did not shape the development of the Common Law. For his pains, his tortured argument was shredded by Joseph Story, who was a great legal scholar—which Jefferson was not. The fact remains that neither Jefferson, nor Franklin, nor anyone else of importance doubted that some version of Christian morality had to support the Republic, if it were to survive and prosper.

The equality proclaimed by Christian doctrine is, in the first instance, the spiritual equality of all "men" (understood to mean human beings) in the sight of God. It is, therefore, nonsense to assert that the signers of the Declaration were thinking only of white people, much less only of white males. Their notion of equality had little to do with civic or social equality or the notion of equal political rights. Even "equality before the law" rested on the Common Law, not on an abstract philosophical appeal to individual rights. Or more accurately, to the extent to which equality before the law was inherited and sanctioned by public opinion, it reflected adherence to the very Common Law that Story correctly saw as having been informed by Christian doctrine.

Christian doctrine passed to America, in no small part, through the prism of the Scottish Enlightenment. It affirmed the moral equality of all human beings by asserting their common ability to distinguish right from wrong on essential matters, whatever the culture-bound differences in detail. As for the influence of Locke, learned scholars continue to quarrel over where he stood on these issues, and we may bracket the question of "What Locke really meant." What cannot be denied is that his greatest influence in America came through an interpretation that placed his views in harmony with those of the Scottish realist philosophers.

There is more at stake here than a refutation of the notion that the signers of the Declaration and the authors and adherents of the Constitution understood equality in the way that has become popular since Lincoln's rhetorical masterpiece at Gettysburg. Neither the Declaration nor the Constitution focused on individual rights at all. The colonies acted as corporate units in denouncing the tyranny of George III and in asserting their right to go it alone. As Wilmoore Kendall painstakingly demonstrated in *Basic Symbols of the American Political Tradition* and the essays in *Wilmoore Kendall contra Mundum*, the Declaration drew upon the corporatist tradition of the Mayflower Compact and just about every other early American document of importance. The rights of the individual, to the extent considered, were defined within particular corporate structures, to which submission was required. The rights asserted were, first and foremost, the rights of historically evolved communities to which all individuals owed loyalty and obedience.

Nor will it do to invoke the Bill of Rights as a counterpoint in support of the thesis that individual rights were at issue. First, ratification of the Constitution occurred before the Bill of Rights was promulgated. One has to be dreaming to believe that the American people, whose jealousy of their own rights had already become legendary, would have blithely referred a decision on a Bill of Rights to Congress if they had thought such amendments essential to the preservation of their liberties. Congress, in fact, dawdled over passage of the first ten amendments. Madison had to work incessantly just to get the attention of a Congress that, contrary to myth, was feeling no great pressure from its constituents. The Bill of Rights did no more than to underscore what most people assumed the Constitution had already made clear.

As for that much touted First Amendment—what, in fact, did it say? It said, "Congress shall make no law . . ." That is, it prevented only the national government from intervening in matters of speech, press, and religion. No one suggested that government, as such, should not have the power to restrict individual liberties in the collective interest. Various states had established churches at the time. And until well into the nineteenth century, various states barred Jews, Catholics, and especially nonbelievers from holding office. Few people, if any, claimed that the proscriptions violated the federal Constitution. In short, the so-called wall of separation between church and state was never understood as a wall between society and religion. Not even Thomas Jefferson went that far.

The First Amendment was designed to prevent the establishment of a national church. All through the nineteenth century and even into the twentieth, state governments supported religious institutions in all sorts of ways. Most notably, the school systems of the states openly espoused Christian values and gave the churches special recognition. The American people simply assumed that the principal purpose of education was the moral instruction of youth. And they further assumed that, in the specific experience of our own people, the relevant morality had to be Christian. The recent Supreme Court decisions that have tried to legislate a wholly secular society have no foundation either in the Constitution that was written, ratified, and accepted by pubic opinion for more than a century or in anything else except the arbitrary judgment of a Court that has, in effect, usurped executive and legislative functions and has the temerity to pretend that it is merely reaffirming time-honored doctrine and practice.

Here let us review the record of the South in general and of the slaveholders in particular on religion and religious freedom. Contrary to Yankee propaganda, southerners have always been more tolerant of religious differences than northerners. The struggle for religious freedom proved much easier to win in the South than in the North. In early colonial days, when New England was setting the standard for enforced religious conformity, South Carolina was leading the way in religious toleration, with Virginia not far behind. The Anglican Church was the established church in South Carolina and Virginia, much as the Congregational Church was the established church in Massachusetts. But the toleration accorded dissidents was immeasurably higher in the South. Witches were burned and Quakers hanged in Massachusetts. No such atrocities disgraced the plantation colonies.

In the early days of the Republic, the southern Baptists led the fight for religious freedom and the separation of church and state. Thomas Jefferson deserves the credit accorded him for his leadership in the fight for religious freedom in Virginia, but, as he readily acknowledged, that fight could never have been won without the militant agitation and organizational efforts of the

Baptists. It was they, above all others, who delivered the necessary votes, and who thereby set an example for the rest of the nation.

The slave states sent the first two Jews to the United States Senate and would have provided the first Jew to sit on the United States Supreme Court, if Judah Benjamin had accepted the proffered nomination in the 1850s. Jews and Catholics, as they freely acknowledged, found a much warmer reception among the slaveholders of the Old South than among the propertied classes of the North. In the last decades before secession, Catholic convents were burned and nuns terrorized in the cities of the Northeast. Southerners responded with disbelief, the more so since it was no secret that some abolitionist ministers had been encouraging anti-Catholic bigotry. When Protestant hooligans threatened to attack the Catholic Church in Charleston, the city fathers, with solid public support, let them know that they would tolerate no nonsense. The attack never occurred, for no one doubted that when southern gentlemen said they would tolerate no nonsense, they meant precisely what they said.

Historians love to recount every example of religious bigotry they can find in the Old South—and, surely, the South had its share. But something has gone unnoticed. Those examples of bigotry overwhelmingly come from the yeoman regions of the hill country. The plantation South stood like a rock for religious tolerance. The Know-Nothings had their fling in the South as in the North, but in the South, they had to go to inordinate lengths to deny that they were anti-Catholic. In Virginia, when they ran an avowed anti-Catholic for governor in the 1850s, they threw away what looked like a sure victory against a discredited Democratic Party. He went down to a humiliating defeat. In Louisiana, the Know-Nothings made a desperate attempt to clean up their act by nominating a Catholic for governor.

Now it is true that the South remained orthodox in its Christianity while the North was embracing liberal theology and abandoning the fundamental tenets of historic Christian doctrine—from original sin and human depravity to the doctrine of the Trinity. And even today a lot of folks, white and black, still attend churches in Dixie that preach something that approaches

Christian orthodoxy. They nonetheless have lived with others in a spirit of mutual toleration overmatched nowhere else in the country. To be sure, southerners are not about to pretend that they regard another's religion as intrinsically equal to their own, but they have generally displayed strong opposition to attempts to impose religious tests and to inquire into other people's private beliefs.

As for freedom of speech and the press, the Virginians and Kentuckians whose famous resolutions of the 1790s threw down the gauntlet over the Alien and Sedition Acts did not deny that government could restrict those presumed rights. They argued only that the national government was barred from doing so. In the North, the great Joseph Story opposed the Alien and Sedition Acts as unwise and dangerous—he later recanted his opposition—but neither he nor most other legal scholars argued that such laws were unconstitutional, much less that they would be unconstitutional if promulgated in the states.

Southern conservatives, beginning with the slaveholders, adhered to what, in our own century, Richard Weaver called "social bond individualism": a Christian, rather than a bourgeois, individualism that asserts the inviolability of the human personality against the state but that, with Aristotle, assumes that the individual personality can only mature within a community to which one owes allegiance and accepts duties and responsibilities. It is an individualism that emphatically rejects visions of personal liberation—of a New Man and New Woman liberated from the constraints of those rules and prejudices necessary to community life.

For, in truth, the states' rights interpretation of the Constitution was advanced not as a political dogma, but as a constitutional means toward the higher end of protecting community life. During the twentieth century, southern conservatives, picking up a strong hint from Calhoun, have abandoned states' rights and called for a new constitution that would recognize regional, rather than state, autonomy. Their constant theme has been the rejection of the Leviathan national state and its centralization of political and economic power. They demand that, as it were, power be restored to the people.

It ought to be obvious that, to mean anything at all, "power to the people" must mean considerable decentralization of power and, with it, the restoration of power to the smallest units possible, that is, to historically evolved communities. But communities are based on shared assumptions, values, and faith. They are necessarily based on shared prejudices and are exclusive, not inclusive. To put it another way, they will, more often than not, vote against the pet projects of radical democrats and egalitarians, who therefore prefer to express the people's will by concentrating power in the national government. And as all experience shows, that means to concentrate power in an entrenched bureaucracy, bolstered by a judicial system that declares as constitutional right whatever the reigning elite formulates as social policy.

Those on the Left who denigrate the doctrine of states' rights pretend not to notice that it has been inextricably bound up with opposition to finance capitalism and the voracious appetite of big business. From John Taylor of Caroline to John C. Calhoun, and, in our own century, from Allen Tate and the Southern Agrarians to Richard Weaver and the late M. E. Bradford, southern conservatives have proclaimed their hostility to both capitalism and socialism and especially to the concentration of economic and political power inherent in each.

For all that, the doctrine of states' rights never could stand the acid test that the nationalists put to it. For it simply could not sustain a republic that aspired to world-historic greatness—to world power in the context of a rapidly expanding world capitalist market. I confess to thinking that the southerners bested the Yankees in the constitutional debates of the nineteenth century. I am even more strongly convinced that the proslavery theologians bested their antislavery counterparts over the question of whether the Bible sanctioned slavery.

No matter. John Marshall, Joseph Story, and the other great architects of the nationalist interpretation had an unanswerable political argument. The political fate of the Republic depended upon its successful participation in the process of capitalist development—a process that only a strong and largely consolidated national state could facilitate. And, in a world of rival nations, the security of the Republic depended upon a military capacity that required a high level of political centralization.

Hence the struggle between the centralizers and the particularists has bequeathed to us a quandary that the War for Southern Independence by no means resolved. What the slaveholders contributed most of all was their unshakable insight that bourgeois social relations irresistibly generated a self-revolutionizing social and economic system that dissolved family and community and made the marketplace the arbiter of moral and social life. Southerners objected not to a market economy, but to the transformation of that economy into the essence of society itself. They objected, that is, to the transformation of all spiritual and moral values into commodities. The best of southern conservative thought has carried this critique forward in our own century—a theme I have pursued in *The Southern Tradition: The Achievements and Limitations of an American Conservatism.*

In antebellum times, northern conservatives shared much of the slaveholders' hostility to egalitarianism, radical democracy, and the cultural degradation they perceived as accompanying an unbridled capitalism. But they looked to a national government under their own control to ensure the prevalence of republican principles against democratic excesses. That very control was, however, already slipping from their grasp by the end of the eighteenth century, and it disappeared during the Jackson period. Whereas southern conservatives, as slaveholders, presided over an alternate, if unpalatable, social order, northern conservatives like Story and John Quincy Adams spoke for a declining commercial elite that, notwithstanding its own increasing shift into industrial investment, was proving powerless against the juggernaut of a new and more ruthless class of financial sharpies and heartland entrepreneurs.

In one sense, the War for Southern Independence pit two kinds of conservatism against each other, and with an ironic outcome. For, as Lewis P. Simpson has trenchantly argued in *Mind and the American Civil War*, the triumph of the Union army spelled the defeat of those northern as well as southern conservatives who sought to rein in the political and cultural ravages of the industrial revolution and the rise of big business.

Let us waste no time on the obvious: The slaveholders' alternative to bourgeois society was simply not to be borne. And let us concede that the rise of the welfare state has abolished many of the evils complained of. Still, an astonishing worldwide economic integration is now taking place under the aegis of multinational corporate conglomerates, which are inherently and indeed proudly amoral. The emerging international business and technocratic elite blithely accepts a wide array of social policies, to say nothing of "alternate lifestyles," that do not seriously interfere with business and in fact provide new and extraordinary fields for profitable investment. The emerging elite sees no need to assume responsibility for such social and moral problems as the destruction of black youth, the collapse of the family, the prevalence of drugs and pornography. Animality and filth, like everything else, have become commodities, which people are called upon to tolerate as expressions of freedom and feel free to buy as much of as they wish.

The problems remain with us: How do we simultaneously protect the private property upon which, as recent experience forcefully demonstrates, a free society must rest and, at the same time, provide for public participation and ultimate control? How do we recognize the necessity for considerable concentration of political power in a world of multinational corporations and discrete nation-states and yet arrest the homogenization— and destruction—of cultures and communities that provide the only, if increasingly fragile, bulwark against the threat of a thinly disguised totalitarianism and cultural barbarism?

This is not the place to plunge into a debate over possible political solutions to the crisis of our time. But I hope that I have at least indicated that the southern political tradition, for which, alas, slaveholders laid the foundation, has much to offer us in the clarification of issues; that it has been clear-eyed in its understanding of the relation between moral issues and the form and content of property ownership; and that it has been right to insist that any solution must be based on a republican Constitution that leaves a wide swath for individual freedom while giving priority to the collective interests of the community.

Southerners may—and should—be called upon to repudiate their legacy of slavery, segregation, and racism, but they have every reason to insist that the Old South stood for a lot more than that. They have every reason to honor the memory of their forefathers' heroic struggle to create and sustain the modern world's first great republic and to refuse to repent in sackcloth and ashes for the finest and most wholesome features of southern life. In the juxtaposition of the wholesome side of the southern legacy with the ghastly lies the tragedy of southern history.

And that lesson of the evil that honorable men may do our prescient Founders took to heart. They left us a Constitution well designed to resist the invention of countless and presumed individual "rights," which in practice end as a justification for a massive concentration of power in hands of socially irresponsible elites. And they left a legacy that recognizes as legitimate the claims both of society and of the individual—the legacy of a society that deserves to be called "free" because it places the burden of proof on those who would restrict individual expression, not because it places individual expression above the common interest. May we, as a people, prove worthy of that legacy.

Religion

There was a time when you held
it a mark of special courage to
cast off partially the restraints of
inherited dogmas. You were still
willing to discuss particular subjects,
though it were only to efface one
of those notions. Such a figure as
religion moving gracefully, adorned
in eloquence, still pleased you, if
only that you wished to maintain
in the gentler sex a certain feeling
for sacred things. But that time is
long past. Piety is now no more to
be spoken of, and even the Graces,
with most unwomanly hardness,
destroy the tenderest blossoms of
the human heart, and I can link the
interest I require from you to nothing
but your contempt. I will ask you,
therefore, just to be well-informed
and thorough-going in this contempt.

—*Friedrich Schleiermacher*

11

Christendom under Siege

The abolitionists, in launching an ultimately successful crusade, assaulted a social relation that had been ubiquitous in world history and continued to infect every corner of the earth during much of the nineteenth century. The dominant religions everywhere accepted slavery as part of the social order. Only in the West did a great movement arise to assert everyman's right to freedom, and it arose primarily on Christian foundations. Notwithstanding the centuries-long complicity of the Christian churches in slavery, the abolitionists were able to mount an ideological challenge based on Christian theology. They advanced a doctrine of individual freedom based upon a doctrine of the immortality of the soul and of sin as a direct offense against God, not merely the community of men. Not always skillfully or even honestly, the abolitionists interpreted the Bible as antislavery, and we may thank God and the big battalions that, whatever their sins against intellectual integrity, they prevailed.

The slaveholders and their theologically conservative allies fought back, citing chapter and verse to prove that slavery was divinely ordained. Those who think that the Word of God ought to mean what the Bible says it does must give the defenders of slavery high marks for their learned, intellectually acute argumentation in a ghastly cause. Fortunately, learned discourse counts for much less in historical crises than intellectuals prefer to think, and the slaveholders went down to a deserved and overdue defeat.

Under the circumstances, we should expect a book on the historical relation of Christianity to slavery and racism to file an indictment against the churches for their long complicity with slavery.
Forrest Wood opens *The Arrogance of Faith* with a discussion of
Christianity's historical engagement with slavery and racism and
then proceeds to his main subject, the Christian experience in
the United States and especially the South. Accordingly, we might
have hoped for a solid synthesis that could steel us for the battle
against today's resurgent racism.

Alas, we have fallen under the Chinese curse, "May you live
in interesting times," and ideological outrages in ostensibly good
causes are becoming a way of life in Academia. William Bennett,
neoconservative hero of the Right and bête noire of the Left,
deserves to have his knuckles bloodied for his sadly un-Burkean
defense of a narrow and bigoted literary canon, but he deserves
gratitude for his blunt and accurate definition of the central issue
in the enfolding cultural war. He has told a truth that few wish to
hear: Those who are today attacking the canon have no interest in
reforming it to include the great black, female, and other voices
ignorantly and maliciously excluded. They are not so much attacking courses in Western civilization as attacking Western civilization
itself. And they are doing so dishonestly.

Wood files an indictment not merely against the principal
Christian churches, which have a lot to answer for, but against
Christianity itself. "The central thesis of this book," he writes, "is
that Christianity, in the five centuries since its message was first
carried to the peoples of the New World—and, in particular, to
the natives and the transplanted Africans of English North America
and the United States—has been fundamentally racist in ideology,
organization, and practice."

Wood claims originality especially for his thesis that the Christian churches provided politically valuable rationalizations for
slavery, racism, colonialism, and imperialism. In fact, the story of
the complicity of the churches has been told often and well. Even
his ideologically charged formulation has its pedigree as well as
its grain of truth. More to the point, Wood goes to great lengths to
try to show what he palpably cannot show—that Christianity and

Western civilization indulged in horrors that other religions and civilizations never dreamed of. All that he actually does show will not come as news: The great technological, economic, and military breakthroughs—the commercial and industrial revolutions that made world conquest possible—came in Christian countries and with much church support. That rival religions would not have accommodated a Chinese, Indian, Zulu, or Malaysian conquest of the world may be doubted.

Wood tries to cover his tracks by writing, "One can never be sure if Hinduism, confronted by the irresistible lure of capital and power, would have compromised its fundamental integrity, because it was never in a position to do so." If, however, the lure of capital and power was indeed "irresistible," we may ask just what the question reduces to, and we may, at the least, note that the periodic bloodletting of Hindus, Muslims, and Buddhists in Southeast Asia invite an unpleasant speculation. The rhetorical burden of this book and much of its craftily ambiguous argumentation constitute a condemnation of Christianity as a faith especially oriented toward racism, slavery, imperialism, and mass murder. Wood adds to his remarks about the last five centuries: "But one can say that, good works notwithstanding, there has been no greater religious force in the dehumanization of humans than Christianity, the self-proclaimed religion of peace, brotherly love, and fellowship."

In the end, then, Christianity and the West stand condemned as the great enemies of the world's peoples, whose traditions ostensibly have been more freedom-loving and less ethnocentric and arrogant. If so, we need to hear the reason that those very peoples look to the political theories and institutions of the West every time they raise the banner of freedom against tyranny.

No wonder that courses in Western civilization are in disrepute among the enemies of Western civilization. If taught with a modicum of honesty, such courses could hardly deny that the very concept of individual freedom, as generally understood and cherished even by the noisiest radicals, arose in the West and on Christian foundations. They could not deny what Wood labors to obscure in his muddled excursions into theology—that Christian doctrines provided the moral ground on which the exponents of freedom could stand.

Wood's romance with the Third World generates its own problems. He squirms on Islam as on much else, for he must explain the racist and oppressive features of non-Christian religions while underscoring his judgment that, for savagery, Christianity remains in a class by itself. The Muslims, we are told, "eschewed forced conversions and the persecutions of religious dissent" in their great jihads and territorial expansion. Christians and Jews who refused to convert "only had to pay higher taxes." That the laying of tribute on whole communities qualifies as a bagatelle may be questioned, but let us not quibble. Still, Wood forgets to mention the third choice offered: Those who refused to convert or pay tribute were, in the language of the day, put to the sword.

Wood pursues the theme of a gentler slavery in Islam in his customary fashion. He admits that racism also emerged in Islam, but he gives it short shrift, noting that manumission rates in Muslim countries were higher than in Christian countries. (A more appropriate comparison would be between the plantation regions of both sets of countries.) And he acidly refers to "the American situation, first established by the law of southern colonies, where children always assumed the status of the mother." Those awful Christians again. And no matter that they were following not canon law, but the precedent of pre-Christian Roman law. Well, almost no matter. For what are we to make of Wood's remark that "English North Americans embraced slavery *because* they were Christians, not in spite of it"? (Original emphasis here and throughout.) Perhaps Wood does make a just claim for his own originality after all. I myself had not been aware that the English colonists embraced slavery either because or in spite of their being Christians.

Wood advances some strange notions in a constant conflation of intent and result. Thus he writes of the missionary work among Africans: "Whether or not the Christian realized he was disrupting traditional life was probably irrelevant because he almost certainly would not have cared anyway. The dogmatic mind claimed exclusive access to the truth and thus was inherently incapable of compromising because it saw no reason to." The history of the Jesuits, among others, may be read more generously. For that matter, though I hate having to say a good word about Protestant missionaries, their history may also be read more generously. The history of the Christian missions has not been uniformly glorious, and a harsh judgment may be rendered on much of it. But it has been a complex terrain of struggle among warring tendencies within the churches themselves, and that part of the story must be told if we are ever to understand the continuing power of Christianity among decolonized peoples.

In a typical observation, Wood reveals his method of argumentation: "If anyone needs a vivid lesson in the expansive power of Christianity, he has only to reflect on the fact that on the eve of the twenty-first century the largest Roman Catholic edifice in the world is in Yamoussourko, Ivory Coast." Yes, indeed we should reflect. But it would be useful for reflection to recall that a secular national government built that edifice to celebrate its own glory, and that it did so over the protests of the Catholic Church, which thought the money would be better invested in economic development and relief for the poor. Wood also fails to mention that when the Church made its plea, the Ivory Coast's cynical politicians wittily charged it with "racism" for allegedly trying to prevent an African country's having the world's largest church building.

In advancing his claim to originality, Wood loves to pour it on. He finds Reinhold Niebuhr guilty of "pontification"; he dismisses William Jennings Bryan as "the Bible-thumping populist from Nebraska"; and he slyly files a blatantly stupid suggestion of racism—or does he mean "insensitivity"?—against David Brion Davis, the greatest living historian of slavery, whose monumental scholarship breathes an unrelenting hostility to racism in every form. Presumably, a man who loves to pour it on may be expected to respond with a good-humored chuckle when some of it gets poured back.

Historians, in reviewing each other's books, often pass lightly over factual errors. I know I do. I have never read—or written— a book that does not contain some embarrassing errors, some of them real dumb. Self-interest aside, compassion for human frailty, common decency, and a sense of humor intervene to temper justice with mercy. The unwritten rules of our profession require that we point out only those errors which undermine the author's thesis, or are likely to cause serious mischief, or, when taken together, are likely to undermine confidence in his competence. When many of the errors are howlers that make us wonder if he knows his subject at all, even the most merciful reviewer cannot pass lightly without prostituting himself.

For a start, Wood's paraphrase of documents and secondary works cannot be trusted, especially on the numerous occasions when he writes the words *of course* and *in other words*. As a typical illustration, he writes: "Shortly before the Civil War the Rev. B. M. Palmer claimed that God had entrusted the black race to the care of the white—a 'trust providentially committed to us'—which meant that the South was obliged to *'conserve and to perpetuate the institution of slavery as now existing.'*" Palmer, an important man much discussed by historians, ranked among the South's best-known and most-respected divines, and the widely circulated published version of his famous fire-eating sermon set the Southwest ablaze for the secessionists.

Wood interprets Palmer's words and those of other leading divines as advocating the permanent enslavement of blacks by divine command. That interpretation lies at the heart of Wood's subsequent discussion of the mythical sin of Ham. The problem, however, is that neither Palmer nor the other leading divines with whom he was most closely associated preached such a message. Quite the contrary. Led by James Henley Thornwell of South Carolina, Palmer's mentor and the acknowledged giant of the southern clergy, they preached a doctrine of ultimate deliverance under Christian tutelage. (How effectively they preached it is another matter.) Wood does not tell his readers what he himself ought to know if he read the books he cites in his bibliography: Members of Palmer's church challenged him to clarify his meaning on that very point. He replied by emphatically denying the imputation made by some of them and here repeated by Wood. He insisted that his remarks were being wrenched out of context, as indeed they were.

Or consider Wood's excoriation of Calvinism: "In other words, it was through commitment to Christ, economic abundance, and purity in conduct that one was assured of election. Hard work (the Protestant ethic) and clean mind (Puritan morality) were tickets to salvation." Calvinism has been caricatured many times at many hands by people who know nothing about it, but rarely if ever in so asinine a manner. It should be enough to note that Wood attaches to the idea of predestinarianism a totally unassimilable doctrine of salvation by works. That small matter aside, my first thought was that Wood was confusing John Calvin and James Henley Thornwell with Oral Roberts, but I reminded myself that I could not be right since Roberts is not a Calvinist. Then, still rubbing my eyes, I noticed that Wood's text and footnotes refer to Paul Tillich, not to Calvin or any American Calvinists. Notwithstanding the problems I have with Tillich's theology, I could not recall his ever having peddled such rubbish, so I went back to his *History of Christian Thought*, which Wood cites. No. Whatever one may think of Tillich's critique of Calvinism, it never remotely descends to the gross caricature that Wood invokes.

Yet even this gaffe does not much matter. For Wood goes after Calvinism hammer and tongs, giving the impression, as many historians are fond of doing, that the Old South wallowed in predestinarianism. He seems not to reflect upon what he surely knows—that the Arminian and harshly anti-Calvinistic Methodists emerged as the strongest denominational contingent among the whites of the slaveholding South. For that matter, even the Baptists, as well as the adherents of other denominations with Calvinist roots, were in steady retreat from predestinarianism, and the Methodists were justly celebrating the victory of their Arminian doctrines of free will and salvation for all repentant sinners. Wood might profit from reading the theological works of Thornwell, the most intransigent spokesman for the Old School Presbyterians, for even there one finds some surprising concessions to human agency.

The list of howlers in this book is daunting. Wood describes Daniel O'Connell, the great leader of the Irish emancipation movement, as an Irish-American. He denounces the northern divines for being racists and soft on slavery and cites two cases as representative, describing Frederick A. Ross as a "prominent northern Presbyterian minister." Ross certainly was a prominent figure, important enough to draw fire from Abraham Lincoln and praise from Andrew Johnson. But a northerner he was not. The son of a slaveholding planter, he was born and raised in Virginia and served as a pastor in Tennessee and Alabama.

Another of Wood's attributions ranks as my favorite. Wood goes on for pages in a pompous and biased assault on the Roman Catholic Church's complex engagement with slavery and racism. It is a story that has been much better told by any number of others, including some fine Catholic historians who have not shrunk from exposing their church's worst offenses. The measure of Wood's account may be taken from his singling out several bishops as particular culprits, among them George Foster Pierce of Georgia. Again, Pierce does deserve careful attention. He was an influential figure in the political as well as religious life of the Southeast, and for good measure he served for a while as president of Georgia Women's College in Macon, which pioneered in higher education for women. He may well have qualified as a racist, but Wood might have mentioned that he also fought for laws to protect slave families, enable slaves to read, and punish cruel masters.

After a few years Georgia Female College was transformed into Wesleyan Female College. The name might have made Wood thoughtful. Even in our own ecumenical times the Catholic Church does not name its institutions after John Wesley. And Pierce was the son of the well-known Reverend Lovick Pierce, as Wood should know since almost all the sources that mention George Foster Pierce mention his father. The curiosity of an allegedly Roman Catholic bishop's having a reverend for a father might also have made Wood thoughtful, but it did not. In any case, George Foster Pierce did indeed rise to become a bishop of his and his father's church: The Methodist Episcopal Church, South.

Time and again Wood leaves his readers with ideologically loaded false impressions. Thus he implies that the southern divines, in defending slavery, defended the African slave trade. In fact, the overwhelming majority of the leading divines opposed the trade vigorously. Wood here confuses two separate issues: their speculation on God's providence in initially having permitted the slave trade, and their theological and political response to the demands to reopen it. Or to take an even more flagrant example, Wood claims that the proslavery divines could only make a scriptural case "by ignoring certain important features of Old Testament slavery." He then refers to the six-year limit on servitude of fellow Israelites and to related matters that, in fact, the divines ably discussed in sermon after sermon, pamphlet after pamphlet.

Wood's attempts to intervene in the disputes over the meaning of biblical texts are simply embarrassing. Especially so is his discussion of the Golden Rule, which both proslavery and abolitionist writers invoked. He misrepresents the proslavery argument, missing its main point: If, as the abolitionists alleged, the Golden Rule condemned slavery on the grounds that no one would want to be treated as a slave, then, by extension, it must have condemned virtually all forms of authority and subordination. Do you, then, the proslavery divines asked, mean to invoke the Bible in the manner of the few confessed anarchists in your ranks, whom most of you denounce as infidels and Jacobins? In such terms did the southern divines link the defense of slavery to the defense of social order and to Christian principle itself.

We may, if we wish, judge their arguments politically odious and unacceptable, but, contrary to Wood's superficial polemics, intellectually contemptible they were not. And indeed, the southern divines' powerful case proved politically and ideologically irresistible in the deeply religious South. Southerners read their Bible and earnestly sought God's sanction for their social and political relations. The tragedy of the divines' performance resulted not, as Wood would have us believe, from its intellectual shoddiness but, to the contrary, from its impressive intellectual force in defense of a towering social evil.

For an index to Wood's polemical style, turn to his discussion of Thornwell's view of the Golden Rule. Thornwell insisted that under the Golden Rule a master must treat his slaves as he would feel he ought to be treated if legitimately enslaved. Wood comments:

"Apparently it never occurred to Thornwell—or he never publicly acknowledged it—that the *first* thing he would 'feel' that he ought to receive if he were enslaved would be his freedom." But the question certainly did occur to Thornwell, who went to considerable lengths to establish the legitimacy of the enslavement of whites as well as blacks and therefore the illegitimacy of the complaint. And so did Ross, Thornton Stringfellow, George Armstrong, Thomas R. R. Cobb, John Fletcher, and numerous other proslavery writers, clerical and lay. They cannot fairly be accused by anyone who reads them of an unwillingness to reply to arguments they met head-on and at great length.

Thornwell was a great man who, according to his understanding of the light God had given him, lived and spent his last breath in an unrelenting struggle to lead his flock in the ways of God and to uphold a proper Christian social order. However unworthy the social cause to which he devoted his extraordinary talent, he scorned to indulge in evasions in his carefully honed sermons and discourses, which may be read with profit to this day. But one claim for Thornwell that even his most ardent admirers have never made is the very claim that Wood does make. By no stretch of the imagination can Thornwell be called "the real leader of American Presbyterianism." Perhaps he deserved to be, but just about every Presbyterian north of the Mason-Dixon Line would have roared with laughter at the assertion. Wood is here quoting Alice Felt Tyler's generally useful *Freedom's Ferment*, and we should be grateful that he quotes no further from her short paragraph on the Presbyterians in the sectional crisis, for it is riddled with errors that would be spotted immediately by anyone who has read the relevant works in Wood's bibliography.

Considerations of space forbid the cataloging of sundry other atrocities—gems such as the grave warning that churches which refuse to ordain women thereby expose themselves as racist. This dreadful book should nonetheless be taken seriously as a sign of the disarray in Academia and at our most distinguished publishing houses. Anything that comes with a cri de coeur for the poor, the oppressed, and the downtrodden passes muster and may be expected to be greeted with hosannas, no matter how absurd the arguments and blundering the scholarship. In its own way, *The Arrogance of Race* does constitute an important event. It stands as a testimonial to the standards that have been reigning in the historical profession since the Establishment capitulated to the demands for political and ideological conformity that were championed by the McCarthyites of the 1950s and have been carried forward by leftwing radicals ever since.

12

Religious Foundations of the Constitution

Within the historical profession most celebrations of the Constitution and the founding of the Republic have proved gloomy affairs, remarkable primarily for the promulgation of sectarian political agendas. Suffice it to recall that the *Journal of American History*, apparently determined to confirm "political correctness" as the guiding spirit of the Organization of American Historians, published an issue on the Constitution from which it coolly excluded such accomplished conservative scholars as Forrest McDonald, not to mention various unreliable liberals.

There is a bright side. Never before have the luminaries of our professional Establishment, who capitulated to the McCarthyites in the fifties and are now capitulating to their leftwing counterparts, displayed so rich a sense of humor. Taking a page from Orwell, they have solemnly offered their mean-spirited repression of dissenting voices as a contribution to "diversity." And there is a grim side. Once again, the Establishment has anointed its favorite spokesmen for the Left, but this time with unprecedented justification. Radical chic has triumphed because our leftwing colleagues have declined to dissociate themselves publicly from those anointed and from the reigning practices of political correctness, although many of them privately express dismay with much gnashing of teeth. So be it. But let us hope that those who censor themselves on grounds of *pas d'ennemis à gauche* are

142

prepared to accept full responsibility for their complicity in the dishonoring of the frail remains of their political movement.

Meanwhile, admirable studies of the Constitution are being published and will be studied long after the trash has been forgotten. Occasionally one comes from the Left, as evidenced by Jennifer Nedelsky's fine *Private Property and the Limits of American Constitutionalism*. Yet, however much some of us may wince, the conservatives whom our profession is treating as nonpersons if not lepers are publishing much of the work that promises to provide the basis for an intellectually and politically honest reassessment of our constitutional history—for example, Forrest McDonald's *Novus Ordo Seclorum*, Thomas Pangle's *The Spirit of Modern Republicanism*, and Paul Rahe's *Republics, Ancient and Modern*.

Here, we are concerned with yet another: Ellis Sandoz's *A Government of Laws: Political Theory, Religion, and the American Founding*, which like Pangle's study, sheds much light on the original impact and continuing influence of classical thought on the course of the American Republic, and which, like such earlier work as M. E. Bradford's *A Worthy Company* and related essays, strives to restore the religious dimension of American republican thought. Sandoz, like Bradford and McDonald, is a southerner and, notwithstanding a regrettable effort to distance himself, he is heir to an impressive conservative tradition of a special if largely ignored type. A professor of political science at Louisiana State University, Sandoz speaks in the accents of his mentor, the great philosopher-historian Eric Voegelin, whose works may yet achieve their rightful place as required reading in our graduate schools. Director of the Eric Voegelin Institute for American Renaissance Studies, Sandoz studies the Constitution in an illuminating transatlantic framework, but he weakens his effort by bypassing the distinctly southern contribution to it.

A Government of Laws begins with first principles. Even before Aristotle, Sandoz insists, all discussions of political and social order have been about "the nature of human beings and human existence itself." He contrasts the various forms of "radical man" in Comte, Marx, Bakunin, and Nietzsche with his preferred "liberal man" of Locke and the Founders. The Constitution appears here as a practicable instrument for a rational politics that avoids the calamitous error of having humanity try to solve most if not all its problems through politics.

The founding of the Republic emerges as a "unique anti-modernist rearticulation of Western civilization," deeply responsive to classical and Christian influences. It reaffirms "the central principle of medieval constitutional theory by establishing limited government and rule of law in direct opposition to modern tendencies toward statism, absolutism, tyranny, ideological politics, and totalitarianism." In Sandoz's cautiously optimistic view, this fundamental tendency remains dominant in American political life. Since he here concerns himself with the founding, he does not discuss the continuing political struggle to keep that tendency alive, let alone dominant. But he clearly intends his discussion of origins, theory, and spirit as a contribution toward the strengthening of that tendency.

A Government of Laws offers rich fare, to which no brief account could do justice. The opening chapter on political obligation mounts a telling attack on moral relativism and "the shattering of the 'givenness' of existence as symbolized in the hierarchical representation of being." It includes an especially good discussion of the reification of "property" and the reduction of social relations—of society itself—to the marketplace. Sandoz carefully distinguishes the ideals of the Founders from the subsequent perversions introduced by the free-market liberalism that today passes for conservatism. In vigorously defending private property as necessary for a just social order that respects individual freedom, he scorns to celebrate the marketplace as a veritable substitute for society itself. And to his credit, despite his aversion to Marxism he does not hesitate to draw upon the scholarship and insights of C. B. Macpherson to bolster his case. Regrettably, he does not draw upon the contributions of the many southern conservative theorists who engaged this problem with direct reference to the Constitution.

Subsequent chapters discuss the "civil theology" of American constitutionalism, the "classical and Christian dimensions of American political thought," civil rights, and much else. The chapters invite challenges and quarrels, as they were doubtless intended to. The book as a whole is nonetheless open to the charge of excessive abstraction, of questionable intellectualization, and of silence about the specific social and political struggles through which the principles Sandoz upholds have been sustained. For myself, I am distressed by his inattention to the great sectional conflict over the interpretation of the Constitution and the slavery question that lay at its root, for they were prefigured in the early constitutional debates on which he focuses. Others will find themselves distressed over other matters. But one of the great strengths of this unusually learned and thoughtful book lies in the light it indirectly sheds on the very questions it does not directly engage.

In America the Constitution has often been criticized as an instrument of an antidemocratic counter-revolution, but at the time of the founding and for long after most revolutionaries and radicals throughout the world viewed the republic it created as a beacon. In defending the essentially democratic character of the Constitution, Sandoz forcefully draws attention to the resonance of the great philosophers of ancient and medieval Europe in the Founders' concerns, thought, and practice. He argues, "The founders consciously, explicitly, and shrewdly sought within the limits of the practicable to establish a just political order, one fully attentive to the demands of human nature and its differentiated ontological existence." He suggests that the Founders' *novus ordo seclorum* "continues to serve as the pulse and standard of American reality in the contemporary world, and, equally, to be experienced by the affected community as a particular historical embodiment of the enduring truth of universal reality."

The Founders, Sandoz approvingly writes, regarded man as "capable of virtue and faith but inclined to vice and sin." He notes the claims of democracy in the Christian doctrine of equality, understood as everyman's possession of a common nature bestowed by God, and—*pace* those who rail against Eurocentrism—he argues cogently that modern ideas of freedom and democracy would be incomprehensible if abstracted from the Christian inheritance of Western civilization.

That the notions of freedom and democracy now embraced throughout the world are of Western origin can be contested only by those for whom the clear historical record may be deconstructed so as to be read as its opposite—that is, by crooks. That the separate meanings of freedom and democracy may be conflated, as Sandoz does in his weaker moments, is another matter. Sandoz offers a serviceable if one-sided critique of Marx, which falls short of Voegelin's own but adequately shreds the monstrous fantasy of a New Man, New Woman, and New World. The decks cleared, he proceeds to a respectful discussion of Locke in which he demonstrates less a shift from a religious to a secular discourse than a fateful shift within the religious discourse itself. He thus stresses the Christian foundations of Locke's defense of property and natural law. Sandoz's appreciative yet deeply critical appraisal of Locke and his influence on American thought deserves careful discussion, as well as comparison and contrast with that offered in Pangle's *The Spirit of Modern Republicanism.*

Laying considerable stress on Locke's influence, Sandoz wisely warns against any effort to transform the Founders into mere disciples. Rather, he notes their eclecticism, which especially expressed itself in a readiness to draw upon the whole of the Western tradition, most notably its classical and Christian texts, in a manner that rejected a single philosophical standpoint and incorporated the spirit and wisdom of their ancient and medieval forebears. Sandoz protests against the short shrift given the classical and Christian moorings of the Constitution by historians, and an important part of his purpose is to initiate a reappraisal.

Toward that end he puts his erudition to work to show how those philosophical moorings prepared the Founders to grasp "the hierarchical structure of democracy." Here as elsewhere he ably connects religion and politics both theoretically and practically. But here as elsewhere he becomes obscure on the relation of political democracy to an acceptance of the necessity for hierarchy in the social as well as natural order.

The perspective that Sandoz brings to his interpretation of the Constitution, the founding, and the spirit of American republicanism flows from certain theological and philosophical premises.

He writes in the opening sentence of the introduction, "I wish to begin by reflecting on the question of man: 'Human Nature, Politics, and Democracy.'" He proceeds to identify "the contemporary crisis of the spirit . . . the crisis of the intellectual integrity of human existence" as at the root of "the closely related political and socioeconomic crisis of our time."

Sandoz seeks a Christian solution to the crisis of Western civilization, but his quest bears no trace of a bigoted attitude toward non-Christian and non-Western cultures. To the contrary, he apparently approves of Voegelin's remark in *From Enlightenment to Revolution,* which he might have done well to quote: "The first step toward a solution of the very real problem of difference in civilizational structure between East and West lies in a recognition that the 'stagnation' of the East is quite as unfounded an idea as the 'progress' of the West. If we drop the category of western 'progress,' the category of Eastern 'stagnation' will disappear automatically."

Much of *A Government of Laws* constitutes a critique of the despiritualization that marked the radical Enlightenment's dethronement of God and deification of man. The specifics of the critique are Sandoz's own, but the general features recall the analyses of a long list of conservatives, including such recent ones as Voegelin, Richard Weaver, and T. S. Eliot. Eliot and probably even Weaver would, however, have had a hard time with Sandoz's celebration of the beauties of liberal democracy, and he has not begun to reply to, say, the arguments made by Eliot in *Christianity and Culture.*

The special quality of Sandoz's insistence upon a Christian solution to the crisis of Western civilization flows from his assessment of the sinful nature of man. He makes a reasonably good job of it, but not good enough. For his stalwart defense of representative democracy and an essentially liberal polity accompanies a certain philosophical, not to say theological, uneasiness. Basically, he takes the same ground as he did in his searing study of Dostoyevsky's parable of the Grand Inquisitor in *The Brothers Karamazov* (see Sandoz's *Political Apocalypse*), but he does so here with some fudging around the edges. In *Political Apocalypse,* Sandoz was on the attack against radicalism, and his defense of Christian principles did not require the direct confrontation with liberalism that he is forced into here. It did not require, that is, so specific an attempt to reconcile the Christian doctrines of original sin and human depravity with the optimistic temperament of modern democracy—a temperament Sandoz shares to a disquieting degree.

Sandoz is hardly alone among Christian conservatives in defending and even celebrating democracy. But many Christian conservatives stand with C. S. Lewis and defend democracy on the grounds that man is so depraved as to render socially dangerous any system that gives some men more than a minimum of power over others. Thus Lewis, in *Present Concerns*, refused to contradict Aristotle's dictum that some men are fit only to be slaves, but he rejected slavery because he found no men fit to be masters. Sandoz's concessions to liberal political theory, in contrast, follow from his subtle concessions to liberal theology.

The learned Sandoz has no trouble in trotting out appropriate quotations from the great Christian theologians to argue that man is "a little lower than angels" and exists as an intermediary and is neither brute nor God. Others would argue, in contrast, that man is simultaneously both brute and angel. Were we to work through the appropriate dialectics, the two formulations might be reduced to a common denominator, but the rhetorical shift exposes more than a difference of nuance.

The substance of politics for Sandoz is psyche, that is, the soul, understood as passion and reason or, in fashionable parlance, consciousness. Thus he analyzes the crisis of our time—the latest and most terrifying phase of the crisis that unfolded with the breakdown of the medieval Christian order—as at bottom a disorder of the soul. Following Aristotle, Sandoz explores "reason" to reveal the tension between the good and evil in man, but here, and in his other work, he takes pains to emphasize the good as an element of divinity that distinguishes man from other earthly creatures. Sandoz has good reason to emphasize, as Voegelin did before him, the divine aspect of human nature, for the greatest horrors of the modern world have flowed from the widespread contempt for that aspect—a contempt that, with supreme historical irony, has proceeded in tandem with the deification of man in the wake of the much celebrated death, or murder, of God. However understandable, praiseworthy, and politically efficacious this emphasis may be, it strengthens the case for democracy primarily by diluting the sense of evil and makes concessions that threaten Sandoz's hoped-for spiritual renewal.

Consider Sandoz's reference to "the core understanding in Christianity of sin as making an error or mistake about the good we seek; sin is a missing of the mark." He invokes Thomas Aquinas and Bernard of Clairveaux to support this formulation, which could not readily be disputed as a legitimate expression of Christian doctrine. For that matter, neither would a serious Christian be likely to dispute his appeals to "love, faith, and hope." But Sandoz might ponder the regular invocation of "love, faith, and hope" by, among others, the radicals of the Critical Legal Studies movement in support of a contrary worldview and a politics he surely must find abhorrent.

The words *error* and *the good we seek* open the gates to liberal theology by drawing attention away from sin as a direct offense against the God of Wrath who proclaimed himself "a jealous God." As Sandoz doubtless knows, during the nineteenth century Harvard Unitarians, New Haven Theologians, and numerous other worthies marched through those gates to lay low the idea of sin, after first having redefined original sin virtually out of existence and then reducing the depravity of man to an unpleasant tendency in not-as-yet-perfect creatures.

Curious results follow from Sandoz's concessions. There is something charming in his defense of Thomas Paine against Theodore Roosevelt's characterization of "a filthy little atheist" and in the suggestion that since even Jefferson qualified as a believer, so must his contemporaries have. The charm wears off when his strained discussion of Jefferson's murky religious views ends with the judgment that Jefferson was "a nontrinitarian Christian." Reminding myself that it is not my place to define proper Christian doctrine, and recalling the droll claims to Christian orthodoxy made by the early Harvard Unitarians and assorted other heretics, I must confess to regarding the term "nontrinitarian Christian"

as an oxymoron. Besides, we know how quickly the successors of
those self-proclaimed Christians ended as apostates.

Sandoz's decision to distance himself from the southern conservative tradition takes its toll here. An intellectually impressive
array of antebellum southern theologians, culminating with James
Henley Thornwell and Robert L. Dabney, bolstered their own
version of social and political order with an uncompromising
opposition to what they reasonably perceived as a capitulation to
heresy and an invitation to political radicalism and social chaos.
Were Sandoz to engage the southern conservative tradition, the
ideas of which resonate in his own thought, he might not find it
so easy to settle for his formulation of the Christian doctrine of
sin. But in that case, he would not find it at all possible to assert
what he must do much more to prove—that liberal democracy
represents the political order best attuned to the preservation of
Western civilization. For one thing, he would have to confront
the issue he lamentably sidesteps throughout his book: slavery,
the southern defense of which rested on theological foundations.

From John Randolph through Thomas Roderick Dew, John C.
Calhoun, Albert Taylor Bledsoe, James Henley Thornwell, and
other leading southern theorists, on to Allen Tate and Richard
Weaver, the southern critique of social and economic equality,
which Sandoz echoes, has included a critique of democracy itself,
which Sandoz ignores. Hence he is least clear and convincing
precisely where his standpoint demands the utmost clarity, elaboration, and defense. C. S. Lewis's teasing remarks on the relation
of Christian doctrine to political democracy suggest, after all, a
commitment only to the bare minimum—to an extended version
of an ultimate appeal to the popular will that even Calhoun and
Thornwell accepted. Between that commitment and the liberal
democracy Sandoz invokes without a clear delineation of limits
lie all the practical problems of our era and the era into which we
are mindlessly plunging.

Sandoz's willingness to play the Yankee game of making the
great southern conservative theorists disappear is especially irritating since it weakens the best parts of his own case. One would
never know from this book that William Henry Trescot pioneered

in the conservative interpretation of the American Revolution and its legacy; that John Randolph and John C. Calhoun forcefully challenged the constitutional distortions Sandoz insists must be challenged; that Thomas Roderick Dew, in his stunning history of Western civilization, carefully linked the classical and Christian traditions to the emergence of American constitutionalism; that Albert Taylor Bledsoe exposed what Sandoz calls the "false dichotomy" between liberty and order. I am less concerned here with doing belated justice to an admirable phalanx of all but forgotten southern theorists than I am with the overwhelming problem they grappled with—the social foundations necessary to sustain constitutional liberty. For, with the partial exception of Randolph, they could find those foundations only in some form of slavery, and, if we are to avoid that dismal outcome, we shall have to reply to their arguments more honestly and skillfully than the abolitionists and free-soilers ever managed to do.

The humane and generous spirit that shines through Sandoz's Christian worldview and estimate of the American founding sets a noble standard toward which we would do well to strive, if only because the alternatives promise physical as well as spiritual death. But it will require maximum intellectual and political discipline to realize the promise of that spirit. As a nonbeliever who nonetheless has long accepted the essentials of the doctrines of original sin and human depravity and their tragic consequences for human history, I fear the worst. That fear need not generate paralysis, despair, and cynicism. It may, instead, steel us with the wisdom of Romain Rolland's great dictum: "Pessimism of the intellect! optimism of the will!" For on the principal point Sandoz is right: Individually and collectively, as Saint Paul unforgettably warned, we are accountable both for our acts and for our failure to act.

It would be tempting to have sport with Sandoz by denouncing him as a "liberal" or assailing him for trying to combine incompatible philosophical and political notions. But he could reasonably reply that the astonishing plethora of revolutions and counterrevolutions through which we are living compels honest men to return to first principles and to recognize that the healthiest aspects of modern liberalism continue to offer the soundest political

foundation available to those who seek a civilized outcome—
that we have to build upon the constructive achievements of the
Enlightenment while resisting those perversions which corrupted
the spirit and spawned the doctrines that have made our century
one of mass murder on a hitherto undreamed of scale. Sandoz
might, that is, remind us of the truth of the witticism offered
by John Lukacs, another outstanding conservative historian who
has been treated as a nonperson by our profession: "The isms
have become wasms." Sandoz's problem is ours. We need to find
ground on which to stand in a persistent struggle to reconcile
the claims of social justice, individual freedom, and a respect for
human dignity in an age in which the moral as well as intellectual
foundations of the requisite social consensus have crumbled.

Sandoz would have us reassess the course of Western civilization
in a manner that defends its world-historical achievements, most
notably its achievement of freedom within social order, without ignoring or minimizing its terrible crimes. He would have
strengthened his book immeasurably had he paid more attention
to those crimes, especially to slavery. But he is right to honor
the Founders for their creation of a republic based on institutions
and informed by a spirit that make possible a constant struggle
for the maximum possible realization of human goodness. And
he is convincing in his effort to root their thought and action in
Western classical and Christian traditions.

For contrary to current lying, Western civilization has been distinguished not by racism, imperialism, and the denigration of
women, which have disfigured all civilizations, but by its extraordinary and partially successful movements of opposition to
those enormities. Sandoz should be seen as searching for a way
to discipline the magnificent impulses of Western civilization, as
manifested in our own national experience, while combating the
mendacity that today passes for criticism of Eurocentrism. This
impressive book speaks to our times.

13

Abolitionism's Black Prophets

In *Black Prophets of Justice: Activist Clergy before the Civil War*, David E. Swift provides a vivid account of the painful yet inspiring struggle of six Presbyterian and Congregationalist divines who made an inestimable contribution to the emergence of the black church in America. The lives of the six—Samuel Cornish, Theodore Wright, Charles Ray, Henry Highland Garnet, Amos Beeman, and James Pennington—intersected in a heroic effort to build the black church and to enlist it in a protracted and often discouraging campaign to liberate their people.

These men of different backgrounds, slave and free, and of different talents and temperaments shared a determination to transform church and society. Toward that end they organized support for fugitive slaves and militantly fought for civil rights and racial equality. As crusading editors of early black newspapers and as educators, they challenged racism on all fronts. Among their accomplishments, they pioneered in African and Afro-American studies to combat appalling ignorance and malicious bias. Each step of the way they suffered ostracism, economic deprivation, and the constant threat of violence, not to mention the more mundane problems that fall to any minister who tries to build a church among a beleaguered people.

The black contribution to American abolitionism is no longer a well-guarded secret, and neither is the terrible struggle that blacks had to wage against racism in the abolitionist movement itself. Swift therefore does not break ground here, but he does add substantially to the story. His account of the indignities these men suffered and of the unsparing way in which they fought back adds much to what we thought we knew. In short, Swift does a fine job in sketching the lives of some extraordinary men and in enriching our understanding of the black experience, the development of the churches, and the most turbulent era in our national history. In particular, he illuminates the evolution of the black church as a socially engaged institution.

Black Prophets of Justice nonetheless contains some dangerous silences. Swift writes as if these black divines showed little concern for the theological and ecclesiastical issues that were wracking the churches. Indeed, it would appear that they did not pay much attention to those issues, but their course nonetheless deserves careful attention. For Swift writes: "Being Christian meant for these ministers preaching a biblical message—a liberation theology based on the Exodus, the Old Testament prophets, and Jesus Christ." Yet he tells us virtually nothing about that theology. It is as if social and political activism itself constituted a theology, as I very much fear many today assume.

The silence amounts to an obfuscation and threatens to undermine essential features of the history of the struggle over slavery. The debate was, in the very first instance, a debate over the Bible, over Christian teaching, over the substance of the Word of God. For Presbyterians, especially, the ramifications were far-reaching in an age in which James Henley Thornwell and his impressive phalanx of southern divines were raising the banner of "the spirituality of the church" in part as an effort to keep the church out of politics. To be sure, even Thornwell could not avoid social questions. His great sermons "On National Sins" and "The Christian Doctrine of Slavery" advanced powerful interventions in political debates and, alas, constituted an intellectually formidable scriptural defense of slavery. Yet he did not thereby violate his own precepts; rather, he cogently defined terms and delineated limits.

Unfortunately, Swift proceeds in a manner that has become de rigueur among historians of the religious dimension of the sectional crisis. Whether influenced by the current rage for social history, by ideological fashion, or by entirely different considerations, he largely bypasses theology. Or rather, like almost all recent writers, he blithely assumes that which needs to be demonstrated— that the abolitionists, black or white, successfully repelled the proslavery argument from Scripture. In fact, he shows only that the black divines, like their white abolitionist counterparts, refused to take the scriptural defense of slavery seriously.

The various head-on debates between proslavery and antislavery divines—Wayland versus Fuller, Blanchard versus Rice, Pryne versus Brownlow—and the hundreds of published tracts on both sides make depressing reading. In truth, the abolitionists took a fearful drubbing. And let it be noted that many eminent northern divines emphatically agreed that the Bible did not condemn slavery as sinful. It should be enough to recall the great Charles Hodge of Princeton, who opposed slavery politically and voted Republican. Time and again, those who denied the sinfulness of slavery challenged the abolitionists to cite a single passage in either the Old or the New Testament. Time and again, the abolitionists failed miserably, notwithstanding elaborate efforts that sometimes bordered on intellectual dishonesty.

In the end the abolitionists fell back on the Spirit rather than the Word, and, regrettably, the Spirit in question turned out to be the spirit of modern man—that is, of themselves. They insisted that slavery was an enormity not to be borne by an enlightened people. They were right. But they never did make their case from the Bible, any more than the early antislavery southern divines had been able to. In consequence, white southerners, a deeply religious and Bible-reading people, rallied to the proslavery standard with an easy conscience.

This debate constituted part of a larger debate over religious orthodoxy and the steady retreat of the northern theologians into a watering down, not to say abandonment, of the doctrines of original sin, human depravity, and the nature of God as a God of Wrath—"a jealous God." From the perspective of the leading southern theologians, the increasingly liberal religious doctrines of the northern divines—those "baptized infidels," as they were known in the South—complemented the cancerous doctrines of radical democracy and egalitarianism, even as they confirmed the southern conviction that the root of the grand religious and political heresy lay precisely in the free-labor social system and its attendant marketplace morality. Thornwell, among others, slighted the specifically racial arguments based on the myth of Ham and defended slavery as the labor system best suited to a Christian society among Europeans as well as Africans. Thus the proslavery ideologues taunted the abolitionists with the charge of planning genocide against the black race—of threatening to hurl black people into a competitive market in which they could not hope to survive.

Swift's silence on the black divines' theology and its relation to political economy and political science proves frustrating. We need to know what, if anything, the black divines had to say, especially if we are to know just what a "liberation theology" is supposed to consist of. For surely, that story, too, needs to be told if we are to understand both the black experience and the religious history of the American people and if we are to assess the challenges and resources that black people had to contend with as they passed from slavery to freedom.

14

The Theology of Martin Luther King, Jr., and Its Political Implications

I

Heroes are hard to acknowledge in this era of moral decadence and failure of national nerve. A mushrooming cult of self-expression paradoxically feeds the childish notion that individuals count for little in history. So let us pity those harsh rightwing critics of Martin Luther King, Jr., who abhor the excesses of an individualism devoid of civic discipline and nobly plead for the proper recognition of national symbols: How they must gag at seeing King the only hero to command much national recognition.

King's memory has been coming under rightwing fire, but it has also been suffering under a more insidious denigration by those for whom no flesh-and-blood human being deserves to be considered great, lest his greatness cast doubt on the equality of all "persons" in the marketplace of egalitarian dreams. The civil rights movement nonetheless effected a revolutionary change in America, and no amount of postmodernist blather or rightwing fulmination is likely to dim our memory of the man who emerged as its greatest leader, symbol, and martyr.

The long-awaited publication of King's *Papers* has begun, and the quality of these first volumes fully justifies the deliberate pace at which the editors have chosen to work. Clayborne Carson and his staff at The Martin Luther King, Jr., Center for Nonviolent Social Change deserve congratulations for a splendid job. The long biographical and analytical introduction in volume 1, bolstered by fine charts on genealogy and chronology, is fresh and instructive. The "Statement of Editorial Principles and Practices" lucidly describes the procedures for selection of representative documents from a massive archive, and the annotations for each item are painstaking. Coretta Scott King, Christina King Farris, and the advisory board have every reason to be proud of their general editor and of the staff he put together. Congratulations too to the University of California Press for handsomely printed, illustrated, and produced books.

The first volume contains letters and other documents that confirm the main features of King's early life as depicted by his biographers. Most of the volume, however, consists of his early term papers from Morehouse College and Crozer Theological Seminary, which provide invaluable material on his intellectual development.

These early volumes may legitimately be read from different perspectives. Here we shall focus on King as a young seeker of God and an aspirant theologian. Respect for his life's work requires that, at the least, we consider seriously the questions that haunted him throughout his life. His career as a theological liberal paralleled his career as a man of the political Left, but with a twist that is not as surprising as it might at first appear to be. In time he made important concessions to theological conservatism while he became politically more radical. The link may be found in his shift toward a greater appreciation of inherent human sinfulness. As he tempered his theological liberalism in this respect, he took a more sober view of political possibilities, relying less on spiritual appeals and moral suasion and recognizing the necessity for a large measure of force in the struggle for social justice.

King grew up in a strong and loving family, embedded in a solid, law-abiding, churchgoing black community in racially segregated Atlanta. He descended from a long line of dedicated Baptist preachers who, at considerable risk, helped to guide their people in a dangerous struggle against segregation and racism. The Atlanta into which King was born in 1929 had burgeoned into a city of 270,500, more than four times its size as of 1890. Quintessentially, Atlanta represented the "New" South then, as it still does. Very much a product of the post-slavery era, its leaders pushed it toward economic and political participation in an industrial and bourgeois United States. They paid lip service to the chivalrous old regime—their successors no longer bother—while they barely hid their embarrassment and contempt. Atlanta, a veritable frontier town before the War for Southern Independence, had been known more for desperadoes and men-on-the-make than for ladies and gentlemen. The gentry viewed it as a Yankee town, and to this day conservative southerners may be heard to say, "Even General Sherman had some good in him. After all, he did burn Atlanta."

After Reconstruction whites prided themselves on Atlanta's racial peace and especially pointed to Booker T. Washington's famous "Atlanta Compromise" speech of 1895. Not all blacks agreed, and by 1900 even the redoubtable Washington faced rising criticism from militantly anti-segregationist blacks. The explosions came, the worst in 1906 with one of those savage white assaults on the black community that have euphemistically been called race riots. In the aftermath, blacks concentrated on building up their own communities, drawing upon a solid middle and working class to strengthen their churches, schools, and businesses. Combining political prudence with fierce pride and dedication, they scored impressive if limited successes.

The Reverend Martin Luther King, Sr. ("Daddy King"), followed in the footsteps of his Baptist preacher forebears. A political realist who eschewed suicidal adventures, he preached a social gospel that combined a theologically conservative message of personal deliverance with a politically militant demand for racial justice. His son, even as a boy, had trouble with the theology but not with the principle that the church had to speak for the political and social aspirations of the community.

Not quite fifteen, Martin, Jr., emerged as a prizewinning orator at Booker T. Washington High School and held forth on "The Negro and the Constitution," declaring, "Black America still wears chains." Two years later, as a sophomore at Morehouse College, he wrote and saw published a letter to the *Atlanta Constitution* in which he protested against racial inequality. Consisting of two short, powerful paragraphs, the letter, in its style and content, announced the man in the making. After giving short shrift to the latest expressions of white fear of miscegenation, King wrote: "We want and are entitled to the basic rights and opportunities of American citizens: The right to earn a living at work for which we are fitted by training and ability; equal opportunities in education, health, recreation, and similar public services; the right to vote; equality before the law; some of the same courtesy and good manners that we ourselves bring to all human relations."

Thus even as a teenager King proved worthy of his family tradition by bravely and eloquently entering the struggle, speaking out in a manner few were then wont to do. At the same time, as his earliest autobiographical reflections show, he struggled successfully with himself to overcome reactive feelings of hatred against whites, which arose from his experiences as a student on prolonged visits to a bigoted North as well as in a segregated South. In 1945, for example, in New Jersey, King and some friends were refused service at a tavern and threatened at gunpoint. Then too, King grew up during the depression and witnessed with indignation the suffering of working people, black and white. Raised in a Republican household, as most blacks of his generation were, he turned toward socialism early in life.

Family life had its share of internal tensions. Relations with his father were especially taxing, with evidence of an Oedipal struggle that should delight Freudians. His father, like his mother, demonstrably loved his children, but he ruled his household as an old-fashioned disciplinarian. King's early letters breathe a deep and well-requited love for father, mother, and family, as well as a respect grounded in both personal feeling and a healthy sense of filial duty.

While he chafed under considerable paternal strictness, his respect for his father, if anything, became stronger over time in a way fraught with significance for his own theological and political development. Daddy King was a bright and courageous man and a powerful preacher but with limited learning and little inclination to challenge biblical authority. As such, he offered a splendid target for condescension and even embarrassment from the son for whom he was providing a substantial education. Young Martin recoiled from the content as well as the style of his religiously orthodox forebears and sought a more cerebral religion that could pass muster according to scientific criteria and modern sensibility. He was not above treating much southern (black and white) Baptist belief and church practice with an edge of contempt, which he would slough off slowly as he came to recognize how much their product he was.

Attracted to fashionable liberal theology, political radicalism, and intellectual sophistication, King distanced himself—but never meanly or decisively—from his father and his community. In later years he remained a theological liberal but an increasingly chastened one. As he became more critical of his own theological liberalism, his understanding of and respect for the more traditional religious tendencies of his father and of the black community steadily deepened. In particular, he came to appreciate, even if he could not fully embrace, their dogged insistence upon The Word. He also came to appreciate, as well as to embrace, their insistence upon an inherent sinfulness in all men that cautioned against utopian expectations.

At Morehouse, which he entered in his midteens, probably earlier than he should have, he encountered admirable teachers whose own intellectual boldness encouraged his rebellion against orthodoxy but curbed any incipient disrespect for the traditions of his people. The best of his teachers, led by the scholarly and politically engaged Benjamin Mays, Morehouse's distinguished president, were intellectually talented men who stressed scientific method, historical accuracy, and empirical investigation and who cautioned against received wisdom, prejudice, and dogmatism. King learned a great deal at Morehouse, where his professors rated him as intelligent and promising but not brilliant. Prone to partying and not yet an especially dedicated student, he displayed considerable intellectual curiosity and concern for both sociopolitical and religious questions. For better or worse, his years at Morehouse strengthened his radical tendencies in religion as well as politics.

The recent revelation that King plagiarized his doctoral dissertation at Boston University ("A Comparison of the Conceptions
of God in the Thinking of Paul Tillich and Henry Nelson Wieman") came as a painful shock, although some scholars previously
glimpsed the truth but preferred to remain silent. Here we may
note the intellectual and professional integrity, as well as the tact
and good sense, that the editors of the *King Papers* have brought
to the disagreeable task of exposing the story to full view. Their
careful notes reveal that King's susceptibility to the charge of
plagiarism began with his term papers at Morehouse and Crozer.

This early plagiarism contains no few curiosities. By and large,
his professors, who at least at Morehouse were heavily overworked,
let him get away with it, although not without occasional chiding
about the carelessness of his citations. Yet King does not seem
to have tried to get away with much. He usually indicated the
works he was cribbing from, thereby leading his professor directly
to the scene of the crime. He misquoted frequently in a manner
that suggests impatience with scholarly procedures and just plain
sloppiness rather than an intent to deceive. And he aroused few
suspicions of laziness or unwillingness to do the required work.
His papers suggest an inquisitive mind, a genuine interest in the
subject matter, some hard work, and a strong effort to organize
the ideas of leading scholars and theologians so as to work out a
point of view of his own.

King, by his own admission, worked eclectically, borrowing
from hither and yon those ideas and expressions that he could
arrange in a pattern compatible with his own developing thought.
With one or two exceptions, his papers would pass muster as good
work if only he had taken fifteen minutes or so to straighten out
his references and put in the requisite quotation marks. For he in
fact made the nature and extent of his borrowing clear to anyone
who knew the literature, as his professors surely did. The best of
King's youthful essays, on the relation of the ancient pagan cults
to Christianity or the problem of God's relation to evil, are worth
reading, at peak moments for their intrinsic content and generally
as evidence of a fine mind engaged in a struggle to find God as
well as himself.

Full justice to King's religious thought would require a critique of the course of the liberal theology to which he generally subscribed and of the theologians to whose work he most often responded. "Liberal theology" is a rubric that covers a multitude of sins and, presumably, virtues and can become an easy catchall for derision or approbation aimed at various tendencies that should be considered discretely. For immediate purposes suffice it to recall that the Unitarians captured Harvard and much of the Boston elite early in the nineteenth century and that the defenders of Christian orthodoxy in the principal northern churches slowly surrendered so much ground that their white southern brethren dubbed them "baptized infidels." The concept of original sin went down in flames early, and that of human depravity followed suit, although more often than not these concepts were not so much repudiated as reinterpreted so as to render them meaningless. Much else followed, until today it is difficult to know what of Christian doctrine, if anything, remains in the professedly Christian "mainstream" churches. Some important sections of the Episcopal Church, for example, proudly invite nontrinitarians, Jews, Muslims, and even atheists into their House of Many Mansions. And why not? The only God left standing so loves the world that He forgives all our sins and welcomes all of us into the Kingdom of Heaven—if, that is, He really exists, which moderns are entitled to question even as they amble up to take Communion.

During the nineteenth century the battle raged with mounting fury and considerable bitterness. The more genuinely orthodox, most notably the Old School Presbyterians at Princeton, fought a determined rearguard action. But a rearguard action is what it turned out to be. The southerners put up a better fight, as they generally have, but their theological cause became intertwined with their defense of slavery and went down with it.

Science provided much of the heavy artillery against orthodoxy, but the battle was less between scientists and believers than between divines who at any cost were determined to render theology compatible with scientific method and divines who increasingly insisted upon a separation of spheres. At that, before the War for Southern Independence even the orthodox theologians denied any possible contradiction between science and religion, insisting that they were mutually supportive. Geology especially caused problems, but they proved manageable. After the War, Darwinism and the remarkable development of the sciences in general proved more difficult to assimilate. Step by step the attempt to render theology and science compatible led to the rout of Christian orthodoxy and a bunker-like Fundamentalism on the one hand and to the repudiation of essential doctrine on the other.

The southern black churches have had their own history in relation to these questions, which has yet to be studied with anything like the care it deserves. In many respects the southern black churches have ranged close to those southern white churches that still try to hold the line for the Word, but they have always espoused a social gospel of their own, which also still awaits adequate theological study. Daddy King, like his forebears, stood astride that tradition, holding its tensions within himself as best he could. His son, attracted to the modernist theology of the wider European and American Christian world, almost instinctively tried to resolve the tension through acceptance of a liberal theology committed to social action. Despite his best efforts, he never completely shook off the theological orthodoxy that constituted a critical part of his people's religious inheritance. Those who view Martin Luther King, Jr., as a Christian prophet have a point. For by returning to his father's ground, if haltingly and only to a limited extent, he staked out claims to having been called by the Lord. At any rate, his ultimate acceptance of the tension between his own liberal theological inclinations and a gnawing sense of the reality of a God of Wrath and a world of sinners led him to a stern view of human frailty and thereby to a political realism that his people have generally preferred to recurring utopianisms.

Among the liberal theologians who influenced King, Edgar Sheffield Brightman stood out even before King went to study with him at Boston University's Divinity School. Certain features of Brightman's thought seem especially to have impressed the youthful King and reinforced what he presumably learned from the views of his professors at Morehouse: a determined effort to render Christian theology consistent with the demands of scientific method; and an insistence that God has limited power and is a progressive being capable of moral and intellectual growth over time. Thus Brightman wrote in *The Problem of God*, "Frankly, I believe in a God who has more to do than he has yet done, and so is capable of growth."

Another feature of Brightman's thought was probably the most important for King: the emphasis on personal experience as a way to God and, by extension, the defense of a personal God against those theologians who were sliding toward a notion of depersonalized Spirit. For some years King echoed Brightman's projection of a God of Love to the virtual extinction of a God of Wrath.

Brightman, like everyone else, tried to account for evil in a world presided over by a God understood as omnipotent and perfectly good. He repeatedly insisted that only a perfectly good being could be God and worthy of being worshiped. King held to such a view all his life, although even as a youth he was more deeply disturbed by the orthodox insistence upon human depravity than most of his favorite theologians were. Brightman solved the problem to his own satisfaction by denying the omnipotence of God and postulating a "Given" that God himself had to come to terms with.

Liberal theology, including the versions that initially attracted King, has generally been embarrassed by the Old Testament's God of Wrath, to whom it has counterpoised Jesus as Pure Love. Brightman went so far as to refer to "Jesus the crucified Son" and to "God the loving Father." Indeed, despite all disclaimers, liberal theology has been embarrassed by the Bible itself, for, among other difficulties, no one has yet refuted the evidence that the Bible sanctioned slavery. On what grounds, then, can God be defended as perfectly good? The invocation of God's perfect love solves nothing when His love, like His will, emerges as an expression of the individual's own experience and understanding, that is, of every individual's moral standpoint. In such readings, "Thy will be done on earth as it is in heaven" becomes a version of the Spanish lords' oath to obey their king so long as he respected their self-determined rights and privileges: "If yes, yes; if no, no."

Even as a teenager, King became troubled by the relation of faith to reason and by the riddles of theodicy. If God's will is not ultimately inscrutable, faith must yield to science and a deified Reason on all essential matters, and nothing prevents His will from miraculously conforming to our own politics. But if God's will is ultimately inscrutable, then it is revealed to us partially, only in such doses as He chooses to reveal. And if that revelation cannot be found in the Word, however great the difficulties of interpretation, where can it be found? The Bible offers Jesus simultaneously as Redeemer and as Judge who presides over the law He came to fulfill. The God who gave us the law did not forswear vengeance. He declared it His own monopoly: "Vengeance is mine, saith the Lord." Jesus did not come as one more prophet but as the Christ—as Lord, Savior, Redeemer.

For Brightman and the other liberal theologians whom King followed, Christianity joins Judaism, Buddhism, Islam, even philosophy and science, as ways of finding God. But if Christianity surrenders its special claim to being Spirit and Word-become-flesh and as "final revelation" (in Paul Tillich's sense) why not prefer Buddhism or Hegelian philosophy? King's student essays suggest that he was by no means sure that Christianity could in fact claim superiority. Indeed, throughout his life he veered perilously close to embracing Hegel's project of subsuming theology under philosophy. King offers a Jesus who is a man especially touched by divinity but considerably less than the Second Person of the Trinity. And King himself does not seem to have believed in the Trinity at all. Brightman, for his part, cried out in *The Finding of God* that liberalism in both politics and religion "suffers, above all, from the incapacity of the ordinary man to think." Maybe. But other explanations, less flattering to liberals, come to mind.

King recoiled at orthodoxy. He never took the doctrine of original sin seriously, and he later recalled how, as a thirteen year old, he upset his Sunday school teachers—and Daddy King?—by scoffing at the bodily resurrection of Jesus, which like the doctrine of the virgin birth and much else, he continued to regard as unscientific and therefore as merely metaphorical. His view of Jesus appeared vividly in an essay at Crozer that betrays misgivings about his all-too-human picture of Jesus but nonetheless concludes: "The divine quality of this unity with God was not something thrust upon Jesus from above, but it was a definite achievement through the process of moral struggle and self-abnegation." King only rarely mentioned the Holy Spirit and then he did so not as the Third Person of the Trinity but as little more than an abstract morality.

His professors heartily approved these plunges into what Daddy King probably regarded as rank heresy. Indeed, according to Taylor Branch in *Parting the Waters,* the standing joke told by the students at Crozer about Professors James B. Pritchard and M. Scott Enslin was that "Pritchard destroyed the biblical image of Moses in the first term and Enslin finished off Jesus in the second." We are entitled to ask how Arianism and Socinianism came to qualify as Christian theology in Baptist seminaries.

In these early essays King already shows considerable uneasiness and seems to have turned to Brightman's theological "personalism" as a way of holding on to some semblance of a personal God. In the doctoral dissertation he would throw down the gauntlet to the leading theologians of the day.

No doubt Christianity should be considered both as concern for the afterlife and as engagement here on earth, and, historically, the black churches have insisted upon both with special vigor. But today one has to search diligently, especially in the principal ("white") denominations, for a serious effort among the theologically liberal to meet the first half of the challenge. Worse, one increasingly finds a tendency to reduce the second half to some fashionable political agenda. Not surprisingly, the most fashionable political agendas cast Jesus and the Bible as the spiritual font for social and political radicalism.

King's early essays signaled the beginning of a lifelong struggle with such problems, marked by an increasingly critical stance toward his own liberal presuppositions. An early fascination with Hegel, combined with his indignation at the breadlines of the 1930s, led him toward Marx or, more directly, toward a Christian socialism that drew upon Marx in a manner recently espoused by some radical exponents of a theology of black liberation. But

Hegel also offered King a dialectic of God, which, curiously, led him to follow Brightman's non-Hegelian projection of a finite God subject to an internally contradictory "Given" that is prior to God and that contains the evil for which He is not personally responsible. God, as perfect goodness, is therefore engaged in a ceaseless struggle to guide humanity (and Himself?) away from the evil He did not create and lacks the power to eradicate. Such a God exists in time and therefore, according to Brightman and King, satisfies the demands of science. As such, God is a progressive being.

No wonder, then, that in the more specifically political formulations of a subsequent host of radical theologians, God the Father implicitly yields to Jesus, understood less as the Second Person of the Trinity than as the Son of Man. And that Son of Man, in the hands of those who would push King's notions to their logical extreme—as he himself did not—looks disquietingly like the General Secretary of the Central Committee.

Almost at the very moment that Brightman was publishing *The Problem of God* (1930) and *The Finding of God* (1931), upon which King drew heavily, John Crowe Ransom, the poet, literary critic, and spokesman for the Southern Agrarians, published a haunting, idiosyncratic excursion into theology. Apparently, King never read *God without Thunder;* probably, he never even heard of it; certainly, his professors were not about to recommend it, if they knew it at all.

Although *God without Thunder* is subtitled "An Unorthodox Defense of Orthodoxy," its interpretation of Jesus revealed Ransom as a closet Unitarian and surely must have struck orthodox Christians as flagrantly heretical on many counts. It is safe to say that King would have been appalled by it. Still, one wishes that a spirit of diversity had prevailed in the schools he attended and that he had been compelled to respond to the challenge mounted by his fellow southerner.

Ransom scorned to question God's omnipotence and asked: Why bother to worship a God we need not fear? Did Ransom thereby surrender the idea of God as perfect goodness? Not exactly. He argued that only hubris would insist upon our capacity to understand God's will beyond the dictates of His Word. Human goodness lies precisely in submission to His will. God, for Ransom, thereby does emerge as responsible for that which human beings experience as evil, the purposes of which lie beyond our understanding.

When, years ago, I finished reading *God without Thunder*, I muttered that I would rather burn eternally in Hell than submit to the will of such an arbitrary, not to say monstrous, God. But then, as an atheist, I am at liberty to indulge in such grandstanding. Were I in grace and in fear of the wrath of the God who proclaimed Himself "a jealous God," I would not be able to afford the luxury. Liberal, not to mention liberationist, theology, whether in white or black, should warm every atheist's heart. For if God is a socially conscious political being whose views invariably correspond to our own prejudices on every essential point of doctrine, He demands of us no more than our politics require. Besides, if God is finite, progressive, and Pure Love, we may as well skip church next Sunday and go to the movies. For if we have nothing to fear from this all-loving, all-forbearing, all-forgiving God, how would our worship of Him constitute more than self-congratulation for our own moral standards? As an atheist, I like this God. It is good to see Him every morning while I am shaving.

Toward the end of his career at Crozer, King was already beginning a brave reexamination of his own most cherished views, notably in the doctoral dissertation, published in volume 2, on the theologies of Paul Tillich and Henry Nelson Wieman. Most of the dissertation is open to a graver charge of plagiarism than might be leveled at the Morehouse and Crozer essays, for by then King had been well instructed in the requisites of scholarship in contradistinction to those of preaching. The dissertation, despite its plagiarism, constitutes a serviceable if uninspired exposition of the thought of Tillich and Wieman. But the last chapter, notwithstanding some heavy doses of plagiarism, is easily the most arresting and valuable part. In it King subjects the theology of Tillich and Wieman to a forceful critique from decidedly more conservative ground than he had occupied earlier. Specifically, he protests against their abandonment of a personal

God and the doctrine of personal immortality and moves toward a more orthodox Christianity. In particular, he moves at least a few inches toward a doctrine of sin that his father might have been more comfortable with. And, if I am reading him properly, he also implicitly takes a much more critical view of Brightman's theology.

How much King's reading of Reinhold Niebuhr influenced his critique remains in hot dispute, but here and elsewhere he was clearly influenced by the thought and practice of the southern black world in which he was raised and which has always exhibited some strongly conservative, not to say fundamentalist, theological tendencies. A vigorous debate has been raging over the specifically Afro-American sources of King's thought, and it is even being asserted that much of his invocation of European theology and philosophy was largely a tactic to gain the respect and attention of white Americans for his political message. There is probably a grain of truth in this assertion, although those who push it hard might recognize that they inadvertently come close to accusing him of hypocrisy and deceit. They also implicitly if unintentionally reintroduce the accusation of Uncle Tomism leveled against the many black parents who, like W. E. B. Du Bois, have long encouraged their children to study "the classics" without in the least denigrating their African heritage. King's early essays and the dissertation do not support such a charge. Rather, they suggest that he invoked white European and American theologians and philosophers primarily because they raised questions he considered vital to an honest search for a Christian understanding of God. In consequence, by the time he left Crozer he had prepared himself for a more realistic appraisal of political possibilities and for a skeptical view of the utopianism that disfigured his earliest hopes for racial and social justice.

King became a great preacher but hardly a significant theologian. His gifts as a preacher appeared early, as if in the blood that coursed through generation after generation on both sides of his family. Like father, like son: His preaching resonated an extraordinary black sermonic tradition, and careful study is beginning to suggest a significant impact of specifically Afro-American

Christian thought as well as sermonic style on the stronger features of King's own theology. But his genius as a preacher as well as a political leader rested largely on his peerless ability to blend Euro-American and Afro-American theology and folk religion in a manner that remained firmly rooted in the particularism of his people and simultaneously in the universality without which Christianity loses all meaning.

The influence of a genuine religious quest—a search for God and the meaning of life—on King's emergence as a great political leader is already apparent in these youthful efforts, which support King's declaration in 1965: "In the quiet recesses of my heart, I am fundamentally a clergyman, a Baptist preacher. This is my being and my heritage for I am also the son of a Baptist preacher, the grandson of a Baptist preacher and the great-grandson of a Baptist preacher." One might wish that his theological training had been as rigorous and as broad as he seems to have been ready to welcome, but he struggled manfully and with impressive results to use the tools that lay to hand. A reading of his earliest essays strengthens the sense that his commitment to nonviolence flowed from a deeply held sense of God's will and the demands of a Christian life and was no mere matter of political strategy and tactics.

These volumes provide a revealing glimpse of the qualities that, notwithstanding all caveats, led King to greatness. If I may recall Gibbon on Belisarius, albeit with an emendation Gibbon might not have liked: King's faults were those of his age and of the sinful nature to which all human flesh is heir. His virtues, rooted in the traditions of his people, were largely his own.

II

In the editing of the second volume of the *King Papers*, as in the editing of the first, Clayborne Carson and his associates at The Martin Luther King, Jr., Center for Nonviolent Social Change have demonstrated exemplary scholarship, industry, and integrity under extraordinary difficulties. Volume 2 largely chronicles King's career as a theology student and the development of the religious views upon which we shall focus here. But it also includes valuable information on the National Baptist Convention, local black churches, the early response of southern blacks to desegregation, and much else of interest.

King's stature as an American and world-historical, as well as a discretely black, political leader remains secure. No amount of idol-smashing is likely to dim his luster. Our immense debt to the man and our respect for his memory do not, however, provide the slightest excuse for a political agenda that credits him with virtues he did not have and successes he did not achieve. Historians, at least those not mesmerized by postmodernist claptrap, ought to know that sooner or later the truth will out.

In the long run, King's personal and professional lapses are not likely to diminish his stature any more than assorted revelations are likely to diminish significantly the stature of others who deserve to be revered as constructive historical figures. Great men, more often than not, commit great sins and must be prepared, even more readily than others, to go to their death as Pushkin's Boris Goudonov went to his, crying out, "Forgive a poor sinner." The unfolding tragedy lies elsewhere. Those who foolishly think they protect his memory by denying or explaining away his lapses from his own highest moral standards render difficult a sober assessment of his legacy.

The scandal of King's well-documented plagiarism reveals only part of the even greater scandal of an academic career that will not bear scrutiny. Theodore Pappas has chronicled that scandal and the even worse scandal of the reaction of the media and Academia in *The Martin Luther King, Jr., Plagiarism Story*, which deserves much more attention than it has been getting. King's plagiarism began while he was an undergraduate and culminated in the revelations about his doctoral dissertation. Unflinchingly if tactfully, Carson and his associates have documented the plagiarism in excruciating detail. It is not a pretty story. From his undergraduate papers at Morehouse, to his papers at Crozer and Boston University divinity schools, to his dissertation, King plagiarized constantly and blatantly. And he got away with it.

To take only two of the more egregious examples from the dissertation: King's account of Tillich's view of "methodological correlation" was, like much else, lifted from Jack Boozer's doctoral dissertation, "The Place of Reason in Paul Tillich's Conception of God," which had been written under the same professors at Boston shortly before; and some of King's most telling criticism of Tillich was lifted from Rafael Demos's 1952 review of the first volume of Tillich's *Systematic Theology* in the *Journal of Philosophy*. King had taken a course at Harvard with Demos, whose work was surely well known to the professors at Boston.

There is a curious feature to King's plagiarism—and other cheating—for he constantly wrestled with difficult subject matter. The laziness and indifference that usually mark plagiarists do not seem to have been at issue here. From his undergraduate days he displayed a deep thirst for a knowledge of God, making a constant effort to understand God's nature and his will. Plagiarized or no, his papers, from Morehouse to Crozer to Boston, provide ample evidence that he was thinking hard and trying to find Christian ground on which to stand. The plagiarism, that is, consisted of his collecting other people's words and thoughts to buttress a viewpoint that he was formulating through a good deal of work and reflection. It is noteworthy that King passed over the chance to take courses on social Christianity, Gandhi, race relations, and other trendy subjects, preferring courses on Plato, Hegel, formal logic, and modern philosophy. It is also noteworthy that he was active in the black students' Dialectical Society at Boston, which met regularly for what appears to have been intellectually demanding work.

In any case, King's student papers and doctoral dissertation remain required reading for those who would understand his life's work. For the moment, forget the plagiarism and the many jejune formulations of his student papers. After all, how many among us would want our graduate school papers read today? I doubt that I am alone in having burned mine. What remains striking is the extent to which the essentials of his early theological and philosophical ideas survived to influence his religio-political course to the very end. Those ideas, honed by experience and maturity, proved a tower of strength, as well a source of some dangerous weaknesses.

In struggling to understand God, King focused on the work of those liberal theologians who bent theology to the exigencies of philosophy. Too bad. For a religion based on the relation of each individual to a God who has promised to render judgment cannot readily surrender its theology (its basic concepts of God, nature, man, sin, and salvation) to a discipline based solely on human reason. I do not mean to suggest that theologians may proceed in a manner indifferent to philosophy and human reason. The best and most "orthodox" of theologians do not make that mistake. Karl Barth, among the neo-orthodox theologians of King's day, was suspicious of the claims of philosophy, but, when push came to shove, even he had to make an attempt at constructive engagement. In any case, Christians may argue endlessly over the specific meaning of the Word, but when, as is now the fashion, they are brought to question whether the Word, as manifested in the Bible, constitutes revealed Truth, they run the grave risk of restricting themselves to arbitrary ethical pronouncements that atheists could readily share. At that point they no longer have much if anything to contribute specifically as Christians. For King, as for others, political consequences follow.

On the plagiarism: No explanations, qualifications, or fancy interpretations can excuse or mitigate it. King wrote the dissertation while he was meeting heavy responsibilities as the full-time pastor of Montgomery's prestigious Dexter Avenue Baptist Church, and he encountered the temptation to cut every corner. But nothing required him to do so, and he was at his most eloquent when preaching the example of Jesus' resistance to temptation and excoriating those who lived by what he sardonically referred to as the Eleventh Commandment, "Don't get caught."

Nor will the plea that the "black sermonic tradition" permits extensive borrowing without attribution serve, for it comes a cropper of the obvious objection that the same plea might be made for the "white sermonic tradition." Since a preacher of "Christ and Him crucified" is trying to convey the Word of God, not his own words or those of another interpreter, he need cite only the Bible, which until a century or so ago American Protestant preachers could assume their parishioners knew reasonably well. At that, King sometimes stepped over the bounds of the permissible by lifting sermons virtually wholesale from others.

Whatever excuses might be made for the many liberties King took, none could possibly serve for the doctoral dissertation. By then he had been well instructed in the requisites of scholarship, including the professional norms appropriate to the critical and historical study of the interpretations of others. King clearly understood and accepted the distinction between preaching and scholarly criticism.

Although it has gone unnoticed even by King's most hostile critics, his academic career was also rife with cheating of other kinds. He pretended to have done work he clearly had not done. That, too, he got away with. Boston University has indignantly denied that its professors relaxed their standards for black students in the spirit of the racist paternalism that is now running wild on our campuses. They seem unaware that, in mounting this denial, they convict themselves of something perhaps worse—of cheating all students, white and black.

King barely read German, a language regarded as indispensable for serious students of theology and the language in which Tillich's early theology had been written—and not translated into English. He failed his German examination during the year in which he was taking Edgar Sheffield Brightman's seminar on Hegel. It is not even clear that King carefully studied the English translation of the crucial *Phenomenology of Mind*, for he relied heavily on W. T. Stace's *Philosophy of Hegel*, a useful book on which many of us cut our teeth as undergraduates but which can hardly substitute for a reading of Hegel. No matter. King's papers on Hegel, which his professors praised, were heavily plagiarized anyway. The dissertation cites the German texts of Tillich's first book and other early writings, but the editors' notes show that in each case King is quoting translated passages he lifted from secondary sources.

An understanding of King's intellectual development requires a glance at the professional standards at Boston and the temper of the leading theological seminaries of his day. L. Harold DeWolf, who took a particular interest in black students, became King's dissertation adviser when Brightman died. The editors of the *King Papers* remark that DeWolf and other professors had little reason to suspect plagiarism in King's papers since King did well in examinations written in class. Fair enough—so far as it goes. But we may question how responsible King's professors were in reading those papers, which were full of theological blunders. Alternatively, we may question how well grounded they themselves were in the subjects in which they purported to be specialists.

As the result of poor training, King's serious weaknesses as a student of theology become more readily explicable, although hardly excusable. King's pretense to a knowledge of German led to serious problems and claimed an especially high price in his work on the theology of Karl Barth. To make matters worse, his reading of the English translations of Barth's books was hasty and wooden. His discussion of the concept of "God as wholly other," for example, raises doubts about how well he grasped Barth's central concepts. In "Karl Barth's Conception of God," another largely plagiarized paper that won DeWolf's praise, King interpreted Barth's notion of God as "unknowable and indescribable" in a manner that reduces it to an irrationality with which Barth cannot fairly be charged. And in a thinly veiled swipe at trinitarianism, King disapprovingly quoted Barth on the personality of God without noticing Barth's implicit attack on man's egotistical attempt to make his own personality the center of all things—an attack that, in accordance with King's own views, offered a potentially solid theological basis for a radical politics.

These errors may be dismissed, if lamely, as of a kind to be expected from graduate students or as matters about which interpreters may disagree. The more serious problems concern King's and his professors' scholarly competence. In praising Barth for providing a useful counterpoint to liberal theology, King cited the English-language versions of Barth's books: *The Word of God and the Word of Man; The Knowledge of God and the Service of God; Dogmatics in Outline;* and *The Epistle to the Romans,* the second and drastically revised edition of which came as a theological thunderclap in Protestant and even Roman Catholic circles. In seminary papers and the dissertation, King attacked Barth for rejecting natural theology, and he focused on Barth's reliance on dialectical method. But by the time King was writing, Hans Urs von Balthasar's *The Theology of Karl Barth* had become available in German, as King's professors should have known, and it contained an impressive critique of Barth's rejection of natural theology that compelled a reassessment of the problem.

King's professors failed to recognize a much worse embarrassment: Barth's retreat from the dialectical method he had espoused in his *Epistle to the Romans*. They did know that Barth had long before embarked upon what would become his magnum opus, the multivolume *Church Dogmatics* (1936–1968), which appeared as fourteen separate books, the first of which were available in German at the time of King's work in seminary. (Only a part of volume 1 had been translated.) In the 1950s, Barth's theology was still at the center of spirited controversy in American church circles that were reeling from, among other crises, the departure of the orthodox Calvinists from their long-standing stronghold at Princeton Theological Seminary.

King's professors, notably DeWolf, were keeping up with Barth's work, but, apparently, they did not alert their students to the problems. Calamity ensued, for Barth had radically changed course, supplanting the dialectical method upon which he had previously relied and on which King focused his critique. At that, King should not be criticized too severely, for virtually every erroneous reading he made of Barth's work followed no less erroneous readings in DeWolf's own work.

Had King been subjected to the firm discipline we should expect from theological seminaries, he might well have developed differently. But might-have-beens do not count, and King floundered. His study of Hegel, however superficial, influenced or reinforced his lifelong adherence to the project of subsuming theology under philosophy—a project outlined in Hegel's *Early Theological Writings*. King's careless treatment of Barth, although given an A and praised as "excellent" by DeWolf, had especially regrettable consequences, political as well as theological and philosophical. For King ignored Barth's critique of the Hegelian project and thus bypassed the radical Left's most powerful Protestant theologian. In the event, he lost the chance to ground his politics in a more coherent and promising alternate theology.

King's discussions of Calvin contain worse embarrassments. In a paper that compared the theology of Luther and Calvin, he read Luther as stressing God's love and read Calvin as stressing His justice and power. He thereupon challenged their common emphasis on His sovereignty, insisting that "God is first and foremost an all loving Father." His professors apparently saw no need to demand that he reply to Calvinist arguments against such a dichotomy. Robert Dabney and John Girardeau, among other American Calvinists, had long before offered critiques of the dichotomy worthy of consideration, and, for whatever my opinion may be worth, they shredded it.

In seminar papers, graded high by his professors, King discussed sin and especially original sin and grossly caricatured Calvin's views: "Calvin has very little use for reason in theological formulation. He is forever speaking out against idle speculation." Calvin, the father of a school of theology that has prided itself on its appeal to reason, science, and Baconian induction, certainly did condemn "idle speculation." What estimable theologian has not? King's reading of Calvin will not inspire confidence in those who read the *Institutes of the Christian Religion* for themselves. Among other problems, he dubiously attributes supralapsarianism to Calvin and interprets it as making God responsible for the Fall and for the presence of evil in the world. Most Calvinist theologians have denied that Calvin was a supralapsarian, and all have denied that he made God responsible for sin and evil, a charge Arminians and others have hurled not only at Calvin but at Turretin and every other Calvinist, including such Americans as Edwards, Hodge, Thornwell, Dabney, and Girardeau. At the least, students, even at an Arminian divinity school, should be required to know and evaluate the Calvinist replies.

The retreat from historic Christian doctrine has proceeded apace, with results that—to invoke fashionable liberal incantation—compel one to "understand if not condone" the severe fundamentalist reaction that is taking place in the seminaries of the

Southern Baptist Convention. Here too, an infidel might ask: If Christianity is not primarily concerned with the nature of a triune God, His personal relation to each individual, and the salvation of one's immortal soul, why need anyone become a Christian rather than a Jew, a Muslim, a Buddhist, or even a morally sensitive atheist? The argument from ethics will not do. Indeed, those who, at least since Schleiermacher, try to reduce Christianity to a code of ethics are usually the loudest in insisting that other religions have produced equivalents. And so they have. Which restates the problem. If a code of ethics is all Christianity has to offer, why not rest content with Judaism? Jesus said plainly that He had come to fulfill the law, not to overthrow it. Calvinist theologians have especially been fond of stressing that the Sermon on the Mount clarified the Ten Commandments; it did not institute a new law.

In the early essays at Morehouse and Crozer, King already showed considerable uneasiness over such difficulties, and he turned to Brightman's theological "personalism" as a way of holding on to some semblance of a personal God. But if Brightman treated God as a person rather than as a vague force, he caved in on His omnipotence. He declared that God has limited power over evil and is a "progressive" being capable of growth. An ever-changing God is constantly learning new things from the historical experience of His creatures.

King swallowed a lot, commenting, "According to [Brightman's] view, God is not in perfect possession of life and truth, although He is actually on the way to such possession. The perfect God is future possibility, not present actuality." King nonetheless had misgivings. What evidence, he asked, do we have that God's goodness is triumphing over evil? He characterized Brightman's method as that of "rational empiricism," and approved its echoes of William James's and John Dewey's rejection of the ideal of "finished" truth. Yet, before long, King was gagging. Describing Brightman as a rational empiricist in "the Platonic-Hegelian tradition which defines reason as a principle of coherence," he asked:

> Can one hold to an empirical method of coherence and at the same time make absolute decisions? Certainly religion demands

such absolute decisions. . . . Theoretically we can never make a
claim to absolute certainty and that I accept. But while we cannot
be theoretically certain about any issue, we are compelled to act.
And certainly we have a right to act and accept any belief until
one better is found if it does not contradict our experience. So
that along with a "theoretical relativism," we have the perfect
right to adopt a "practical absolutism."

On this matter King had good reason to believe that he was
protesting out of the marrow of the black churches. In Detroit
in 1954, he delivered a powerful sermon, "Rediscovering Lost
Values," which received a rousing reception. He defined the real
danger as not the admittedly fearful atomic bomb, but "that
atomic bomb which lies in the hearts and souls of men, capable
of exploding into the vilest of hate and into the most damag-
ing selfishness. That's the atomic bomb we've got to fear today."
There are, he averred, absolute truths of right and wrong to which
we must hold firm. He denounced the "pragmatic attitude" that
would reduce ethics to whatever works, and, in words he repeated
in Montgomery and elsewhere, he called for obedience to the Ten
Commandments, not the Eleventh, "Don't get caught."

King's instincts were pulling him toward greater orthodoxy, but
he tried to make the best of Brightman's theology, commenting
that Brightman's "faith in immortality is faith in the goodness
of God. Brightman's belief in a finite God never leads him to
believe that God is so finite that he cannot conserve values." In a
paper applauded by Brightman himself, King wrote, "Brightman
never limits God's ethical nature. God's power is finite, but his
goodness is infinite. At present I am quite sympathetic with this
idea. . . . I am all but convinced that it is the only adequate explanation for the existence of evil." King did not say just how Brightman's musings added up to a solution of the riddle of theodicy
that has bedeviled Christian theology. And in the dissertation, in
which King sternly criticized Tillich and Henry Nelson Wieman
for depersonalizing God, he praised them for arriving, by different
routes, at the concept of a finite God. Yet in the same dissertation
King finally threw down the gauntlet, explicitly to Tillich and
Wieman and implicitly to Brightman. In so doing, he reasserted

the deepest convictions of the black Christian community, which, as Nicholas Cooper-Lewter and Henry H. Mitchell demonstrate in one of the strongest chapters of their *Soul Theology: The Heart of American Black Culture*, has stood squarely on faith in God's omnipotence.

King never did reconcile his demand for an absolute sense of right and wrong, which implied an absolute truth, with his philosophical pragmatism and his insistence that scientific thought is the measure of truth-telling in theology. Rather, he superimposed orthodox pronouncements on a liberal theology that he continued to espouse. Thus in private notes he stressed God's Love as all-inclusive: "This is what distinguishes the New Testament from the Old. The God of the Old Testament was only a tribal God."

King might have pleaded that he was following in the footsteps of distinguished liberal theologians. The nineteenth-century New England Theology had, in effect, shunted God's justice and wrath back on the God of the Old Testament, nicely discarding the "consuming fire" and "jealous God" of Deuteronomy 4:23–24 while celebrating the love and benevolence of the God of the New Testament. And Adolf von Harnack, the renowned historian of church dogma, drove liberal theology to its logical conclusion by calling on the Christian churches to scuttle the Old Testament once and for all.

King reflected, "I have been strongly influenced by liberal theology, maintaining a healthy respect for reason and a strong belief in the immanence as well as the transcendence of God." But by 1952 he concluded that liberal theology was collapsing and that neo-orthodoxy was on the ascendant. And indeed, the assorted challenges to liberalism that were being mounted by Barth, Niebuhr, and others, whether fairly called neo-orthodoxy or no, were re-emphasizing original sin and human depravity with considerable effect. King, in his notes, invoked Jeremiah and commented, "One of the great services of neo-orthodoxy, notwithstanding its extremes, is its revolt against all forms of humanistic perfectionism. They call us back to a deeper faith in God." The dissertation, then, was a culmination of King's effort, begun at Morehouse, to develop a synthesis of the best in liberal and neo-orthodox theology. Trying to find a third way, he acknowledged that he rejected neo-orthodoxy as a body of doctrine, but appreciated it as a corrective for some errors in liberalism. As the editors of the *King Papers* acutely remark, "The significance of King's academic papers lies not in their cogency or originality, therefore, but in their reliability as expressions of his theological preferences."

King nonetheless had a hard time in living up to his own well-taken strictures on the excesses of liberalism. Difficulties plagued his embrace of liberal theology, including some that had immediate political implications. King understood as much, and he struggled manfully to meet his responsibilities. Throughout his life he scoffed at the concept of a triune God, following Schleiermacher and Ritschl in viewing Jesus as a human being with "a unique and potent God consciousness." King justly considered Tillich's formal acceptance of the Trinity and a personal God as little more than the projection of a necessary fiction that could only "point to an impersonal God" and to pantheism. And he criticized Wieman for reducing God's characteristics to a minimum so low as to be beside the point. King's obsession with scientific method led him to accept Wieman's dismissal of trinitarianism as lacking empirical support—a safe gambit since no one ever suggested that the ultimate mystery of the Trinity could be demonstrated empirically. Thus while dissociating himself from Wieman's rejection of a personal God, King wavered on the underlying contention that personality can only arise from a society of interrelating individuals.

On this politically charged theological problem, King slid toward incoherence, apparently unaware of a critical literature his professors did not bother to assign to their students. Thus he sensibly insisted that the personality of God should be understood as absolute and not confused with human personality, but he showed no sense that the concept of the Trinity itself expressed interpersonal relations within the Godhead. If King had read the leading theologians of his native South, most notably James Henley Thornwell and Robert L. Dabney, he would have had to confront a defense of Trinitarian doctrine that asserted a triune God who expressed interpersonality.

No amount of appeals to the superiority of African spirituality over the allegedly Hellenic and overly intellectualized elitism of "Euro-Christianity" can compensate for the deficiency. For the appeal does violence to another and more plausible claim—that African and Afro-American folk culture compel significant revisions in Christian theology itself. To defend that claim, which may indeed have merit, proponents cannot avoid the responsibility to demonstrate specifically how black folk culture compels rethinking of such fundamental problems as the relation of the Creation to the Incarnation, the Fall, the nature of sin, and the Atonement.

The implications of the course taken by King and his successors remain politically troubling, for they suggest a gap between the spirituality of black Christians and the theologians who speak in their name. As a political leader, King came on the scene at a decisive historical moment and proved equal to the tasks his people and, presumably, his God set for him. Even if his theology intrinsically left much to be desired and in some ways abstractly separated his views from the sensibility of his people, the attendant difficulties were as nothing in the context of the exigencies of the great social struggle on which he and they had embarked. His successors, in asserting their own version of a disembodied Socinianism, may not emerge as so fortunate.

Notwithstanding the warm approbation of King's professors, his critique of the doctrine of original sin was appallingly weak. "On moral grounds," he declared, "a person cannot be punished in the place of another." Following in the footsteps of the abolitionist theologians during the slavery controversy, King wrote as if man tells God what is moral and what is sinful, rather than God's telling man. But if so, in what could King ground his appeal to an absolute truth in ethics? That quibble aside, King, in the qualifying examination for the doctorate, insisted that guilt and punishment are not transferable from one person to another. "It seems much more logical," he concluded, "to find the origin of sin in man's free will. Sin originates when man misuses his freedom." The socialistic King seems not have noticed that, in discussing sin, he was sliding onto radical-individualist ground, implicitly rejecting the collective nature of sin as derived from Adam as the representative of humanity as a whole.

Here as elsewhere, King takes Arminian ground, but serious Arminians understand that they must separate two distinct parts of the Calvinist argument if they are to reply satisfactorily: the free will attributed to Adam during the probationary period in which God placed him, and the corruption of the will that rendered man "dead in sin" after the Fall. Apparently, King never heard of such doctrines as "Numerical Identity" or the "Federal Theology," which present powerful challenges to his argument. Let us restrict ourselves to the Federal Theology. King frequently cited Calvin's *Institutes*, which, arguably, contains an interpretation of Adam as the federal representative of a human race that collectively sinned through him. Then and now, any theology student ought to be acquainted with the elaboration, defense, and development of the Federal Theology by a long line of outstanding Calvinists. It should be enough to mention Charles Hodge, whose *Systematic Theology* long held pride of place in American Calvinist circles.

King did ponder the nature and ubiquity of sin, struggling bravely with its political implications. While still in his teens he caviled at liberal theology's rosy view of human nature and admired the neo-orthodox emphasis on man's ubiquitous sinfulness. He criticized the "strong tendency" in liberal Protestantism toward "a sentimental view of man" and rejected perfectionism and the political utopianism it encouraged. Thus in a paper on "Contemporary Continental Theology," he wrote that such optimism has been discredited by "the brutal logic of events"; that man appears to be "more of a sinner than liberals are willing to admit"; and that "many of the ills of the world are due to plain sin." He concluded: "The word sin must come back into our vocabulary." This paper, too, was heavily plagiarized, but, as in his other work, plagiarism or no, King was asserting deeply held views that remained with him throughout his life. And he was developing a language through which he could lay the foundation for an ultimate reconciliation with conservative southern whites, which he knew to be essential to the long-run success of the black cause.

Problems nonetheless recurred. When King wrote of the "logic of events," rather than events, he suggested a theory of inherent sinfulness, but he had no discernible explanation of its origins. He approvingly referred to Reinhold Niebuhr's view that sin arises from man's refusal to admit his creatureliness and from his pretension to being more than he is. But Niebuhr accepted the doctrine of original sin, whereas King, as he himself noted, could offer no alternate explanation for an inherent sinfulness.

King did better with the political manifestations of sinfulness, taking an admirable stance toward burden and responsibility. Reviewing his people's responses to the terrible afflictions they have suffered, he espoused the doctrine, recently espoused eloquently by Cooper-Lewter and Mitchell, that God only demands of us what we are capable of fulfilling—that He places upon us no burdens He has not given us the capacity to bear. Theologically, this formulation may be contested sharply, although it has proved well-nigh indispensable for pastoral work. In any case, the constructive political uses to which King put it remain striking. For he translated it into an impatient refusal to make "oppression" an excuse for avoiding personal responsibility for destructive actions and inactions.

The problematic relation of King's theology to his politics surfaces in his doctrine of nonviolence. The defeat of legal segregation signaled the end of America's formal adherence to racist ideology, for, as Thurgood Marshall and his team of civil rights lawyers forcefully argued before the Supreme Court, the rationale for segregation implied the racial inferiority of blacks. The great struggle that followed the Court's historic decision of 1954 was, therefore, revolutionary, for it overthrew centuries-long constitutional, social, political, and institutional structures and practices. King, boldly challenging the leaders of the older civil rights movement, in effect turned to revolutionary measures, but, in accordance with his deepest religious beliefs as well as his political realism, he demanded that the necessary program, however revolutionary, eschew violence.

Central to King's religion and politics lay the concept of *agape*, which has become especially popular in twentieth-century

American theology as a recapitulation and extension of the nineteenth-century New England obsession with "benevolence." King
defined *agape* as spontaneous, uncaused, all-embracing, disinterested love indifferent to human merit. Following Tillich, he wrote
in the dissertation:

> All love except *agape* is dependent on contingent characteristics,
> which change and are partial, such as repulsion and attraction,
> passion and sympathy. *Agape* is independent of these states. It
> affirms the other unconditionally. It is *agape* that suffers and
> forgives. It seeks the personal fulfillment of the other.

In an earlier essay on "Reinhold Niebuhr's Ethical Dualism," he
filed a caveat that sheds light on his opposition to any politics
based on class, racial, sexual, or other hatreds:

> *Agape*, which remains a law for the individual as a vertical ref-
> erence, must suffer in purity when taken into social relations.
> *Agape* is at best a regulative social norm. The balanced Christian,
> therefore, must be both loving and realistic. . . . *Agape* is always
> a possibility/impossibility.

Two weeks after *Brown v. Board of Education,* King demonstrated
the seriousness with which he considered nonviolence an expression of Christian faith rather than merely a political tactic. He
devoted a sermon in Montgomery to a theme that he would
return to again and again: "Loving Your Enemies." Indeed, from
his student days onward he exhibited that seriousness in his critique of communism. King, despite a misreading of Marx as an
economic determinist, saw much to praise in his theory of class
power, but he worried much over the lack of a moral perspective
in Marxism. He especially recoiled from the totalitarian tendency
inherent in materialist philosophy and its implicit ethical relativism. In his student days, he flayed the atheistic dialectics of
Marxism-Leninism, and in 1961 he identified "the greatest tragedy
of communism" as its doctrine that the end justifies the means,
which translates into a justification for "lying, deceit, or violence"
in the service of "the classless society."

In espousing nonviolence in his "I Have a Dream" speech,
King called for an imitation of Christ that would reconcile oppressed and oppressors—would lead "the sons of slaves and the

sons of slaveholders to sit down together at the table of brother-
hood." In effect, he invoked the Christian concept of forgiveness,
which should not be confused with the sentimentality according
to which "to understand is to forgive." King always stressed that
Christians must seek forgiveness through confession and repentance, doing everything in their power to undo the damage they
have done. Racial reconciliation therefore requires that whites do
everything in their power to exorcise the legacy of slavery and
racism.

But King was also speaking directly to blacks, admonishing
them to eschew hatred, which, however "understandable," could
only destroy their own souls. King, invoking nonviolence as Christian principle, was offering a therapy designed to prevent the
oppressed from becoming the mirror image of the worst of their
oppressors. He never wavered in his conviction that no just society could emerge from a mere reversal of roles—a theme well
developed by Theophus H. Smith, *Conjuring Culture: Biblical For-
mations of Black America.* In speeches during the late 1950s and
1960s King hammered at the theme that the movement must
seek reconciliation, not the humiliation of adversaries. Speaking
at Lincoln University in Pennsylvania in 1961, he said:

> As I have said in so many instances, it is not enough to struggle
> for the new society. We must make sure that we make the
> psychological adjustment required to live in that new society.
> This is true of white people, and it is true of Negro people.
> Psychological adjustment will save white people from going into
> the new age with old vestiges of prejudice and attitudes of white
> supremacy. It will save the Negro from seeking to substitute one
> tyranny for another.

The principle and strategy of nonviolence proceeded in high
tension with the resort to revolutionary measures, manifested in
mass demonstrations against the law of the land and the juro-
political system itself. King was engaging in high-rolling and em-
barking on a dangerous course. Even Thurgood Marshall initially
condemned him for his mobilization of young students to defy
the law, sneering that the struggle for civil rights was a job for men,
not children, and describing King as a "first-rate rabble-rouser."

However dangerous the course, King grasped its special promise, and he proved Marshall wrong. Digging deep into the religio-political experience of his people, he appealed to the prophetic tradition to invoke symbols that were likely to resonate among the white Americans whose support the black cause desperately needed. King grounded nonviolence in Scripture and Christian ethics. The sincerity of his stern denunciations of violence is clear enough, but his doctrine contains some painful political and ethical problems. No more than Thoreau, Tolstoy, Gandhi, or the more recent figures who, especially since the 1960s, have distinguished force from violence did King squarely face the contradiction in his position. Gandhi preached nonviolence as forcefully as any man, but large numbers of his followers repeatedly resorted to extreme violence. Gandhi condemned them for violating his teachings, but when followers repeatedly slip into violations we must ask whether the teachings themselves do not carry the seeds of opposite doctrine.

Force generates counterforce. If people have a "right" to use force against others and against the state, those under siege have an equivalent "right" to defend themselves. And rights or no, historical experience demonstrates that they usually will defend themselves, invoking the unassailable principle that self-preservation is the most firmly grounded of all rights. When force meets counterforce, violence ensues. When, for example, demonstrators exercise their presumed right to sit down and block entrance to the office of a university president, he may readily claim an equivalent right to walk into his office. If he insists upon walking, he will have to step on those who are sitting down. When his foot meets the body of a demonstrator, we have an act of violence. But whose violence? Those who sit down assume that the president must either surrender his office or accept responsibility for the consequences of his unwillingness to be intimidated.

I imply no equation of the moral positions of oppressors and oppressed. Politically, the presumably oppressed may have a strong case for their action, especially if, as is often the case, they have been denied effective and lawful means of redress. But that is only another way of saying that violence may sometimes be justified. Responsibility inescapably rests with those who initiate the confrontation on grounds of principle, of ethical imperative, of Higher Law. The one thing they cannot do is play Pontius Pilate and wash their hands of responsibility for the probable consequences. And manifestly, King refused to play Pontius Pilate. To his credit, he preached that those who feel compelled by conscience to break the law must be prepared to suffer accordingly.

Still, the example of Tolstoy, whose religio-social views King admired, might have led him to reflect upon the anarchism to which they led. King, like Tolstoy, invoked the Sermon on the Mount, which he interpreted in accordance with his view that God gives us only such burdens as we can bear. King viewed Jesus as a God-conscious man who demonstrated how human beings could resist temptation through strict obedience to God's law. Jesus' sacrifice on the Cross for the redemption of humanity was a supreme act of obedience. Since Jesus as God was impervious to sin, we might ask how could He have experienced temptation in a manner equivalent to that experienced by an ordinary man. Some of the explanations advanced by theologians are ingenious, but it remains doubtful that anyone has yet squared the circle.

Trinitarians surely must cavil at King's doctrine of burden and capacity, for if Jesus is viewed as Incarnation and as a Second Adam born without sin but simultaneously the Second Person of the Godhead, every effort at the Imitation of Christ must fall short of perfection. Men cannot, for example, be expected to turn the other cheek while wife and children are under assault. But then, could any man in this world live wholly in accordance with the words of Jesus? In an implicit rejection of King's formulation, Jaroslav Pelikan has tersely observed that Jesus demanded a perfection beyond human capacity. The very point of the Sermon on the Mount is to reassert and explicate the Old Testament decalogue and thereby to remind us that we are all guilty of sin and that the heart of man is known only to God. The Sermon on the Mount reinforces our awareness of unworthiness and of dependence upon the grace of God for a redemption we have not earned.

The problem arises not from King's invocation of the Sermon on the Mount, but from an interpretation that leads inexorably to the transformation of Jesus into a mere moral teacher and to the secularization of ethics. With that implicit secularization goes a strong tendency, which a worried King tried to resist, toward the abstraction of evils from the nature of man and the attribution of them to social relations and institutions. It is a short step to the demonization of the supporters of those social relations and institutions which we may deem sinful.

King himself tirelessly preached that Christian ethics without Christian love generates self-righteous attacks on the sinners as readily as on the sin, if indeed not more so. In this matter, despite frequent accusations to the contrary, he practiced what he preached. He took second place to none in adhering to the Christian admonition to hate the sin but love the sinner. At issue here is not the sincerity of his moral stance but the contradiction between it and the logic of his religio-political theory. Those who, often while espousing nonviolence, assume responsibility for the initiation of physical confrontations may be more deeply moved by revulsion against injustice than are those who defend social order, but their claims to moral rectitude do not relieve them of the responsibility to have available a tenable alternate social order that promises to eradicate existing evils without creating worse ones.

King confronted the most perplexing problems of our age and led a heroic effort to solve them in a manner worthy of a civilized nation. He achieved as much as he did because he had the precious gift of an intellect and a will capable of bringing an effective politics out of considerable doctrinal incoherence. That gift manifests itself as political genius, and men who have it come along rarely.

The danger today is that we may replay a story that has recurred throughout history. All great leaders are deeply flawed, but their greatness arises from their ability to manifest their best and rein in their worst at those very moments when the world must depend upon their statesmanship. Unfortunately, even talented and well-meaning successors are rarely themselves great men. More often than not, they build as readily on the errors of their predecessors as on their statesmanship. Those who would carry forward King's legacy cannot expect to achieve anything at all if they do not begin with a thorough critique of his thought in relation to his action, distinguishing carefully between those actions which flowed from his nobility, insight, and wisdom and those which flowed from his doctrinal confusions and personal weaknesses.

Martin Luther King, Jr., should be judged, as we should all expect to be judged—on the balance of his life's work. With faith, wisdom, courage, and extraordinary political skill he led a social and political revolution in American race relations and thereby earned the admiration and gratitude of the world. Yes, King had a full quotient of faults, some of them grievous, for, like the rest of us, he was a man. But, unlike the rest of us, he was a great man.

15

Does God Matter?

Cornel West is a rising star among American intellectuals. An eloquent exponent of radical democracy, he brings an acute intelligence, wide reading, and training in philosophy and theology to bear on the irrationalities in all political camps. His civility and respect for the views of opponents make him a breath of fresh air in an increasingly mean-spirited Academia.

Keeping Faith relates modern philosophy and religious sensibility to America's racial crisis, as well as to the arts, law, and philosophical method, and includes critical explorations of important thinkers and schools of thought. Each chapter is lively and thoughtful, although I fear that he has attempted too much. He exposes and clears away much rubbish but is less successful in presenting alternatives.

West couples sharp analyses of racism with a firm opposition to nihilistic responses. He impressively dissects rightwing and leftwing interpretations of the black experience and political agendas for the racial crisis. Thus, in his prayerful effort to civilize the Left, which needs a lot of civilizing, he tempers a staunch defense of the Critical Legal Studies movement with an excellent rebuke to its destructive "trashing" of liberalism. For he distinguishes carefully between the negative features of all ideologies and the positive achievements upon which morally sound leftwing and black movements must build. The Left, the black movement, and all others would profit by a careful reading of this book. But those who would do so effectively must confront its more problematic aspects, on which, accordingly, I shall focus.

West, an acute and respectful critic, scores well when on the attack but does less well when he attempts to provide an alternate viewpoint. Especially weak are his allusions to economic issues. Swimming against the tide on the Left, he bravely identifies the national deficit as a grave problem, but he then unconvincingly attributes it solely to military spending rather than to the extraordinary middle-class entitlements enjoyed by the political constituency, white and black, he identifies with. And since he offers no estimate of the exigencies of foreign policy, he provides no basis for a rational judgment on the appropriate size of the military budget. West risks the ire of the Left by criticizing Jesse Jackson on several important matters, but he, in effect, swallows the budgetary high jinks of Jackson's unsuccessful presidential campaign of 1988. Ed Koch, the cantankerous mayor of New York, screamed that Jackson's budget would bankrupt the country in short order. Koch was right. Those who doubt it need only do the arithmetic.

At issue here is not so much West's foray into economic policy but his concessions to the Left's unrealistic attitude toward world politics and its mindless hostility toward American foreign policy. For, however inured we have become to the irresponsibility of the Left on such questions, it is the last thing we expect from Cornel West. Specifically, the principal concern with ethics and moral accountability that he brings to current debates fades here into one-sidedness. As is common on the Left, West's argument ignores the threats implicit in the proliferation of weapons of mass destruction in the hands of dangerous men and movements. Since hopes for a sensible international control of events remain a will-o'-the-wisp, the United States can hardly avoid unilateral interventions in defense of its national interests, which at least sometimes correspond to the interests of world peace and security. A call for a rollback in nuclear weapons may well be justified, but an implicit call for a rollback in conventional weapons must be defended carefully and fully, if it could be defended at all.

The ethical implications of national policy deserve the close scrutiny West demands, and he is right to focus on Academia, which today influences, as never before, the bureaucracy and media. But he presents a picture of Academia that I simply cannot recognize. In particular, when he claims that it is dominated by conservatives, I begin to wonder if we live in the same world. Every major university of which I am aware is controlled by liberals or by opportunists who call themselves liberals. West here confuses free-market rightwing liberalism with conservatism. His often penetrating critiques of various viewpoints do not in fact include the conservative. The one exception comes in his tantalizing remarks on T. S. Eliot, whose traditionalism he admires—another place in which he swims against the leftwing tide—but whose politics he dismisses as "reactionary." But it does violence to the finest aspects of West's own thought to proceed as if Eliot's conservative politics could be severed arbitrarily from his Christian worldview. In any case, West ignores those conservatives who have mounted the most intellectually formidable assaults on his egalitarian and radical-democratic ideas: Eric Voegelin, Wilmoore Kendall, Richard Weaver, and M. E. Bradford—to name a few. Thus, in discussing the plight of black Americans, West offers valuable criticisms of free-market rightwingers as well as of assorted leftwingers who long ago ran out of ideas, but his critique of "conservatives" contains no reference at all to recognizable conservatives.

Whatever disputes may arise over the setting of our current debates, West does an inestimable service in counterpoising a prophetic Christian vision to secular philosophies and leftwing ideologies, which have failed to furnish humane and viable ethics. He rejects "foundationalism" and "relativism" in favor of "radical historicism," but he is obscure on the content of radical historicism and on its claims to obligation. Here, where he speaks passionately out of the prophetic Christian tradition to which black Americans have laid a special claim, he wavers. This book could have been written by an agnostic:

> I would give up my allegiance to the prophetic Christian tradition if life-denying forces so fully saturated a situation that all possibility, potentiality, and alternatives were exhausted, or if I became convinced that another tradition provides a more acceptable and enabling moral vision, set of ethical norms and

synoptic worldview. I need neither metaphysical criteria nor transcendental standards to be persuaded, only historically constituted and situated reasons.

With this stroke West virtually dismisses the message of Job. A sympathetic reader may ask how one may speak as a Christian if he does not wholly accept Jesus as the Christ (Lord and Savior), accept God's will in the face of any historical enormity, and accept revealed truth. Yet West writes of "a prophetic pragmatism and praxis" that enables us to see the "rich, though flawed" traditions of Judaism and Christianity. Why "flawed"? Because, West replies, they tend toward such dogmatic pronouncements as "Thus saith the Lord." Well, "thus saith the Lord" may contain troublesome ambiguities, but, notwithstanding two centuries of obfuscation by liberal theologians, exactly how do Christians expect us to do without it? The great southern Calvinist James Henley Thornwell was not whistling Dixie when he insisted in 1849: "Let the authority of the Bible be destroyed, and Christianity must soon perish from the earth. Put its doctrines upon any other ground than a 'thus saith the Lord,' and every one of them will soon be denied."

West's claims for religion are distressingly lame. He asks us to turn to religion because secular efforts to explore the relation of "ultimacy, intimacy, and sociality" are simply too new to have proceeded very far. Even if this claim were true—such secular efforts in fact have a long history—where would it leave us? If the contribution of religion is not qualitatively unique, then surely reason, once adequately developed, need have no further use for religion.

West tries to distance himself from "liberation theology," which appears to be little more than a rationale for political preferences. But, following in the tradition of the radical abolitionists, he seems to say that if the Bible proves unable to sustain his politics, the Bible will have to go. I had thought that God tells Christians what is sinful, and that they would not presume to tell Him. Here and in his *Prophecy Deliverance!: An Afro-American Revolutionary Christianity*, West expresses a debilitating impatience with theology. He cannot be allowed to get away with dismissing Karl Barth as "unphilosophical"—a charge no less untenable for its being widespread—or with ignoring Nancey Murphy's *Theology in the Age of Scientific Reasoning*. For, arguably, both offer whatever hopes remain for a theology that can rescue religious radicalism from its current impasse. West assumes that Christianity commands social equality and radical democracy, but he merely asserts what he has to prove.

The validation of claims to knowledge, West writes, "rests on political judgments constituted by, and constructed in, dynamic social processes." And we may note that, at least since Schleiermacher, the inerrancy of the Bible has proved ever more difficult to sustain. But it is one thing to expose the irrationality of a dogged insistence upon the objective truth of every word in the Bible, and quite another to proceed as if, therefore, the Word may be treated as a series of metaphors or stories or discarded entirely. If Christians, while repelling the excesses of Fundamentalism, cannot defend absolute truth as revealed in God's Word, what makes them think they have anything special to say?

By reducing religion to ethics and morals, liberal and radical theologians make a merely utilitarian, political argument for religion. West appears to accept Edgar Sheffield Brightman's droll concept of a "progressive" and "limited" God who is still "learning" from the experiences of the human beings He created. West substitutes philosophy and science for theology, but if they can contradict or supersede theology, then, notwithstanding Hegel's claims to the contrary, rational religion has no prospects.

West calls for an ethical standard in politics, but neither here nor in his valuable book *The Ethical Dimensions of Marxist Thought* does he favor us with a clear statement of its content. Rather, his flirtation with religion-as-ethics risks the surrender of the religious standpoint altogether. A Christian perspective, West writes, requires that we see the world through the prism of the Cross. Very well. But he focuses exclusively on "oppression," "victims," and "victimization" without defining those terms. Jesus said, "The poor ye always have with you." He did not say that we ought to be indifferent to their plight, but neither did He say that their plight necessarily arises from particular social relations or the instrumentalities of power, or the evil doings of others. West, unlike Barth, inspires no confidence that his social radicalism flows inexorably from his Christianity, rather than vice versa.

The closest he comes is the notion of oppression as the deprivation of identity and self-expression. In defense of the school of Critical Legal Studies, he replicates not only its admirable critique of illegitimate authority but its lamentable failure to identify any authority as legitimate. And it will not do to invoke "the people" as the source of legitimate authority, for everything turns on one's understanding of "the people." L'Abbé de Lamennais (the ultramontanist), John C. Calhoun (the slaveholding republican), and Giovanni Gentile (the fascist) invoked the authority of the people as sincerely as did John Stuart Mill, Abraham Lincoln, and Karl Marx.

Everyone subject to authority is tempted to view it as oppressive. For subordinates as well as superordinates self-expressed claims to victimization easily paper over inherent depravity. Abstractly, West rejects the idea, prevalent since Rousseau, that sin and virtue arise from social conditions and pertain to specific social groups. But whenever he turns to specifics, he concedes essential ground to those whose rosy view of human nature he criticizes in a splendid warning to radicals against grand schemes for remaking humanity. West wisely insists that a worldview must be grounded in historical experience, and he cogently rejects teleological readings of history. He applauds Richard Rorty, the neo-pragmatist philosopher, for insisting upon "histories," rather than "history," but he then invokes "world-historical process."

Regrettably, West's own invocation of history is replete with errors and dubious generalizations. Merely irritating are such matters as his questionable chronology of the Cold War. More serious is his wild assertion that for exponents of a bourgeois worldview "the slightest acknowledgment of uncertainty and arbitrariness signifies fundamental crisis." A strong case could be made for exactly the opposite. More important, while West is eloquent on the crimes of ruling classes, he falls silent on those of egalitarian movements, which have repeatedly slaughtered people in ever larger numbers and, for good measure, always generated new elites and sometimes generated even worse tyrannies. And it is depressing to see West peddle such ideological puffery as "the sexist history of the European age." For in truth, Western Christian civilization, and it alone, gave rise to effective mass movements against worldwide sexism, not to mention slavery.

West is having trouble in fighting a war on two fronts: on the one side against bourgeois liberalism and conservatism, and on the other side against what he elsewhere accurately calls "the intellectual crisis of the Left." (He might well have added "moral" and "political" to "intellectual.") He has a lot of work to do if he is to sustain his radical politics and, simultaneously, his prophetic Christian vision. Meanwhile, he has posed urgent questions with an integrity and critical intelligence all too rare these days. West has just turned forty, and we may expect that his best is yet to come. May the Holy Spirit be with him.

Culture
and Politics

Politics is a strong and slow boring
of hard boards. It takes both passion
and perspective. . . . Even those
who are neither leaders nor heroes
must arm themselves with that
steadfastness of heart which can
brave even the crumbling of all
hopes. This is necessary right now, or
else man will not be able to attain
even that which is possible today.
Only he has the calling for politics
who is sure that he shall not crumble
when the world from his point of
view is too stupid or too base for
what he wants to offer. Only he who
in the face of all this can say 'In spite
of all!' has the calling for politics.

—*Max Weber*

16

Herbert Aptheker

I

The first edition of my book *In Red and Black* (1971) brought together essays written during the tumultuous 1960s, including "Marxian Interpretations of the Slave South" (1968), in which I severely criticized Marxist historians, most notably Herbert Aptheker. I stand by the essential argument I laid out there but regret the tone and some of the specifics. In particular, I was unfair to Herbert Aptheker, the Communist Party's longtime principal historian, whose contributions to Afro-American history have been seminal. By the time I brought out the first edition of *In Red and Black*, I was already having misgivings. The tone toward Aptheker in the book as a whole veered from one side to the other, for the essays had been written for discrete occasions and showed signs of their origins. Not until the second edition did I indicate how much I have profited from Aptheker's work and acknowledge that he had been closer to the truth than I on the way slave revolts and black resistance to slavery should be understood.

Aptheker has written a great deal, and his work, like that of the rest of us, is uneven—maybe somewhat more so since he has spent his life in political journalism and party work as well as in scholarship. Having been barred, for flagrantly political reasons, from a permanent professorship in our universities, he could devote to political work the time that academics have to put into their teaching and many other university duties and frivolities.

He comes as close as any man I know to being an exception to the dictum I laid down in my essay "On Being a Socialist and a Historian" (the opening chapter of *In Red and Black*) about the virtual impossibility of combining a career as an activist with sustained, serious scholarship. But he has worked under exceptional conditions and is an exceptional man. Writing for *Political Affairs*, his party's theoretical organ, and other publications, and having to prepare pamphlets for mass education, inevitably led to some compromises with the highest standards of his more leisurely scholarly writing. The same could be said for a lot of people, including the great W. E. B. Du Bois and Marx himself, as well as some of the luminaries of the political Right. It could also be said for lesser lights like Genovese, who, having been through the wars himself, ought to have been the first to understand the "trade-off."

I do not mean that Aptheker's more popular writing is unworthy of respect or trifles with the standards of scholarship. Rereading his work today, I am struck by how good it is—by how much can be learned from even the hastier and more vulnerable efforts. Rather, I mean that he sometimes exposes himself to hard blows he would have anticipated under more relaxed working conditions. His occasional dropping of inspirational one-liners is a case in point. I have had good sport with two of his worst: "History's potency is mighty. The oppressed need it for identity and inspiration; oppressors for justification, rationalization, and legitimacy," and "There is an immutable justice in history, and the law of dialectical development works its inexorable way."

The line about dialectical laws may be the worst he has ever written, and I trust he can chuckle over it now. For his historical writing shows little of the dogmatism and mechanism implicit there. From his doctoral dissertation, published as *American Negro Slave Revolts*, which gets better with each reading, through his subsequent efforts, he has tried to restrict his broad generalizations to matters on which he can array impressive evidence and to warn readers that he is advancing other generalizations tentatively as hypotheses.

Many anti-Marxist critics just loved "Marxian Interpretations of the Slave South" for its broadside attack on other Marxist historians, even if those critics normally did not want to engage the principal positive argument I presented. The trouble with the essay is that, in an effort to establish the grounds for what I and others in a new generation of Marxist historians regarded as a sounder Marxist interpretation, I concentrated wholly on what I thought was wrong. No reader would have imagined that I had learned a great deal from my Marxist predecessors, that I owed them a great deal, that in fact I had long been inspired and sustained by the work they did under adverse political conditions. My essay was written in the heat of some partisan political battles that conditioned the harsh tone, but that explanation cannot excuse the higher insanity: At the very moment when younger Marxists like myself were trying to combat the self-defeating tendency of the New Left not merely to ignore or trivialize Marxism but to act as if the previous history of the Left was of no importance, I mindlessly threw away our most formidable weapon, the evidence of a hard-won, honorable, and invaluable tradition of continuous ideological and intellectual struggle.

I wrote "Marxian Interpretations of the Slave South" at the height of the upsurge in the antiwar and black-liberation movements, and I was primarily concerned with combating, as I had long been trying to do, the mechanistic and dogmatic tendencies in "official" Marxism. That task, which others were also embarked upon, seemed essential if Marxists were to combat effectively the subjectivism and voluntarism of the New Left ideology. We had to put our own house in order. Tactically, therefore, the blows were aimed primarily at the New Left. And to some extent we did manage to demonstrate that Marxism need not be abandoned or dissolved into radical sentimentalism—that purged of its tendencies toward economic determinism and dogmatism, Marxism remained the most powerful worldview available to us.

In my case, the effort led to an unfair treatment of Aptheker. In retrospect—or rather, upon a rereading of his work—it became clear that, notwithstanding polemical flourishes about dialectical laws and the like, he had himself long been embarked upon his

own version of our enterprise. Naturally, as a staunch party man—
something I have always admired and envied him for being—
he has spoken in different accents, written in a different way,
and treated some subjects more frankly than we and some less.
Necessarily so, for specific political commitments entail specific
responsibilities toward specific audiences. If, however, I and others
had taken up his work sympathetically, we would have found
much to build on beyond his extraordinarily fresh researches,
and we would have saved ourselves a lot of time. We would have
found the beginning of the fresh thinking we were determined
to do; a wholesome corrective, grounded in a responsible party
discipline, to our tendency to swing wildly on sensitive matters;
and yet enough to dispute respectfully but sharply in a comradely
spirit.

II

A review of the way in which historians have discussed the
theme of slave resistance in the United States quickly reveals the
seminal character of Aptheker's *American Negro Slave Revolts* and
numerous supplementary studies. The literature falls easily into
categories of "before" and "after." To be sure, as Aptheker has
always insisted, he built on the work of such outstanding black
scholars as W. E. B. Du Bois and Carter Woodson. Still, his own
book broke fresh ground, theoretically as well as empirically, and
it forced itself upon a white Academy that had been able to ignore
those black scholars and would soon wish it had ignored Aptheker
too. By the time the Academy arrived at the conclusion that he
was dangerous, it was too late: Too many respected scholars had
praised his first book, and too many people had read it.

The literature on slavery published since the Second World War
has reflected Aptheker's influence and has, with surprisingly few
exceptions, demonstrated acceptance of his principal theses, notwithstanding ritual disclaimers and signs of acute discomfiture at
being associated with a real live Communist. During the decade
before Aptheker published, rumblings of revolt against the hegemony of Ulrich B. Phillips's racist reading of the slave experience

were being heard even in the Academy, but it was *American Negro Slave Revolts* that openly and effectively challenged that hegemony and prepared the ground for such subsequent works as Kenneth Stampp's *Peculiar Institution*.

Aptheker laid down a straightforward but, at the time, startling and controversial thesis—that blacks never accepted slavery, never ceased to struggle against it, and from time to time carried their struggle to the point of insurrection. Notwithstanding the temporary detour occasioned by the debate over the Elkins thesis of infantilized slaves, we would be hard-pressed to find a reputable historian who has not had to end with a positive assessment of Aptheker's thesis. Indeed, even those historians who defended Elkins against misunderstandings and unfair criticism generally dissociated themselves from his thesis of slave docility and argued, instead, that his psychological model could prove heuristically useful for more limited purposes than he intended.

For the most part the criticism of Aptheker's book has proceeded on a secondary level and has largely filed charges of exaggeration of the number and extent of the revolts. Whatever the merits of such criticism, the implications of which turn out to be much more complex than meets the eye, we confront an astonishing fact. For fifty years, marked by the Cold War and the criminal exclusion of Aptheker and other Communists from the universities by especially fierce red-baiting and by attempts to denigrate the work of Communist Party historians, no one has even tried to replace Aptheker's book with a fresh synthesis and reinterpretation. The book has stood up as the indispensable introduction to its subject, and no broad challenge is in sight. All subsequent work on the subject, no matter how critical of Aptheker on particulars, has had to build on it. It is easy to predict that when a new synthesis does appear, it will represent a deepening and broadening of his book on the basis of new materials and the posing of new questions. There is no hint that a new synthesis will challenge its fundamental viewpoint and principal conclusions. Few books have exercised such dominion over a subject of prime importance. That fact speaks for itself. It provides the context for, and defines the limits of, all criticism worthy of respect.

Aptheker's *American Negro Slave Revolts* and subsequent work on black history present a number of theses and suggestions that illuminate American history as a whole and have yet to receive the attention they deserve. Not all his ideas have panned out as he would have liked, but virtually all have proved fruitful, and many in fact have panned out. Let me settle for a few of particular importance: the thesis of continuity, cumulative effect, and mutual reinforcement in the slave revolts; the thesis of interracial unity and of the relation of the struggle of the slaves for freedom to the struggle of the southern yeomen and poor whites for material advancement and democratic rights; and the thesis of the centrality of the slaves' contribution to the struggle for political democracy in the United States as a whole.

First, Aptheker has been cautious about arguing that the slave revolts were connected and cumulative, warning of a paucity of direct evidence and of substantial methodological difficulties. A half century later the jury is still out and may never be able to reach a verdict. Yet by raising the question of a connection, Aptheker was led to develop a supporting thesis that has steadily been gaining support: his strong but little noticed thesis that the revolutionary philosophies of the American and French revolutions exercised a decisive influence in the encouragement and shaping of slave revolt during the eighteenth and nineteenth centuries. As the evidence in support of this thesis mounts, it renders less important the interesting but narrower question of direct links among the revolts. In other words, the explanation for the dynamics to which Aptheker was, along with W. E. B. Du Bois and C. L. R. James, among the very first to draw attention, appears to have been rooted in an international revolutionary process, so that links between specific revolts need not be established in order to sustain the deeper argument. (I have explored these questions in my book *From Rebellion to Revolution: Afro-American Slave Revolts in the Making of the Modern World* [1979], which built especially on James's work but was also influenced by that of Aptheker and Du Bois.)

Second, Aptheker's thesis of a considerable measure of black–white unity in the antislavery struggle within the South—a thesis he also advanced cautiously—has yielded good fruit up to a point. The excellent new work on the social history of the colonial period, especially in the Chesapeake region, has demonstrated that blacks and poor whites, especially indentured servants, were by no means initially hostile to each other and in fact displayed considerable unity in struggle against a common oppressor. Edmund Morgan's *American Slavery, American Freedom* (1975) argues, in consequence, that the ruling class was badly frightened and that it deliberately promoted racist ideology and practice in order to divide and rule. Morgan's book and the monographic literature, most recently reinforced by Douglas R. Egerton's *Gabriel's Rebellion*, thereby confirm one of Aptheker's earliest theses, although he has not been inundated with credit for having pioneered.

When Aptheker pushes his thesis into the nineteenth century, he fares less well. Unfortunately, the poison of racism, as Aptheker well calls it, did its work. By the Nat Turner revolt in 1831— probably a good deal earlier and certainly thereafter—there was precious little unity of blacks and whites. We shall have to live with that disappointment, but we ought not to scorn the evidence of its feeble and scattered persistence, for that too deserves a place in a full history of the Old South. And we may credit Aptheker's probes for having alerted us to this dimension.

Aptheker's larger argument about class struggle in the South has gained ground steadily. He is being proved right by the new work on antebellum political history. That work supports his conclusion that "growing internal disaffection is a prime explanation for the desperation of the slaveholding class which drove it to the expedient of civil war." As Armstead Robinson's forthcoming book, which I have been privileged to read in manuscript, will stunningly demonstrate, the Confederate war effort collapsed in no small part because of the parallel struggles of slaves and yeomen against the slavocracy. Robinson's great contribution has been to show that those struggles, while parallel and objectively reinforcing, did not become ideologically and politically interlocked. That is, they remained discrete and, in so doing, resulted in a tragic foreshadowing of the defeat of black Reconstruction.

Third, Aptheker scores heavily with his thesis of the centrality of the black struggle to the larger political history of the United States. Here, he makes a beginning—or rather, as often, he develops a beginning blazed by Du Bois, to whose greatness he has consistently paid high tribute: the beginning of a political history of the slaves, however odd the notion of slaves' having had a political history might sound. In *American Negro Slave Revolts* he mentions the Louisiana Purchase, the Ostend manifesto, and other matters, and in subsequent writings he makes some additions.

Further additions come to mind: the censorship of the mails, the gag rule, the collapse of interstate comity in the judicial system, the furor over the Fugitive Slave Law, and the southern insistence on the right to carry slaves into places as far away as Oregon, where no slaveholder in his right mind would have ventured. These and similar actions by the slaveholders drove a deep wedge between them and their all-too-complacent, not to say supine, allies in the northern Democracy. Those actions sealed the slaveholders' fate in the Union and backed them into a corner in which their enemies could isolate, confront, and smash them. Why then, since the slaveholders were hardly stupid or prone to paranoia, did they do it? The answer to that question confirms Aptheker's judgment on the significance of slave revolt and throws into relief the limited value of the attendant numbers game.

For certain problems, notably those connected with the comparative history of slave revolts in the Americas, the numbers game retains some value. It remains striking that if the criterion for a slave revolt is raised from Aptheker's preferred ten participants to twenty, the number of revolts drops precipitously. Hence, critics, myself among them, have accused Aptheker of exaggerating the incidence of noteworthy revolts as distinguished from violent local disturbances. And there is a distinction to be made among a massive rising of thousands in Demerara, a dangerous and nearly successful rising of hundreds in Bahia, and a rising, if it should be called that, of ten in Virginia or South Carolina. Tempered criticism is therefore in order, but I am afraid that there has been little tempered about most of the criticism so far.

And there are problems that concern the interpretation of black history in the United States. Let me settle for one example in which Aptheker may be saying too much—too much, that is, for his own larger argument. I am less impressed than he with the evidence of slave revolt between 1831 and 1861 and would recall Du Bois's observation that the slaves' insurrectionary impulse was largely exhausted by the defeat of Nat Turner. But let Aptheker grant, *arguendo*, that he overstated his argument for this period. He could still point to enough violent actions to sustain his argument that the slaves never wholly lifted the threat of revolt, and, more important, he could still defend his larger argument that slave resistance included explosions of militancy and took new forms, most notably the massive support for the Union during the War.

The wartime refocusing of militant black struggle compels reconsideration of the antebellum slave revolts themselves. Let us turn the question of extent and numbers around and direct it to Aptheker's critics. Just how do we assess the historical significance of those slave revolts and conspiracies, no matter how defined and measured? From this point of view, Aptheker's analysis stands up well in essentials and indeed appears stronger as we learn more about the political dynamics of the period.

The inescapable truth is that the slaveholders plunged into a suicidal course for one reason above all others. Their pervasive fear of slave revolt, rationally based on episodic experience with actual violent outbursts and conspiracies, no matter how scattered and small, convinced them that their slaves must be disabused of any idea that they had prospects, that they had allies, that their masters were politically isolated, and that slavery was increasingly becoming moral anathema throughout the North and the whole civilized world. Thus the slaveholders had to assert a defense of their vaunted southern honor. They had to require that the North silence all criticism of slavery and join in a celebration of its virtues. As early as the mid-1830s, James Henry Hammond of South Carolina, one of the brightest and ablest of the slaveholding congressmen, told his shocked northern colleagues that they had a moral responsibility to hang the abolitionists in their midst. Nothing less would serve. But the measures required to allay the fears of the South necessarily spelled the end of civil liberties and democratic freedom in the North. The only way in which the southerners could meet the challenge posed by the militancy of their slaves was to suppress the freedom of white northerners. The slaveholders' allies in the northern Democracy were being asked to do the one thing their sense of political expediency, if not their consciences, forbade them to do. The abolitionists had long warned that slavery was incompatible with northern freedom and democracy, but few believed them. It took the intransigence of the slaveholders to make that case look good. Thus the slaves, by their episodic direct challenges to the regime, pushed their masters down a political road that led to their destruction as a class.

When, therefore, we finish with the refinements and settle on appropriate numbers for solutions to specific problems, Aptheker's principal thesis is sustained. The slaveholders themselves, in effect, acknowledged a record of revolt and conspiracy adequate to make a decisive impact on the political history that ended with emancipation.

In view of Aptheker's achievements, only some of which I have touched upon, we might profitably turn to the political implications of his career and of his exclusion from the university appointment he so richly deserved. The Academy excluded Aptheker not simply because he is a Marxist and a political radical—during the 1960s those barriers fell—but because he is a Communist. That exclusion constitutes a tribute both to him and to his party. But it has had perverse effects beyond the obvious blow to academic freedom and beyond the dishonoring of the universities and the historical profession. By excluding him and depriving him of a graduate seminar—the training ground for the next generation—the Establishment sought to arrest the development of his point of view. On balance, it did not succeed. There are, after all, less formal ways to influence younger scholars and even to train graduate students. I do wonder how many professors went along without dreaming that their own graduate students were quietly appealing for and receiving Aptheker's guidance. The exclusion nevertheless took its toll. By excluding Aptheker from a university post, the Academy minimized the opportunities for a full airing of his specific viewpoint. For a long time, and to some extent even now, he could be treated as a nonperson, with his work sometimes cited and more often mined but not seriously discussed.

To make matters worse, he has had more than his share of the Establishment's customary catch–22. When he is judged to make a mistake or perform poorly, he does so because he is a Communist, a Marxist-Leninist. When he is acknowledged to write a seminal book like *American Negro Slave Revolts* or to perform well, as he usually does, then he does so in spite of his being a Communist, a Marxist-Leninist. Either way, Marxism-Leninism loses, and so does Aptheker. To get out of this bind, all he would have to do is to announce that his Communist politics and Marxist-Leninist theory are irrelevant to his work as a historian. The Establishment will wait a long time to hear that announcement. (Conservative historians might not wish to be associated with Aptheker, but, alas, they can hardly avoid it since they get the same treatment.)

When the time comes to evaluate Aptheker's lifework, his accomplishments and limitations will have to be encompassed within a framework that pays equal attention to his individual talent and performance and to the particular kind of Marxism that has informed his thought and guided his action, and to which he has contributed significantly. That full and proper evaluation can wait until his productive years are behind him. But even now, we cannot avoid a partial discussion without risking unprincipled compromises with the overt and subtle red-baiting to which he has always been subjected. What must be insisted upon is that his admirable work on black history and other subjects not be divorced from his effort to interpret history from a Marxist-Leninist viewpoint. Accordingly, permit me to suggest a few relevant themes.

Aptheker's emergence as our country's first great white historian of the black experience cannot readily be separated from his development as a Communist. We may dismiss with contempt the attribution of political opportunism to the Communists for their concern with black people. We should also reject the honest error of attributing leftwing romanticism, which may well have merit when applied to some radical historians but misses the point when applied to the Communists. Not that special apologies are necessary for leftwing romanticism when it is embedded in a demand for justice for black people and for an end to racism: There are, after all, worse crimes, most notably the original injustice to black people and the racism that has accompanied it. But the criticism nonetheless misses the point.

For inherent in Aptheker's stance and manifest throughout his intellectual labors has been a critical political insight that has deep roots in the international Communist movement. I refer to the insight articulated in the Comintern as early as 1924 by Ho Chi Minh, subsequently the leader of the Communist revolution in Vietnam, who made the Negro Question, as it was called, central to the struggle against American imperialism and for a socialist America. In general political terms, the Communists saw, before anyone else except an occasional prophet like Du Bois, that no effort to effect a deep structural transformation in American society or to challenge American imperialism could arise in the United States without a great upsurge of the black-liberation movement. The Communist Party did not consistently adhere to its own insight and did make serious mistakes. These inconsistencies and mistakes have repeatedly evoked harsh criticism from liberals and social democrats who, never having had the insight in the first place, had nothing to be consistent about and no mistakes to make. We would do well to note the remark of William Styron. Recalling the bitter exchanges occasioned by his novel *The Confessions of Nat Turner*, he has written in his book of essays, *This Quiet Dust and Other Writings*: "I bear no ill will against Aptheker and keep trying to remember—as it might behoove us all to do— that in the horrible dark night of racism at its worst in America, the 1930s, the Communists were among the few friends black people had."

The point at issue, as Aptheker has tirelessly insisted, is that the struggle for peace, democracy, and socialism cannot advance except in relation to the black-liberation movement; that such a relation can only be based upon an uncompromising war against racism; and that a war against racism requires a clear view of the historical experience of black Americans. Thus, those who accuse Aptheker and all serious Marxists, whether Communists or no, of bringing a political commitment to their work are right. But what that proves, contrary to the assertion of such critics, is that political commitment, when properly disciplined, sharpens historical writing and strengthens the search for truth. For the record shows that the politically committed history of Du Bois and Aptheker or John Hope Franklin for that matter has not, at its best, transformed black history into ideology. To the contrary, it has made a decisive contribution toward overthrowing the flagrantly ideological history to which the Phillips and Dunning schools often descended.

In the masterwork we honor here, but also in his pathbreaking work on the maroons, the black contribution to militant abolitionism, the postslavery development of the struggle against racism and imperialism, and other subjects, Aptheker has demonstrated that the struggles of black people have had a double aspect throughout the course of American history—as distinct struggles for black liberation and as an integral part of the struggle of the American people against reaction. The historical profession has found it possible, and indeed increasingly necessary, to accept this first aspect, but it has for the most part wanted no truck with the second. Instead, it has tried to absorb the black-liberation struggle into the mainstream of American liberalism and thereby to pull its political teeth. [Since these words were originally written a reversal may seem to have occurred. In the next essay in this book— on Black Studies—I shall try to demonstrate that the apparent reversal is in fact nothing of the sort.] Thus, to do full justice to Aptheker's achievement requires the concentration of our efforts on an explication and deepening of the second aspect, which has always pointed toward the unity of thought and action— toward the indissolubility of the search for historical truth and the responsibility to make clear the political meaning of our historical research.

The emergence of assorted radical schools of thought since the 1960s has not solved the problem. Some of these schools and such individual efforts as Vincent Harding's stunning *There Is a River* have in fact contributed toward a restoration of the political dimension to social history. But much of the current work in black history, like that in social history in general, is in retreat from its own political implications. Let me offer a single illustration. The fine, often outstanding, work on the cultural struggle of the slaves—on their family life, religion, and community solidarity—bears heavily on the historical tension between the integrationist and black-nationalist tendencies in the black experience. Among other things, it buries the thesis, made popular by Theodore Draper and widely subscribed to in the Academy, that black nationalism should be understood as a pathological response to oppression rather than as an authentic expression of the black experience. The political uses to which this history will be put are not foreordained and may safely be left to the black-liberation movement. I am not even sure that Aptheker and I would agree on the specifics, but I am sure that Aptheker has always insisted upon a politically responsible reading of history—upon the responsibility of the historian to draw out, analyze, and risk judgment upon the political implications of his intellectual work. To reread his work today is to recognize that it contains a powerful antidote to the political neutering of black history and to the distressing tendency to make social history a substitute for political history instead of an indispensable part of it.

There is one important matter, which concerns this relation of history to politics, on which I part company with my Marxist comrade and with the Leninist development of Marxism: the thesis that the black experience has extruded a revolutionary tradition, in contradistinction to a tradition of determined opposition to enslavement and racism. And on this matter I must frankly concede that Aptheker's Leninism, like Lenin's own thought, is closer to Marx's viewpoint than my own Marxism. Aptheker would insist, I am sure, that a straight line runs from Marx's philosophical writings, which he produced early and never repudiated, to Lenin's *State and Revolution* and other political and philosophical writings. I object neither to the pedigree nor to the orthodoxy. Rather, I object to Marx's philosophy of humanity, which I think wrong, inconsistent with his philosophical materialism, and a superimposition on his interpretation of history. Obviously, this is a big quarrel, which I have pursued in spurts in other writings and which cannot be pursued here. For the moment I merely wish to indicate the nature of the family quarrel that I have with Aptheker and with other Marxists, including the great historian Eric Hobsbawm, the communist character of whose work the American Academy also pretends not to notice whenever it feels compelled to praise him.

The very notion of a revolutionary tradition is elusive and requires an act of faith. That is not a point against it. For if it opens the way to the self-fulfilling prophecy that some interpret as scientific prediction, it also provides an estimate upon which to base a hard politics. And perhaps more important, it fuels militant partisanship in struggle in a way that alternate views cannot readily do. As Aptheker knows, a tradition is not something static, something inherited, something to be applied. It is a living cultural force that can only remain living if developed in constant struggle. Hence, no ultimate empirical test will ever be possible, and the quarrel will continue.

I would not belabor this point if there were not embedded within it two radically different historical psychologies. According to the first, which Marx suggested and Lenin defended unambiguously, and which I believe informs Aptheker's work, the destruction of class exploitation will lead to the destruction of racial and gender oppression, not as an automatic reflex—only simpletons have ever believed that—but as a result of historically inevitable victory in struggle. The Marxist-Leninist theory of the withering away of the state and of a free communist society devoid of coercion rests on the psychological premise that the destruction of class exploitation will liberate human beings to relate to each other naturally—where the view of what is natural is one of intrinsic goodness and harmony with others. I see no scientific or historical basis for such a view, although I wish I did. If, to the contrary, one regards human beings as a historical product of intrapsychic struggle—if, that is, one posits an inherent and ultimately irreconcilable antagonism between self and society— radically different expectations follow, including abandonment of any hopes for the withering away of the state under communism.

And indeed, there are other problems, such as the overcoming of the social division of labor, which Marx insisted upon and Lenin made the foundation of the ideological edifice he built, but which has little to recommend it today and increasingly looks absurd.

If I am correct in this sketchy criticism, then the development of Marxism, to which Aptheker, like Hobsbawm, has contributed much that is rich and powerful, remains flawed and, at the least, requires extensive comradely discussion. I raise this question here in order to illustrate a serious weakness in American Marxism as a whole—a weakness that Aptheker has himself always tried to combat.

For too long American Marxists have been forced to respond to questions posed by bourgeois historians. Up to a point, we have had no choice. Even Aptheker, who obviously saw the trap early in his career, had to devote much time and energy to demolishing racist arguments and clearing away ideological rubbish before he could get on with the task of posing fresh questions. Even now, we collectively suffer in this way, although with less and less excuse. It is time to compel our bourgeois colleagues to respond to our questions, and especially to address those larger questions of historical process, in both its objective and subjective aspects, to which I have alluded. A rereading of Aptheker's work shows that throughout his career he has fought to do just that.

Let me elaborate by reference to one of Aptheker's principal themes. He ends *American Negro Slave Revolts* by saying that discontent and rebelliousness were characteristic of American slaves. In a simple, straightforward reading, I would certainly agree, but his statement is in fact much more subtle and multileveled than it might appear. I would also agree with Aptheker that "passivity" and "docility" did not characterize the slaves in any historically meaningful sense. (Aptheker counterpoises "discontent" and "rebelliousness" to "passivity" and "docility," the terms invoked by previous historians.) But Aptheker, like most Leninists, might not accept my own formulation in response to what I perceive to be the deeper and more nuanced meaning of his concluding statement. For I add that the slaves of the Old South, like all people everywhere, combine a will to rebel with a will to submit;

that the claims of individual freedom or expression run counter to the claims of submission to authority, which are also deeply internalized; and that throughout history, as a function of the human condition, the latter claims have, on balance, manifested themselves regularly and the former episodically. It was from this point of view, the Freudian cast of which will elude no one, that I wrote *Roll, Jordan, Roll* and *From Rebellion to Revolution* as complementary books. In fact, the latter was originally written to be a section of the former.

It may not matter much whether Aptheker's viewpoint or mine prevails. Obviously, they cannot both be right, and could both turn out to be wrong, for there are other possibilities. What does matter is that Aptheker has always met his responsibility to bring these problems to the forefront of discussion and to try to force a confrontation with the political implications of his historical work and that of others. In meeting our own responsibility to connect our historical work to our politics without ideological superimpositions and wish fulfillment, we have Aptheker's work, thought, and political action to build on. In the end, our willingness and ability to build well will constitute the most appropriate tribute we can pay him and the only way in which we can render permanent what he has done for us.

17

Black Studies

Academic Discipline and Political Struggle

Within the last quarter century Academia has gone through a series of struggles, always painful, often bitter, sometimes violent, over racial segregation, exclusion, and discrimination. Until well after the Second World War the record of our universities, professional associations, and scholarly journals constituted a racist outrage, the extent of which has not yet been properly assessed. It should be enough to recall that even the great W. E. B. Du Bois could not teach at a "white" university despite his Harvard doctorate and outstanding academic record; that his work and that of numerous other black scholars now recognized as of high quality went unnoticed or was denigrated; that the professional associations went to great lengths to exclude blacks from participation and promoted flagrant racist propaganda under the guise of science; that black authors and work in Black Studies were unwelcome in the leading professional journals. In short, the professions disgraced themselves, perhaps none worse than the historical profession.

Much has changed for the better, but some of the deepest problems remain not merely unresolved but undiscussed. Here I wish to focus on a problem that arose during the 1960s and 1970s and remains with us: Black Studies as an intellectual discipline and the programs instituted to promote it. Black Studies programs may not rank as the most important racially charged problem on our campuses, but they may well be the most revealing. For unless the stagnation and ghettoization of Black Studies programs are arrested, we shall, however inadvertently, condemn our universities and professions to many years of shamefaced complicity in an increasingly ominous resurgence of white racism and black despair.

In focusing on Black Studies programs I intend a criticism of one feature of Arthur Schlesinger's analysis in *Disunited America*, in which he staunchly defends the principle of an American nation, however much ethnically varied and nuanced, and vigorously combats the ominous attempt to deny the very existence of an American nationality. I heartily agree with its principal thesis and much admire the historical and political argumentation arrayed in its support. But I take issue with its implicit assimilation of the black experience to that of other ethnic groups and minorities.

The black experience in the United States has been unique, not in the trivial sense in which all historical experience may be judged unique, but in the special sense that it has no analogue in the Caribbean, Brazil, South Africa, or anywhere else. A caveat: I shall argue that "black nationalism" is a historically legitimate expression of that unique experience, but I shall invoke that problematic term only because it is widely accepted as a kind of shorthand for a complex reality that cannot accurately be labeled. If my argument here is sound, the term is a misnomer. It nonetheless remains unavoidable because our grossly inadequate political language propels us toward analogies and reference points that generate much more confusion than illumination.

Not until recently were white students in any numbers made aware of the grim realities of slavery, of the achievement of an Afro-American culture forged under conditions of extreme adversity, and of the richness of an African heritage previously and ignorantly dismissed as barbarous and without lasting value. Not until recently could black students in any numbers study their own heritage in a positive atmosphere outside the black colleges.

These hard-won gains are once more at risk. Despite the vast changes of the last quarter century, the typical white student cannot avoid imbibing heavy doses of racism. America's history,

culture, traditions, socioeconomic realities—just about everything—conspire to that effect. If the universities do not accept
a social responsibility to educate our young to reject racism, what
social responsibility would they accept? Simultaneously, if black
students are to be welcomed on predominantly white campuses,
they must be offered a stable environment in which they are not
patronized as perpetual victims whose every weakness is someone
else's fault and may be excused as the result of vast if vague
objective forces. That environment must include, among other
things, academically competent black professors and a curriculum
that takes account of their heritage.

Black Studies programs are today being undermined by self-
proclaimed supporters, white even more readily than black. Notwithstanding the honorable record of some campuses, most Black
Studies programs have been condemned to ghettoization. Three
reasons—or, better, excuses—are advanced for treating Black Studies programs as an intellectually worthless political plaything or
for absorbing them into jerry-built programs in "Ethnic Studies,"
"Urban Studies," or something else.

First, we hear complaints about a decline in student interest.
Are we to suppose that if our students decide to avoid courses in
mathematics or physics, to say nothing of art history or classics,
those subjects should be abolished or reduced to a skeleton existence? Educators generally recognize that certain subjects are a
necessary part of the curriculum and must be allowed to remain
viable despite the vicissitudes of enrollments. The argument from
enrollments reduces to a polite way of saying that the subject
matter of Black Studies programs need not be taken seriously.

Except for those who wish to become teachers, professional
scholars, and perhaps ministers, black students sensibly prefer
to major in law, medicine, the sciences, business administration,
engineering, or some other subject. Many readily cite potential
income, but even the most militant and politically committed will
acknowledge that their communities need doctors, lawyers, and
businessmen. In 1968 a gifted black student at Yale, an English
major with a special interest in Shakespeare, explained: "We have
a big job to do in our communities to educate black people, and

whites too, about our heritage and problems. Even if it only comes to participation in a local PTA, black professionals, businessmen, and workers have to know black history and the specifics of the black condition in America. We have to be able to respond to the needs of the people in our communities and be able to convince whites to respond."

Second, it is widely assumed if less widely expressed that Black Studies is just not a proper academic subject—not an intellectual discipline with a manageable subject matter and discrete methods. This argument was leveled at many other programs now accepted as legitimate, for almost every interdisciplinary program, most notably American Studies, had to face the same charge when first launched. In its most benign aspect, it represents merely the institutional—not necessarily the ideological—conservatism of those who constantly struggle to keep maximum resources and prestige attached to their particular departments. Yet the best of the older interdisciplinary programs have demonstrated the advantages of combining the methods of discrete disciplines. The strength of American Studies programs, for example, has always lain in their combination of traditional methods of historical inquiry, sometimes fortified by mathematics and economic theory, with the methods of literary criticism and art history as well as, increasingly, those of folklore, archaeology, and other branches of the humanities and social sciences.

The charge against Black Studies, therefore, concerns the intellectual content. Is there a legitimate subject with appropriate data? This question immediately reveals itself as ideological projection—a charge that Black Studies is merely a political enterprise designed to develop and disseminate Afrocentric and black-nationalist ideology and propaganda. The argument that Black Studies is not a proper subject reveals a breathtaking ignorance of an enormous body of excellent scholarship. A long list of our country's most respected scholars, to say nothing of outstanding scholars in Africa, the Caribbean, Latin America, Israel, and Europe, have created, by all reasonable criteria, a distinct subject. Even the sourest of critics do not deny the high level of much of the work on the black experience. Let that much be duly registered.

The argument has nonetheless become more subtle. It denies the validity of anything that might be called the black experience. More precisely, it seeks to assimilate that experience to the experiences of European, Asian, and Latin American immigrants and thereby to deny its claims to being unique.

Hence, the argument concedes only that the activities of black people should command attention in such traditional disciplines as history, economics, sociology, and literature or should be included in Urban Studies or Ethnic Studies programs. In this view, the demand to study the black experience only makes sense on allegedly discredited black-nationalist assumptions and is therefore merely a political stratagem. It never seems to occur to those who make this argument that their own position only makes sense on integrationist assumptions and is therefore not one whit less ideological and open to the charge of being a political stratagem.

Academia normally defines as political that which lies beyond its ideological consensus, which is generally if not always accurately perceived as "liberal." And Academia defines as objective and scientific that which expresses its own prejudices and viewpoint. At least rhetorically, integrationism is "in." Indeed, in discussions of Black Studies, integrationism is "in" even for those who show little enthusiasm for it in their own communities. Black nationalism is "out"—and that is that, with "that" defined as objective, scientific truth.

To speak of a black experience implies that the African diaspora offers a body of subject matter worthy of discrete study. It does not imply any particular concept of Negritude or Pan-Africanism or the assertion that black peoples everywhere in the world have more in common with each other than they have with the whites of their particular countries. Such ideological constructs should not be rejected out of hand, for they do lend themselves to respectable intellectual defense. But within the universities they ought to be seen as hypotheses to be investigated along with alternate hypotheses and subjected to rigorous empirical investigation in an atmosphere of mutually respectful intellectual discourse. Any serious Black Studies program ought to be viewed as a terrain of ideological as well as scientific contention. But then, the same might be said of the humanities and social sciences in general.

Consider for example the vigorous and salutary storm over *Time on the Cross* by Robert W. Fogel and Stanley L. Engerman. The debates over econometric methods and scientific calculations of economic growth and labor productivity accompanied harsher debates over their bold attempts to analyze black culture in slavery. Basically, they argued that the slaves absorbed bourgeois values, especially a bourgeois work ethic. Their opponents challenged these theses and insisted that a growing body of work on black work habits, religion, family life, and folklore pointed in an opposite direction—that a distinctly black culture had arisen from the slave quarters to resist not only slavery but the attempt to impose white culture and values.

Fogel and Engerman, whatever else they had in mind, knew that they were writing an integrationist tract, and, indeed, they said as much in response to criticism. Yet most of their critics have maintained an embarrassed silence over the implications of their counter-argument, which emphatically provided aid and comfort to those who build on the premises of black nationalism. These questions cannot be fudged without a plunge into rank intellectual dishonesty and political irresponsibility. But there is virtually no place in the traditional curriculum and departmental structure for a full-scale airing of such urgent problems. They can only be taken up in a program that simultaneously studies black history, religion, folklore, and family life together with the more familiar problems of political economy, anthropology, political theory, and social psychology.

To put it another way, Black Studies has emerged as quintessentially interdisciplinary. And it is wonderfully funny to notice how, at one and the same time, so many educators are pleading for increased interdisciplinary studies while frowning upon a body of subject matter that has proved especially amenable to the combination of methods and data across a wide spectrum of discrete disciplines. It may be doubted that any other subject has so successfully lent itself to the highest quality of work in such "hard" disciplines as econometrics and such "soft" disciplines as folklore.

Black Studies has emerged on the cutting edge of the long sought integration of the humanities and social sciences. For a quarter century it has flourished on the frontier of creative scholarship, as exemplified by Fogel's Nobel Prize in 1993, to say nothing of no few Pulitzer, Bancroft, and other prizes. Specifically, no longer does the historical profession satisfy itself with the study of elites and politics, narrowly defined. A broad consensus has proclaimed the need to study "popular" as well as "high" culture and the relation between the two. But nowhere, not even in the burgeoning studies of working-class and women's history, have the achievements in Black Studies been matched.

The study of religion may serve as an illustration. Building on the pioneering work of W. E. B. Du Bois, Carter Woodson, Melville Herskovits, Roger Bastide, and others, black and white scholars in the United States, Latin America, Africa, and Europe have been unraveling the religious experiences of slaves throughout the Americas. Among other accomplishments, they have demonstrated the links between traditional African religions and Afro-American variants of Christianity and have been exploring the relation of religious values and movements to economic performance, resistance and accommodation to slavery, family life, and other subjects. In so doing, they have made methodological advances in the study of the history and sociology of religion. What knowledgeable scholar would today deny these achievements?

Comparative history offers another example. American historians have finally recognized that the history of their country cannot be understood in isolation; that its economic development, political institutions, constitutional history, class structure, and national culture must be studied in relation to those of other nations and peoples; that in no other way can specific theses, broad interpretations, or claims to uniqueness be tested. Again, no subject has taken longer strides in the application of the comparative method than Black Studies has.

American history has itself been enormously enriched by the creative work in Black Studies. Yet somehow we are expected to believe that this work deserves prizes when done outside the structure of Black Studies programs but poses a threat to the

Republic when done inside. Indeed, we face the absurdity that as Black Studies takes great strides forward, Black Studies programs are increasingly scorned.

The problem is political; the facade is academic. The problem concerns professional and institutional politics, which largely reduce to struggles for turf, but, more ominously, it also includes national politics. To be blunt: more than a few universities either designed their Black Studies programs to fail or caved in to political pressures in a way that everyone knew could lead only to the failure of the programs. To meet political demands, administrations and faculties allowed hastily constructed Black Studies programs to appoint many professors who could command little respect on campus, and then they crippled the programs on grounds that they did not measure up to standards that were not applied in the first place. Some universities have established quality programs, and there is no reason other than political maneuvering that others cannot follow suit even at this late date. But to do so would require that universities educate their faculties on the intrinsic intellectual value of Black Studies.

It may be objected that blacks brought the worst on themselves. It was, after all, they who called for separation in autonomous all-black departments, often with separate recreational as well as professional facilities. And in truth, much might be said about the scenarios that in the worst cases have resulted in cadre-training schools for those committed to the irrationalities of Afrocentrists, to say nothing of quasi-Hitlerian demagogues. It was apparent in 1968, when the political agitation for Black Studies programs burst upon us, that our leading universities were caving in to preposterous demands in order to ride out the storm. Whether deliberately or no, they effected a ghettoization that rendered the programs worthless or worse. In precious few cases, if indeed any, was a good-faith effort made to separate the reasonable and just demands of black students from the irrational and self-defeating.

The rage over Afrocentrism is merely the latest version of this decades-old story. No time need be wasted on blather that aims to denigrate the great civilization of the West while it presents a child's version of Africa as well as Asia and precolonial Latin

America. But once again the unwillingness of universities to promote full, open, honest debate has had ironic results. For not only are integrationists, black and white, being silenced: It is by no means clear that Afrocentrism, as normally preached, contributes to a serious black-nationalist interpretation of the black experience in the United States. Arguably, it encourages a black racism that would assimilate the black experience in the United States to a transnational racial myth and thereby render incoherent all attempts to construct a rational black-nationalist perspective on American history.

How far separate facilities for black faculty and students may legitimately and wisely be extended in predominantly white state universities and private universities is another question. Let us be frank: Without a strong dose of separatism, even the best Black Studies programs would have been swallowed whole by entrenched white faculty members, who would certainly have imposed an integrationist ideology on them in the guise of promoting nonideological and value-free social science. To correct centuries of injustice on campuses that were dominated by ideologically biased, if sometimes well-meaning, whites, a new generation of black intellectuals had to take possession of their heritage and of the training of black youth. Black Studies could never have advanced without the emergence of fresh black voices, as well as the willingness of whites to hear any black voices at all. That intellectual project was necessarily political, and the disorder, mistakes, and tactical extremism that went into the making proved a necessary if disquieting price to pay for the results.

The implications for university structure and governance await sober discussion. But when we have worked through the hesitations, excuses, and confusion and have made due allowances for honest doubts, we come to the heart of the matter: the unwillingness of the white Academy even to consider the possibility that black nationalism represents an authentic tendency within black America, rather than a pathological response to oppression. To the best of my knowledge, no university that has set up a Black Studies program or that has refused to do so has ever openly and frankly debated the issue. And now some universities have retreated before the bluffs mounted by a handful of black racists who spout virtually national-socialist doctrine thinly disguised as Afrocentrism. Accordingly, the initial refusal to treat Black Studies with respect is turning into a self-fulfilling prophecy and a marvelous excuse to pander to campus bullies while ignoring the responsibility to create academically viable programs with high intellectual standards.

The question remains: Why do the powers-that-be refuse to do their simple duty—refuse, that is, to carry through a thorough depoliticization of Black Studies programs that would provide a forum for respectful debate between integrationist, black-nationalist, and other ideologies, demanding only that all hypotheses and theses be subject, so far as possible, to proven methods of empirical investigation? Why, that is, do not our universities strengthen the academic performance of existing programs by adequate financing and an insistence upon professional standards as high as those demanded for any other subject? The answer, I fear, lies in the ultimate scandal in a generally scandalous story. Black Studies programs will remain sources of black-nationalist sensibility and ideological formation because Black Studies as an intellectual discipline is increasingly revealing itself as containing a strong black-nationalist component.

It does so not only or primarily in response to the political strong-arm tactics and brutal psychological warfare that are in evidence and must be combated, but also in response to the findings of the most respected, painstaking, and disinterested scholarly work. For the hidden truth of the matter, which the white Academy pretends not to notice, is that such recent work as the much praised studies of slavery overwhelmingly support a generally black-nationalist interpretation of the black experience in the United States. Consider such masterly work on black history as that of John Hope Franklin and such general studies of slavery as those of John Blassingame, Leslie Owens, George Rawick, and Sterling Stuckey; add some of the more widely praised books on specific aspects of the black experience in slavery—Lawrence Levine and Charles Joyner on black culture, Amiri Baraka on music, Douglas Dillard on language, Herbert Gutman on the family, Vincent Harding on political struggles, Leon Litwack on the onset of emancipation, Albert Raboteau on religion. When taken together, these books and no few others in essence reveal an overwhelming consensus on the emergence of a distinct black culture in slavery. Some of the authors are black, others white. Some sympathize with the integrationists, others with the black nationalists. Yet all, in one way or the other have documented the emergence of a black community that lived in intimate contact with whites, contributed to a general southern and American culture, absorbed much from whites and Indians too, and, withal, forged a black culture significantly distinct, significantly autonomous, significantly African-influenced, and nonetheless specifically American.

The black-nationalist interpretation of the black experience is by no means "proven," much less sanctified, by this scholarship. No such work in itself could prove the general superiority of black-nationalist over integrationist interpretations. What it does do is bury the "pathology" interpretation of black-nationalism and establish beyond reasonable doubt the claims of the black-nationalist interpretation to a fair hearing. At issue here is historical authenticity, not political correctness. Nationalism is a political process, not an intellectual abstraction. Blacks could take full account of the duality of their national development and its black-nationalist component and yet reject separatism in favor of integrationist politics. Or vice versa: They could take full account of their "Americanness" and strongly prefer integration and yet decide that some form of separatist politics is necessary to protect the interests of the great majority of their people. All such questions they can and will decide for themselves, and whites would do well to withhold gratuitous advice.

Black Studies programs are no place to settle such political matters, any more than, say, American Studies programs are the place to settle disputes between liberals and conservatives. Rather, they are the place to do the scholarship and conduct the debates that can lay the foundation for rational political decisions made in an appropriate arena. Academic freedom, not political correctness in the service of one ideology or another, must become the order of the day in Black Studies programs as in all other programs. And note the irony: The cowardly administrations that have in many places permitted black nationalists, Afrocentrists, and other ideologues to harangue students and hire faculty according to political criteria have thereby expressed their utter contempt for the legitimate claims to a measure of autonomy for black Americans. For what else are they doing except using the power of white-dominated institutions to determine the outcome of political struggles in the black community?

Recognition of the legitimacy of black claims to a measure of autonomy in the larger society can be served within the universities in only one way: by a firm commitment to the highest academic standards in an atmosphere of maximum academic freedom. But to achieve that goal the universities would have to adhere to their own endlessly professed principles—the one thing they once again seem incapable of doing.

18

Eugene Rivers's Challenge

A Response

The Reverend Eugene Rivers, as is his wont, has posed hard questions "without horns" in his welcome open letter on "The Responsibility of Intellectuals." And the *Boston Review* is to be congratulated for publishing the valuable responses by leading black intellectuals. In a graceful and prudent style designed to discourage phrase mongering and posturing, Rivers challenges, implicitly as well as explicitly, a good many reigning shibboleths. In response to his call for an honest reassessment of all ideological positions, I should like to risk a plunge into what may seem airy historical observations far removed from the travail of black people that he and the respondents have properly brought to center stage. For I do believe that the matters I wish to raise bear directly on those painful day-to-day problems.

The customary discussions of the black experience as a "class," "national," or "colonial" question each offer useful insights but invariably prove partial and inadequate. The black experience in America has been unique, that is, without parallel in the experience of other peoples. Others were absorbed into an American national culture that they enriched by their Old World experiences. Blacks came as slaves whose masters imposed a strange new religion; assaulted their family relations and indeed denied them legal sanction for any family at all; and did everything possible to destroy their African cultures while denying them access to much

230

in white American culture. As a rich and many-sided scholarship
has demonstrated, blacks survived not only physically but also
spiritually. Against all odds, they forged a culture that interpen-
etrated with white culture and yet emerged as an Afro-American
culture apart.

The Irish, Jews, Italians, and others, also faced harsh, even
brutal, discrimination, but they did steadily force their way into
business, the professions, and positions of political power. They
did not face anything analogous to the kind of racism that would
put them wholly beyond the pale, and, in consequence, they were
able to consolidate every upward movement in the socioeconomic
scale. In the event, they contributed much to American national
culture—face it, we Italians taught Americans what good food
really is—but to speak of an Italian American or Irish American
culture would be to spin fairy tales.

For blacks the reverse was true. Repeatedly, they were hurled
backward from positions won through hard struggles. Thus, paradoxically, when freedom came to slaves in northern cities, they
found themselves deprived of the measure of protection that their
masters provided along with flagrant exploitation. Skilled blacks
of all kinds were driven from their trades by white violence. This
widespread northern pattern recurred during Reconstruction in
the South, when a nascent black leadership, formed in the inter-
stices of the slave regime, was crushed by legal and illegal methods designed to maintain racial dictatorship. Indeed, until recent
decades, most if not all of the so-called race riots in American cities
were actually white assaults on black communities. And those
singled out for the hardest blows were not the antisocial elements
accused of some offense or other, but precisely the successful,
upwardly mobile, "respectable" blacks who had accepted the standards of the white middle class—who had become "uppity" and
forgotten their "place." Until recently, there was virtually no room
at the top—or in the middle—for blacks who tried to play by the
rules of the marketplace and of bourgeois society.

The enforced segregation that replaced slavery did provide room
for a small professional and middle class within the black community itself but virtually no such room in the larger society. In

consequence, the black cultural development of slavery times was able to flower and combat the tendency toward cultural disintegration that constantly threatened to overwhelm a people trapped by an unparalleled racial enmity and with little hope of rising above poverty. Segregation, however deplorable, did strengthen the cultural striving for an autonomous cultural and community development.

And by no means just cultural striving. For as W. E. B. Du Bois emphasized in his famous critique of Booker T. Washington, blacks were entering the world of cities and modern industry at the moment at which the triumph of big business was aborting the possibility for the creation of a substantial black big bourgeoisie. The tragedy of Booker T. Washington's efforts, from this point of view, lay not so much in his accommodation to white power, which could be defended as a necessary tactic for a people at bay, but in his illusion of black participation at the top of a business society that no longer had much room at the top. It is noteworthy that Du Bois himself ended not only as a Socialist and then a Communist, but also as a strong supporter of essential features of the black-separatist program he had once opposed.

There is, nonetheless, as great a danger in yielding to a black-separatist repudiation of American nationality as there is in yielding to a one-sided integrationism. Recall that Du Bois himself never wavered in his allegiance to Western civilization while he pioneered in African studies. And here we need to take the measure of the nihilistic denigration of Western civilization, which would deprive all Americans, white and black, of a precious heritage. Today, from the heart of the Establishment that controls our universities and media, we hear calls for the repudiation of Western civilization itself as something uniquely horrible. Our children are being taught that the West has been racist, sexist, and imperialist. They are not being taught that the same could be said about every other great civilization and no few not-so-great civilizations. The undeniable truth is that the West has been unique in only one respect. It alone, thanks largely to its Christian heritage and a derivative doctrine of freedom without parallel anywhere in the world, has generated mass movements against racism, sexism,

and imperialism and exported them across the world. The struggle
of black people for equity and justice, notwithstanding all defeats
and frustrations, has constituted an inseparable part of this legacy.
Does, for example, anyone in his right mind advocate a separate
black path of development unillumined by the Christian tradition
of spiritual freedom, to say nothing of the personal and political
protections of the Common Law?

In any case, it is true that today room is appearing for a minority
of blacks in the professions and lower ranges of the corporate
structure. Simultaneously, we are witnessing the renewed threat
of the disintegration of an authentic black culture. On this matter we would do well to ponder Rivers's sober and penetrating
observation :

> As entry into the labor markets is increasingly dependent on
> education and high skills, we will see, perhaps, for the first time
> in the history of the United States, a generation of economically
> obsolete Americans.
>   But remarkably, the tragedy we face is still worse. Unlike
> many of our ancestors, who came out of slavery and entered this
> century with strong backs, discipline, a thirst for literacy, deep
> religious faith, and hope in the face of monumental adversity,
> we have produced "a generation who [do] not know the ways
> of the Lord"—a "new jack" generation, ill-equipped to secure
> gainful employment even as productive slaves.

Even discretely wholesome changes are occurring in the worst
possible way and with ominous effects. Religion provides a case
in point. Blacks have not only preferred to worship in their own
churches and in ways that reveal African influences. They have
developed distinct theological perspectives on Christian doctrine.
From slavery times onward, their preferred doctrines of sin and
soul have also revealed strong African influences that have served
as counterpoints to Euro-Asian Christian orthodoxy. For example,
they slighted the doctrine of original sin while southern whites
remained strongly attached to it, and they reinterpreted the nature
of sin and of the soul so as to reduce the emphasis upon a
one-on-one relation to God and to include a strong emphasis
on the relation of the individual to the collective spirit of both

earthly community and the kingdom of the other world. The political aspects of these African-based adaptations of Christianity contributed enormously to the ability to survive the rigors of slavery and racism. But they came at a price. It is not at all clear that the implicit rejection of some traditional Christian themes has served constructively beyond its original purpose of fortifying black people against the rationale for slavery. Nor is it clear that serious black Christians can maintain such doctrines within a genuinely Christian theology. The resistance to theological liberalism and the dogged adherence to more "orthodox" versions of Christianity that we are seeing in the black churches are widely dismissed as the primitive responses of poorly educated yahoos, but we may yet come to honor them as a healthy corrective to the spiritual disorder of the "mainstream" churches. I am prepared to be corrected, but I do see some such healthy tendency toward orthodoxy implicit in the stance taken by Rivers, who displays a theological depth and seriousness all too rare these days in both white and black church circles, to say nothing of our theological seminaries.

To be sure, these differences with white Christians have been increasingly obscured, for the white churches have, for better or worse—I fear mostly worse—abandoned orthodoxy for massive concessions to basically Unitarian, Universalist, and other doctrines once regarded as flagrantly heretical. I do not wish to ruffle anyone's religious sensibilities, but too often when I hear preaching in the mainstream churches these days I cannot help thinking that Flip Wilson's Reverend LeRoy and "The Church of What's Happening Now" satirize white churches more readily than black.

Many aspects of family life, sexual mores, and the work ethic that represented necessary and often admirable black adjustments to a painfully oppressive reality seem much less startling to whites today than they once did. For, superficially, similar attitudes are now the rage in middle-class white communities. But what constituted strategies for survival for a people at bay in the one case have now emerged, in a radically different context, as celebrations of self-indulgence and the abandonment of time-honored moral standards.

The specific manifestations of the intrinsically praiseworthy destruction of legal segregation threatens a disaster for black communities everywhere. Since the 1960s American society has been increasingly open to a minority of blacks who have access to the suburbs and white society. In consequence, the great majority of blacks are being stripped of their natural leaders and most solid elements, with their communities left to fend for themselves in what are euphemistically called "inner cities"—inundated with unprecedented levels of drugs, crime, hopelessness and supported by a soul-destroying public dole. Counter-currents are appearing, as the splendid efforts of the Azusa Christian Community demonstrate, but recovery presents a staggering task with unprecedented difficulties.

Throughout American history, the black response to slavery, segregation, and racism has been two-edged: integrationist and black-separatist. And neither has worked. For reasons I need not belabor, the demands for a separate national-state have proved absurd in a country in which blacks hold no contiguous territory. But blacks have always struggled to combine the elements of the two responses—to project a black "national personality," to borrow a suggestive term from General de Gaulle—while fighting for equality in the life of the American nation. It should be enough to recall that Martin Luther King rejected separatism and black nationalism and promoted integration through a movement based upon black communities and their churches, with black leadership, and, for that matter, a black following, however many whites were allowed to participate as spear-carriers. Had King taken any other road, he would have faced defeat.

In these and many other ways, blacks continue to assert their claims as a nation-within-a-nation, no matter how anti-separatist their rhetoric and pro-integrationist their genuine aspirations. They do so because the black experience in this country has been a phenomenon without analogue. It has uniquely forged a people at once culturally and politically American and yet a people apart in discernible ways that provide a legitimate basis for demands for a measure of self-determination.

So far we have proved unable to confront this paradoxical historical development and political reality. We lack both an adequate political language in which to interpret it and a coherent ideological framework in which to construct solutions. It should be clear that any effort by the black community to combat social decay and mobilize for an effective political struggle depends upon that community's ability to impose considerable social discipline and to rein in antisocial elements. As Rivers has suggested, the struggle to restore a stable family life may well prove a sine qua non, and, if so, the necessary measures may not comport well with the endless demands for individual rights and the arrogant pretensions to such newly invented constitutional protections as envisaged, for example, in the program of the gay and lesbian movement. Whites have no business in trying to tell the black community, or specific black communities, how to resolve these problems and would do well to keep their preferences and prejudices to themselves. But to speak of "community" at all means to recognize as unavoidable the existence of community prejudices, whether grounded in a historically or religiously sanctioned sensibility or in response to an immediate threat to survival. Whites have a responsibility to support the efforts of black communities to solve all such problems in their own way and in accordance with their own preferences and prejudices, so long as standards of common decency prevail.

In this critical respect, among others, those who would respond constructively to the kind of agenda that Rivers is projecting are being deserted by those whites who most loudly proclaim support for justice to black people. Especially sad is the irrationality that today constitutes the bedrock of the virtual merger of leftwing radicalism with left-liberalism on a program of personal liberation, thinly disguised as a neo-communitarianism—a program that incoherently invents a constitutional right to privacy in matters that are clearly of social concern and simultaneously assimilates it to government intervention in institutional and indeed private life. (And by the way, it is time to recall that the slogan "The Personal Is Political" received its clearest and most intellectually sophisticated formulation from Mussolini and Giovanni Gentile, the foremost philosopher of the Fascist Party.) The left-liberals have, to all intents and purposes, simply sloughed off the restraints formerly imposed upon them by religious convictions or a sense of civic responsibility. To be sure, the Left continues to speak the language of groups, collectivities, communities, but as Elizabeth Fox-Genovese, my favorite feminist, has demonstrated in her *Feminism without Illusions*, these "communities," once scratched, turn out to be political associations of those who claim individual rights and entitlements against the collective interests of anything recognizable as a community.

Who on the Left, for example, is willing to show the slightest respect for the collective will of communities that choose to restrict abortion or oppose affirmative action or provide even a modicum of religious instruction in their schools? The struggle for community autonomy and social justice cannot be sustained by such backing-and-filling. The contributors to the debate in the *Boston Review* paid proper tribute to the historic role of the black churches and seemed to agree that those churches have an indispensable part to play in the salvation of their communities. Very well. But the same could be said about other communities. Why, then, do so many white and black progressives succumb to the nonsense that the American Constitution erected "a wall of separation" between religion and society. It did no such thing. Until well into this century virtually everyone agreed that our schools ought to teach basic moral values and that, in the specifics of our own historically developed nation, those values had to be rooted in the Judeo-Christian tradition. The Left has done a wonderful job of purging our schools of Christianity. But just what has it put in its place, except interminable chatter about the beauties of self-expression? Could anyone argue, with a straight face, that we are better off in the event?

Speaking as an atheist, I would not feel threatened by having a teacher called upon to read from the Psalms of David to open school assemblies. I was not, as a Roman Catholic boy in Brooklyn, hurt by having to listen to our Protestant principal read from the King James version of the Bible. To the contrary, for working-class Italian American boys and girls it was our first introduction to great poetry and to the astonishing power and beauty of the English language. And I do not recall hearing of a boy or girl whose moral sense suffered a setback while listening to the recitals. Yet we are now called upon to revile Pat Robertson for making these simple points and to cheer on the sanctimonious ideologues whose primary contribution to the morals of our youth consists of encouraging nihilistic and increasingly life-threatening sexual mores.

The left-liberals who now hold power in Washington have issued a Serious and Devout Call to replace marketplace individualism with individual responsibility within community solidarity. Splendid. But all such morality has always been derived precisely from community tradition, experience, and faith and is intrinsically exclusive, discriminatory, and prejudiced. To pretend to respect community autonomy while denying each community its own exclusiveness is the last word in intellectual incoherence. I say nothing of hypocrisy. That does not mean that, as a nation, we must tolerate any and all forms of discrimination. Racism has cost us dearly and should be put beyond the pale everywhere. But that minimal demand is no excuse for a broadside program of reducing all communities to a single set of rules—that is, to the obliteration of communities altogether.

Without clarity on these matters the case for the discrete national personality of the black community in America reduces to rubbish—to a blatant illogic unworthy of respect and support. Consider Cornel West's perceptive remarks on the critical importance of law and order to black survival. It should be enough to ask: Could this nation, without losing its soul, tolerate the realization of the statistical projections of a substantial majority of black males dead, on drugs, or in jail by the age of twenty-five? And with 50 percent of black teenagers out of school and 40 percent—three times the rate of whites—out of work, no one need be surprised at this statistical projection. Behind these statistics, as we all know but somehow cannot discuss openly, lies not merely the problem of the unemployed and underemployed, but also that of ever larger numbers of the unemployable.

If Americans are as yet unwilling to confront these issues, so are we unwilling to confront their flip side. A government—any government—that cringes in the face of massive looting, rioting, and defiance of social order does not deserve to survive and probably will not long survive. If the American people are forced to choose between urban terrorism and authoritarian repression, it would be surprising if they did not choose the latter. And they would have every moral as well as political sanction for doing so. For if any "right" is well grounded in human nature, historical experience, and common sense, it is the right of self-preservation.

The imposition of the law and order necessary for the survival of the black community cannot be effected from without. In a racist society such an imposition would take predictable forms with predictable results and would be bitterly and properly resisted. But if so, then black communities have good reason to demand considerable political autonomy and the power to deal with their antisocials in their own way. Community survival and healthy development require considerable discipline and, necessarily, considerable repression. The essential demand ought to be that these specific communities solve their own version of what is now a general problem for America in accordance with their own experience, traditions, and collective sense of imperatives. Must, for example, black communities, to say nothing of white, exclude the churches from their schools and affairs if they conclude that their inclusion and close cooperation with the polity are essential for the reestablishment of moral order? And if the churches, following scriptural and historical authority, declare homosexuality sinful and a threat to community reproduction, discipline, and good order, are they to be told that their autonomy stops there? If so, on what grounds? What, exactly, is the "self-evident truth" at issue here? To whom is it self-evident? We can have a wide measure of self-determination for black America or we can have the insufferable romance with individual rights demagogically paraded as group rights. But let us not delude ourselves: We cannot have both.

Consider another and closely related shibboleth—that poverty causes urban crime. First, the poverty that plagues the United States is nothing as compared to that of many African, Asian, and

Latin American countries which suffer no such ravages. Second, everyone knows that only a small portion of urban crime results from desperate attempts to get food for the family. Third, during the horrors of the Great Depression of the 1930s neither blacks nor whites responded with the kind of crime rate that we now accept as normal. The problem, as Rivers bluntly said—in implicit agreement with William Bennett, Pat Robertson, and a few other unmentionables—lies in the destruction of family and civic discipline. The trouble with Bennett, Robertson, et al., but not with Rivers, is that they refuse to recognize that a self-revolutionizing capitalist system and its attendant marketplace mentality have been history's greatest solvent of "traditional values." If so, we have good grounds for a respectful debate with those gentlemen and the political tendencies for which they speak. And we have no grounds at all for dismissing them as "reactionaries," "fascists," and "bigots," while we pretend that radical and left-liberal liberationists are offering any alternate insights worth a damn.

I confess that I have to laugh when I hear leftists, black and white, run on about community solidarity in opposition to marketplace savagery. Here, note Glen Loury's excellent distinction between a marketplace society that reduces human relations and values to commodities and a market economy that has historically been proved necessary to both prosperity and freedom. Loury may be faulted for the specifics of his analysis and program, but his astute observations should be taken as evidence of the need to include all voices in open and vigorous debate, including the voices of those "black conservatives" who have usually been shut out.

Neither Loury nor anyone in the black movement or on the Left seems to notice that this distinction and an attendant critique of finance capitalism have long been the common coin of the "traditionalist" (primarily southern) wing of the Right. It is true that the southern conservative movement has had a long history of white racism. It is also true that it has been manfully struggling to exorcise that legacy and to purge its ranks of racist demagogues. There is little in the Left's strong and valid attacks on marketplace morality and finance capitalism that has not marked the southern conservative tradition. But unlike the ideologues of the Left, the principal voices of traditionalist conservatism have never fallen into the trap of radical individualism. To the contrary, they have insisted that all communities must be allowed their prejudices and discriminations; that the state must take full account of human depravity; and that respect for the inviolability of the human personality—a concept rooted in Christianity—must not be confused with the endless assertion of individual political and social rights against the collective exigencies of the community.

I say my piece on these matters in my book *The Southern Tradition: The Achievement and Limitations of an American Conservatism.* Here, I merely wish to say what everyone knows but few seem willing to say: The historical categories of radical, liberal, and conservative—of Left and Right—have spent their force, and future political alliances with a prayer of success will have to recruit from every portion of the ideological spectrum.

I fear that I have been staging *Hamlet* without the Dane, for it should be clear to all that none of these problems can be discussed seriously outside the context of the emerging new world order of corporate conglomerates. Here I shall have to settle for a few brief observations, elaborated upon, if also briefly, in my recent book. The international conglomerates are not in a conspiracy against black America. They do not favor genocide. They do not want to see the Third World savaged. They do not have a vested interest in the moral degradation of society and the spiritual crippling of our youth. Let us leave all that to paranoids.

The truth is immeasurably worse. The conglomerates simply feel no responsibility for the solution of such problems unless they interfere with business. Thus they can live happily with the whole agenda of the radical liberationists and their egalitarian dreams, secure in the knowledge that even raw filth constitutes a field for economic exploitation. (Those who doubt it need only turn on their TV sets.) The primary counterforce to the sinister tendencies of our times lies in the reassertion of autonomous national and local communities that are strong enough to prevail politically. And on these critical matters the mainstream of the Right waffles every bit as badly as the mainstream of the Left. Worse it tolerates, when it does not encourage, a smug indifference to the travail of those who are being programmed as the losers in the New World Order.

The reassertion of community life requires for the American nation as a whole, and for the black nation-within-a-nation, social discipline and a willingness to restrict individual rights to those which are proved to be socially safe. The struggle for black autonomy requires the struggle for American national self-consciousness and identity—and vice versa. The many-sided implications of this formulation require a lengthy and careful debate, which will take place, if it takes place at all, at the grass roots—the kind of debate that Rivers has opened so ably.

19

John Shelton Reed

John Shelton Reed occupies a special place among American social scientists, and not only because he ranks among the handful who write English admirably. At home with the methods of sociology, his chosen discipline, he knows southern history and culture, "high" and "popular," as few historians do, and he displays a discerning eye and a sensitive ear worthy of a poet. His style would compel gratitude these days for its clarity alone— for its disdain of jargon and methodological obfuscation and for its respect for readers, who, he assumes, can grasp theoretical complexities when they are presented, as they should be, in strong, clear prose. Beyond that, he writes with a wonderful wit, which he sustains and controls as only a fine writer could. Here too, Reed is something special, for, however frank, and tough-minded, he remains good spirited. As a Christian should, he does not confuse the sin with the sinner.

Reed comes from the middling folk of East Tennessee, that bastion of Unionism from the days of Andrew Johnson and Parson Brownlow and of the Republican Party ever since. He writes, nevertheless, as a special kind of conservative: a southern conservative. Now, the South is full of people who are southerners and think of themselves as conservative, in accordance with the crazy political language of our times. Whatever they are, they are not necessarily southern conservatives. It should be enough to recall that what southern conservatives call the "Southern Tradition" has always been antibourgeois. From John Randolph of

Roanoke and John Taylor of Caroline to Thomas Roderick Dew
and John C. Calhoun and on to the Agrarians and Richard Weaver,
southern conservatives have taken a firm stand against the consolidation of economic and political power inherent in capitalist
development. They have espoused, instead, a peculiarly republican
communitarianism of their own. Recently, these poor chaps have
found themselves locked, with shrinking room to maneuver, in
a Reaganite coalition that celebrates the very "free market" they
distrust. Their miseries may yet inspire a great satire by a latter-day
Jonathan Swift.

Alas, the news from eastern Europe reminds us that the Left has
its own miseries worthy of satire. Here, we need only concern ourselves with the positioning of Reed's thought within the Southern
Tradition. Reed is no ideologue. He displays a healthy skepticism
toward his own worldview and an impish sense of humor toward
the frailty and foibles of humanity. But then, that much, too, is
classically southern. In any case, he emerges as a powerful critic of
the main tendencies of American and modern life without giving
way to cynicism and despair. His folks have been through the wars,
and they lost the big one. They, Reed among them, have learned
that the human race is tough and resilient and that tomorrow is
another day. Reed declines to give the "inevitable" any help and
defends the "old values" to the extent that they remain defensible.

Not all of the "old values" remain defensible, and Reed provides
unsparing criticism of those which do not. Specifically, he has
fought racism relentlessly and well in his own political camp,
where it has been dying much too slowly for his and our comfort.
I know Reed well enough to know that, in true southern style, he
does not cotton to condescension, and there appears something
inescapably condescending in our praising a man for having the
"courage" to insist upon common decency. Accordingly, it might
be well to note his political record and let it go at that.

Reed's primary subject is the South and its (his) people, and he
is as acute a student of that subject as any man alive. His interests
and scholarship range widely, but the same might be said for most
of the intellectuals who have written within the Southern Tradition and who therefore interpret the South in a broad political

perspective. [See Reed's new and fine *Glorious Battle: The Cultural Politics of Anglo-Catholicism.*] It was certainly true of Allen Tate, John Crowe Ransom, Richard Weaver, and M. E. Bradford, and it remains true for their successors. In writing about the South, Reed challenges received wisdom and reigning stereotypes. He makes no effort to disguise the extent to which "modernization" and Yankee values are penetrating the South. He knows that the South is changing, both for the better and for the worse. If Reed is ever tempted into nostalgia and romance, he does a good job of resisting the temptation.

Rather, Reed rejects the superficial fatalism that engulfs contemporary scholarship, not to mention journalism. He has done more than any other writer to measure and explain the staying power of southern folkways and to appreciate the ways in which a "modernized" South resists the replication of Yankeedom while bending to the powerful winds from the North. Do not let his down-home humor fool you. These essays, like his books on continuity and change in the South, offer an essential primer for those who would understand the course of southern politics—who would understand how a Douglas Wilder could be elected governor of Virginia and had a chance to carry the Lower South in a presidential election until he blew his career—whereas a Jesse Jackson never had a prayer.

The free-marketeers of the Reaganite Right could profit immensely from a respectful reading of Reed's work, although, if I know those chaps, they will not bother. Like their counterparts on the Left, they are terribly modern—perhaps, in keeping with the times, I should say "postmodern"—and have no time for good ol' boys who know nothing of the world. That Reed's essays and books could not have been written by other than a learned man who has reflected deeply on history is likely to escape them. At least I hope so. For while I, too, try to hate the sin and love the sinner, I could not pretend to match Reed's Christian virtue and confess to wishing them ill politically. Besides, they are not my problem.

The Left is my problem. As socialism collapses in Europe and the Third World, the American Left finds itself at sea, theoretically and politically. Whether anything positive comes from the current gnashing of teeth remains to be seen. Much depends upon the Left's willingness to consider points of view it has heretofore dismissed out of hand. Theoretically, it would do well to ponder the critique of socialism leveled by the principal figures in the Southern Tradition: the attack on the leviathan state; the defense of socially responsible property rights; the manful effort to combine the prior rights of society and community with institutionally guarded individual rights. Politically, if it is to emerge from the wilderness in which it now wanders aimlessly, it would do well to put an end to the absurdity that it could bypass the South and expect to prevail.

I am not sanguine about the prospects for a revitalized Left and only marginally more so about the prospects for a realignment that would draw upon the healthiest elements across the political spectrum. But nothing is fated, and much remains possible. If a program worthy of decent men and women is to emerge, it would have to combine the most humane and attractive features of communitarianism with respect for the rights of minorities and individuals in a manner free of the racism, bigotry, and bunker mentality historically associated with the darker side of the southern experience. In any case, the Left will fail, on its own or in a historically unprecedented coalition, unless it comes to terms with the positive side of the southern experience. And to do so, it would have to come to terms with the thought of John Shelton Reed.

A proper evaluation of Reed's place in the Southern Tradition would require a long, leisurely critique of the thought of a man who is still finding his own way. But it seems safe to say that his work will gain in stature as time goes on, for more than any other it lays bare the specifics and conveys the "feel" of the South and its people. These marvelous sallies provide a delightful introduction to the corpus of Reed's work, at least for people who are willing to hear other voices and who retain a capacity to laugh at themselves.

20

The Voice of Southern Conservatism

The untimely death of M. E. Bradford at age fifty-eight invites a long overdue consideration of the southern conservative movement and of its foremost spokesman. Although he was not well known in American intellectual circles, he should have been, for he deserved to rank among our country's preeminent scholars, teachers, and politically engaged intellectuals. At the University of Dallas, where, in effect, he succeeded Wilmoore Kendall as intellectual luminary, he served as chairman of the English department. A specialist on Faulkner and, more generally, southern literature, he had been trained at Vanderbilt University in classical studies, history, political theory, and much else. At Vanderbilt, Donald Davidson, his mentor, and Allen Tate, John Crowe Ransom, Robert Penn Warren, Cleanth Brooks, and others promoted a regionally grounded but nonetheless universal conservative aesthetic and social vision, to which they brought remarkable learning and a broad and deep culture. Bradford, reared in that spirit and under that discipline, proved worthy of his predecessors.

Bradford's studies in constitutional history alone ought to have secured his reputation and guaranteed him a place of honor in Academia's elite. Instead he became a nonperson in all but the southern conservative circles he came to lead. I doubt that his invaluable books are assigned to graduate or undergraduate students at any prestigious university in the country. Nor was he a welcome figure in our principal professional associations, which had employed ideological litmus tests long before they fell into the hands of the time-servers who now exclude, when they do not vilify, those who refuse to toe the reigning ideological line.

Bradford spoke from the marrow of a formidable "Southern Tradition" of conservative thought and action that dates back to George Mason, John Randolph of Roanoke, and one side of the problematic Thomas Jefferson. It was honed by John C. Calhoun and other intellectually powerful if largely forgotten southern- ers and developed by the "Southern Agrarians" who collaborated on the famous manifesto *I'll Take My Stand* (1930). The Twelve Southerners who announced themselves as "Agrarians" included some of America's finest and most influential poets, novelists, and critics: Tate, Ransom, Davidson, and Warren, to name the most prominent. In particular, they and such distinguished suc- cessors as Cleanth Brooks introduced the "New Criticism," which fundamentally altered the direction of literary studies in America. Their political as well as literary work won the admiration of T. S. Eliot, Marshall McLuhan, G. K. Chesterton, and others outside the South.

The Agrarians left a deep imprint upon the intellectual world but never succeeded in building a mass political movement of their own. Bradford carried on their intellectual work and proved more politically adept, immersing himself in Texas politics and, more broadly, in efforts to build a coalition that could have some influ- ence on the course of the Reagan coalition in the Republican Party. In assessing their movement, let us begin by dispensing with the slanders maliciously leveled at them. According to the appalling ignorance that passes for sophistication among the provincials of New York and Academia, southern conservatives are racists, ignoramuses, anti-Semites, religious fundamentalists, and virtual fascists. I shall return to the question of racism. As for the rest, they are not now and never have been any of the above.

People whose ignorance of southern history and culture is breathtaking blithely assume that the South has been an intellec- tual desert. This is sheer nonsense. From the earliest days to the present, the South has produced an intelligentsia that has held its own with that of the North. For what it might be worth, the Old South sent proportionately more of its white youth to college than did the North. The Old South established the country's first state universities in Georgia and North Carolina, its first municipal college in Charleston, South Carolina, its first degree-awarding woman's college in Macon, Georgia. More to the point, in theology, political science, political economy, sociology, and other disciplines, the southern intellectuals matched and sometimes overmatched their northern counterparts.

We are entitled to have some sport with the sly suggestion that southern conservatives are religious fundamentalists and fascists, for anyone with half a brain ought to recognize that religious fundamentalism and fascism are mutually exclusive. The first Republican to demand that David Duke be put beyond the pale as a racist and neo-Nazi was Pat Robertson, who later campaigned effectively against Duke during the gubernatorial race in Louisiana. In any case, few southern conservatives have been religious fundamentalists. To the contrary, they have always displayed a deep distrust of ideology in any disguise and viscerally rejected religious as well as secular doctrines of inerrancy. Conversely, although religious fundamentalists may be politically conservative, many are not. Notwithstanding the silly accounts in the media, in the struggle for power that is now raging in the Southern Baptist Convention many of those who oppose the rightwing effort to politicize the church stand on theologically conservative ground. Their ranks include both political conservatives and liberals. And not all who stand for biblical inerrancy take rightwing ground in politics. As for conservatives like Bradford, notwithstanding their own piety, nothing irritates them more than demands for adherence to theological dogma. Southern conservatives and religious fundamentalists often work together in overlapping movements, but they constitute different tendencies. Thus in the presidential election of 1992 a great many conservatives supported Patrick Buchanan, whereas the fundamentalists overwhelmingly supported George Bush.

The charge of anti-Semitism and fascism, which is generally directed against everything traditionally southern, is wildly funny. The South, especially in the days of slavery, when conservatives held power, ranked as the least anti-Semitic and anti-Catholic region of the United States, as a long list of Jews and Catholics certified. The slave states sent the first two Jews to the United States Senate and would have contributed the first Jew to the United States Supreme Court if Judah Benjamin of Louisiana had accepted the nomination. The slave states did contribute a Roman Catholic chief justice. Convent-burning disgraced the cities of the Northeast, not those of the South. Sad to say, anti-Catholicism flourished much more readily among the abolitionists than among proslavery southerners. If the support for Israel so clearly visible among most southern conservatives and religious fundamentalists marks them as anti-Semites, we are living in strange times indeed.

As for fascism, the record clearly shows that the South raised the banner of anti-fascism before any other section. Congressional support for Franklin D. Roosevelt's foreign policy and military preparations against Nazi Germany received overwhelming support in the South at a time when the Midwest was wallowing in isolationism and the Northeast was announcing that "the Yanks are not coming." More to the point, southerners generally and southern conservatives in particular have always opposed the centralization of political power and the glorification of the state. They gagged on Mussolini's totalitarian doctrine of the personal as political and on Hitler's "One *Reich,* one *Volk,* one *Führer.*" And nothing so readily provokes a southern conservative to reach for his revolver as the demand to rally to an infallible leader.

Here a critical distinction appears between the southern conservatives and their fundamentalist allies. Both supported a hard-line foreign policy during the Cold War, but they did so for different reasons. The fundamentalists have apocalyptic visions and tend to see political and ideological struggles as holy wars. Ungenerous critics have even been known to charge them with an un-Christian Manichaeanism. The conservatives for whom Bradford spoke have by no means been insensible to the moral dimension of international politics, but they have arguably taken sounder Christian ground than their fundamentalist allies. They too accept the Christian principles of original sin and human depravity, but they regard as erroneous and dangerous the notion that one people has the right or power to impose its social and political systems on others. They took a hard line against the Soviet Union and communism because they saw them as aggressive. They hated communism as the embodiment of a gnostic arrogance manifested in a centralized state that subjected the individual to tyranny, but their determination to fight it flowed from their judgment that it posed a direct military threat to our own people and society. Then and since, they have been hostile to holy wars, which they associate with Sherman's march to the sea. Hence many of them denounced Bush's Gulf War as imperialist. Some supported Bush on similar principles, reasoning that Saddam Hussein's regime did indeed pose a threat to American national security or to the security of America's allies. In either case, the ideological rationale was rejected as presumptuous.

At the risk of gross oversimplification and homogenization, their core ideas may be summarized as rejection of finance capitalism's substitution of the market and its consumer values for society and values determined by religious and historically developed moral principles; rejection of a radical individualism that places personal expression above social order; advocacy of broad-based private property in a market economy subject to socially determined moral restraints; and faith in a republic based upon respect for local and national cultures that are free to establish their own moral standards. From this perspective, they have cried out with Richard Weaver, the doyen of post-Agrarian southern conservatives: "There is ground for declaring that modern man has become a moral idiot. . . . For four centuries every man has been not only his own priest but his own professor of ethics, and the consequence is an anarchy which threatens even that minimum consensus of value necessary to the political state."

Accordingly, they have supported capitalism against socialism to the extent that capitalism continues to preserve the ideal and some of the substance of private property, and they have supported a market economy in preference to a state-planned economy to the extent that market mechanisms generate equity and justice. Their adherence to the Reagan coalition has embodied considerable strain, for, unlike Reagan and many of his followers, southern conservatives have no romance with the free market and detest much of the ideology that flows from it. Thus Bradford forcefully insisted that not every southerner who, according to the absurd categorizations of the moment, counts himself a conservative is a "southern conservative." He took dead aim at rightwingers for whom conservatism means little more than market economics and pro-business economic policies, describing them as "centralizers" and as "egalitarians on every subject but money."

Indeed, no one on the Left has overmatched Bradford in shredding equality of opportunity as a demagogic swindle that rests on the preposterous projection of an unattainable level playing field for individuals or groups. The siren call of the Left, he argued, is for an equality of condition that cannot be effected and can only embitter those seduced by its promises. Bradford even filed a caveat on equality before the law, noting that it "is in the American tradition only if we remember how restricted is the scope of the law's authority in most free societies."

Bradford, like generations of southern conservatives before him, called equality the real "opiate of the masses," ridiculing as patent nonsense the allegedly self-evident truth that all men are created equal. No two men, they have replied, have ever been equal in any sense other than in their possession of moral worth in the eyes of God. Hence, without doing violence to the democratic core of their republican politics and constitutionalism, southern conservatives have unabashedly stood for recognition of the inevitability of hierarchy and the legitimacy of firm authority in social and political relations. If this be elitism, it is a curiously populistic elitism that insists upon democratic decision making by communities rather than by bureaucracies.

These views run counter to the radical-democratic premises that have governed political life in the West since the French Revolution, and, perhaps more strikingly, they do not readily comport with bourgeois ideology. From Tate to Weaver to Bradford, southern conservatives have carried forth an explicitly anti-capitalist tradition that dates back to the great figures of early Virginia and South Carolina. They have assailed big business as well as big government as destructive of the individual freedom and the republican polity that must rest on private property. That is, they view the bureaucratization and centralization of big business as a complement or prelude to socialism and political tyranny. For them, a republic that respects individual freedom requires a property-owning citizenry.

The weaknesses in the Southern Tradition have long been exposed to view. The best they have been able to come up with as economic policy has been a return to small business and a vast broadening of property ownership, which looks much like a will-o'-the-wisp in these days of multinational conglomerates and worldwide economic integration. What remains latent in the southern conservative perspective is an economic vision that would subject corporate power and property ownership to conditions and restraints imposed by a republican polity. In truth, the lack of attention to economic policy by people primarily concerned with constitutional and moral questions has hurt their cause badly and helps to account for the tendency even of good-spirited critics to find them quaint or politically irrelevant.

The southern conservatives' attendant hostility to the concentration of power in the federal government has always had much to recommend it, and their strict-construction interpretation of the Constitution remains defensible in its adherence to the plain words of the Constitution, the intentions of the Founders, and the interests of the common people against the aggrandizement of big business and bureaucratic government. Bradford's constitutional studies, most recently his posthumously published *Original Intentions*, make out an impressive case for the traditional southern view of these questions. No wonder, then, that Academia and the fashionable reviews of books have given him the silent treatment.

Here we come to the problem of community versus big government and to the haunting question of race and racism. Most southern conservatives do not advocate the imposition of blue laws from on high. On matters of abortion, homosexuality, and much else they primarily demand that communities make their own rules according to their historically evolved sensibilities, interests, and circumstances. They oppose, that is, the cynical invention of more and more "human rights." And we do have the right—what the hell, why not claim it as one more human right?—to laugh at an endless expansion of human rights that can only be based upon a doctrine of natural rights, which implies a doctrine of natural law, which, especially in the light of modern science, is hard to defend without a belief in the revealed truth of a God few of the leftwing preachers of human rights actually believe in.

Bradford clearly articulated a Christian individualism that has little in common with the bourgeois individualism southern conservatives regard as an invitation to personal license. In opposition to all totalitarian ideology, they insist upon respect for the dignity of the individual and therefore oppose any state intervention in private life that cannot be justified as a matter of overriding social safety. They have therefore always offered no more than one cheer for modernism, especially attacking its tendency to reduce society to an agglomeration of atomistic individuals.

On Aristotelian premises they regard individuality as a product of, rather than prior to, society, and they therefore demand submission to time-honored social norms. As Bradford explained, southern conservatives have always accepted the tension between the just claims of "earned rights and commitment to self-realization through liberty and law" and the no less just claims of historically evolved communities. Especially in several splendid essays on the Roman roots of southern—and early American— thought, Bradford defended "the corporate life," for "man is a social being, fulfilled only in the natural associations built upon common experience, upon the ties of blood and friendship, common enterprise, resistance to common enemies, and a common faith." Bradford observed, "Only men who belong to something are in any durable sense free. And belonging to a society also means citizenship in some kind of commonwealth and submission to some kind of law restrictive of our personal freedom to a degree that goes beyond the mere prevention or punishment of crime."

Notwithstanding much that remains defensible and indeed attractive in the thought of southern conservatives, they have come close to ruining themselves politically. Twice in American history their constitutional interpretation, manifested as a doctrine of states' rights, did battle in alliance with ignoble causes—slavery and racial segregation. No wonder that the American people have found nothing more in a valuable constitutional interpretation than a cheap rationale for enormities. The problem has not been that southern conservatives have been racists, although, in truth, most of them were and some of them still are. For they are today engaged in a struggle to purge the residue of racism from their movement. The problem, rather, has been that, since they support the rights of the community against the claims of the centralized state, they have had to bow to the wishes of racist communities. During the great struggles for civil rights in the South, they proved unable to reeducate their constituencies, and, in consequence, they dug in their heels in support of the right of their communities to settle their own affairs in their own ways.

Abstractly, they had a good case for so doing. But they of all people should need no lectures on the claims of historical experience in a country that has learned the hard way to reject racism at all levels as incompatible with civilized life. They of all people should need no lectures on the duty of any people to say plainly, "We cannot live with it." Bradford, in an especially spirited essay in defense of the Southern Tradition, summed up the reigning attitude by quoting his—and everyone's—grandmother: "*We* don't do *that!*" It has taken his colleagues a long time to understand that injustice to black people is one of the things "we" do not, or should not, do.

For that matter, it is difficult to see how the moral corruption that now runs rife in America can be arrested without the intervention of government at all levels. In the wake of the disappointments of the Bush years, Bradford criticized neoconservatives and others who look to a strong national government to solve our problems. What society needs and what government ought to do, he wrote, are two different questions. Yes. But the problem remains, and it is not at all clear that the defensive posture into which southern conservatives and their northern traditionalist allies have been driven promises an adequate answer.

Bradford was no dogmatist, and we shall never know how far
he might have gone to accommodate those who take a different
view of the proper role of the national government. He certainly
held fast to his principles and was not a man to be bought off
by baubles or by the temptations of power. But he always knew
his priorities and scorned sectarian posturing. Within the limits of
principle, he understood the business of practical politics. Hence
he repeatedly expressed his distress over the hostilities that were
rising between opposing factions of the Reagan coalition and did
his best to effect principled compromises.

Bradford, speaking for southern conservatives, refused to advance a monolithic ideology or political program. Southern conservative ranks include narrow ideologues and political sectarians,
but they also include those intent upon building a broad coalition.
Their soberest elements are not likely to risk another split with
the religious Right in a presidential campaign. As the excellent
performance on the Executive Council of the NEH by John Shelton
Reed shows, many of them are ready, willing, and able to work
with others to defend academic freedom as well as academic
standards.

The "movement" in question remains largely a "network" of
engaged intellectuals, but it would be a serious mistake to consider its participants as politically isolated and ineffectual. Mea-
suring the political influence of professors, journalists, novelists,
and poets is an impossible task. That southern conservative and
other traditionalist intellectuals have a wide following is clear;
that they can command a formidable bloc of votes in national
and statewide elections is moot. In this respect the religious Right
is immeasurably better organized and efficient. Neither the Republicans nor those Democrats who look to Sam Nunn for leadership can expect to prevail as other than one more collection
of worthless centrists who pander to the cultural Left if they try
to exclude the religious Right. If the conservatives prove wise
enough to avoid another split with their religious allies in electoral
politics, they will exert considerable influence. For they do reflect
the sensibilities of millions of people in the South and Midwest
who are beginning to choke on the cultural radicalism of the

Clintonites. It would be easy to isolate and ignore the southern intellectuals and such publications as *Chronicles, Southern Partisan,* and broader journals and newspapers that include their viewpoint. It would, however, be foolish and politically debilitating to ignore the immense constituency for which they speak.

There nonetheless does remain a grave danger. As the less attractive features of the Buchanan campaign demonstrated, any political movement that takes a southern conservative—or more broadly, a traditionalist conservative—stance will attract racists and other destructive types. If southern and traditionalist conservatives are placed beyond the pale and treated as moral lepers—if they are compelled to go it alone—they will have a hard time in keeping dangerous elements out of their ranks. Every part of the political spectrum faces the same problem in one form or another, as the disgraceful concessions of the Democratic Party leadership to that party's own quasi-totalitarian demagogues amply proves. If, in other words, those who wish to build a new coalition but insist upon equating southern conservatives with their lunatic fringe may well create a self-fulfilling prophecy.

Bradford was well aware of this danger to and within his own ranks. He held fast to his principles with iron determination, but he did everything in his power to keep the door open to compromises on policy with people whom he regarded as honest and good-spirited. Thus, for example, Bradford's death was a particularly hard blow to his colleagues in the St. George Tucker Society, which brings together specialists in southern history and culture from across the political and ideological spectrum. Numbered among the Fellows of the St. George Society are several types of conservatives, as well as Marxists and radical leftists, and assorted chaps in between—black and white, male and female—who exchange research and debate interpretations in an atmosphere of civility and mutual respect. Bradford was among the founders, and he served on the critical committee that nominates new Fellows according to professional rather than political, ideological, or other criteria. His example has inspired his many admirers in all political camps.

In referring to Bradford, the man, I confess to being biased. Notwithstanding deep philosophical and political differences, I counted Bradford a dear friend and as fine a human being as it has ever been my privilege to know. He was a big man in more ways than one, standing six foot four, weighing some three hundred pounds, and looking like everyone's notion of a Texas sheriff. And yes, he often wore a Stetson. Intellectually, politically, and morally, he was every bit as big, qualifying as a gentleman of a special kind—a "southern" and a "Christian" gentleman. Those who know the breed will not have to be told that such people are strong, not "tough" in the manner of bullies. If he had a mean or bigoted bone in his body, he kept it well hidden.

A word on the "Christian" part. Bradford was quietly pious. His worldview and politics stemmed from his notion of what God required of him. And that notion conformed to the great dictum of his church: Hate the sin, not the sinner. Despite having been savaged and abused by a long list of academic and political worthies, he maintained his dignity and his head. If he hated any man, that too he kept well hidden, constantly astonishing his friends by his refusal to slip into bitterness or personal recriminations. He forgave the trespasses of others as he prayed to have his own forgiven. Among the cardinal features of the Christian life he led was a respect for others, which manifested itself in an intolerance of anti-Semitism and every form of bigotry, as well as intolerance of ideologies that encouraged racial, religious, and class hatreds. He held fast to his own beliefs but never thought he had a private pipeline to God.

As the intellectual leader of the southern conservative movement, Bradford assumed the mantle of his great predecessor, Richard Weaver, the formidable post–World War II social critic whose work, also, remains unread in Academia. Weaver's *The Southern Tradition at Bay* and *The Southern Essays of Richard Weaver* constitute a searing critique of the principal ideological tendencies in Western civilization and as fine a history of postbellum southern thought as we have. Yet they are unknown to all but a few graduate students in southern history and literature. Our most celebrated southern historians do not mention Weaver's scholarship and interpretations in their books or even list them in their bibliographies. They do, however, crib from him liberally. Bradford's work stands by itself, but a full understanding of it would be aided immeasurably by an acquaintance with Weaver's studies of the crisis of modern society and culture in *Ideas Have Consequences* and *Visions of Order*, and his two books on rhetoric.

That Bradford's formidable scholarship, graceful style, and penetrating insights largely remain outside today's intellectual discourse even on much of the Right is doubly unfortunate. For he had a great deal to say on many of the most pressing issues of our times. His opinions and proposed solutions remain hotly debatable, but he displayed an almost unerring instinct for the essentials. He posed and faced the hard questions and rarely if ever wrote a page that did not contain valuable insights. Bradford had the disturbing habit of backing up his opinions with cool logic and extensive research, which might be open to alternate interpretation but cannot be ignored by honest critics. No less important, he spoke for a talented body of conservative intellectuals who are closer to the temper of large numbers of people than is generally appreciated. Their exclusion from current debates is not merely wrong: It is stupid because politically dangerous. The forging of an effective coalition to combat the dismal regime we are now saddled with requires that such voices be heard.

In Memoriam: M. E. Bradford (1934–1993)

With Elizabeth Fox-Genovese

We have lost a great and good man. And, at the risk of presumption, "we" includes those outside the circle of his southern conservative brethren, for we too were privileged to know him as a priceless friend. We too could always count on his largeness of spirit, generosity, sympathy, and wise counsel. Firmly but gently he contested that which he regarded as our errors: firmly, because he held fast to his principles; gently, because, a true Christian, he embodied the great admonition of his church to hate the sin, not the sinner.

Faced with the contemptible neglect of the political and academic Establishment and deprived of the professional and public honors and positions he had earned through inestimable contributions to American letters, he remained a model of personal and political maturity and dignity. Coming generations will honor him for the courageous defense of the southern tradition he mounted through learned studies of literature, rhetoric, and constitutional history; for his penetrating critique of the cultural and political decadence that disgraces our times; for his vision of the good society that decent people in diverse political camps aspire to. He wrote, spoke, and lived conscious both of human frailty and of that element of divinity in everyman which demands respect for the human personality. His "tolerance" flowed from his respect for others—from his willingness to hear other voices and offer reasoned responses.

Mel Bradford was the quintessential Southern Gentleman, whose life, unmarred by holier-than-thou arrogance, challenged— and implicitly rebuked—those of us who, try as we might, could never match his nobility of soul.

21

Southern Conservatism at the Political Crossroads

We have no reason to believe that Samuel Francis suffers from acute masochism. So we might wonder about his decision to entitle his latest book *Beautiful Losers: Essays on the Failure of American Conservatism* and thereby invite sensible people to skip it. Francis, an able historian and ferocious political columnist, announces: "When T. S. Eliot said that there are no lost causes because there are no won causes, he was probably not thinking of American conservatism. Nearly sixty years after the New Deal, the American Right is no closer to challenging its fundamental premises and machinery. . . . American conservatism, in other words, is a failure." Do not be fooled. These words have been written in the spirit of the ironic warning in Dante's *Inferno*.

Francis admires Eric Voegelin, Leo Strauss, Richard Weaver, Ludwig von Mises, Frank Meyer, and other conservative theorists, but he ruefully concludes that they rendered themselves largely beside the point in political struggles. In his view, they relied much too heavily on the power of ideas divorced from social bases and thereby failed to perceive the shift of class power and cultural hegemony from one elite to another. Simultaneously, "Post–World War II conservatism in its political efforts generally ignored the philosophical contributions of its high-brow exponents and fell back on the more mundane considerations of low taxes and small budgets, anticommunism and law and order." Responsibility for the failure of the post–World War II conservative

261

movement to effect deep structural change lies with the readiness of its political and intellectual leaders to divorce themselves from the "genuinely popular discontents voiced by groups that did represent significant social interests"—that is, "Middle American Radicals" whose interests and sensibilities embrace "economic nationalism" and a determination "to preserve national sovereignty and cultural identity."

As a corrective, Francis, the author of *Power and History: The Political Thought of James Burnham*, builds on the work of Burnham and on Vilfredo Pareto's compelling theory of the "circulation of elites." He criticizes the Old Right, New Right, and neoconservatism by focusing on the locus of social power in a manner that should warm the heart of the few Marxists who bother to read him. He argues that the old bourgeois and entrepreneurial elite entered the twentieth century at bay. It suffered hard blows during the Progressive era and finally succumbed to the New Deal. Part of it remained as an Old Right opposition with a shrinking social base. Much of the rest, tied to corporate capitalism, was absorbed into the new elite, which in effect constituted a new class. The mass support to which it appealed had come from small businessmen, farmers, and, generally, the populace of small-town Middle America, all of whom were in decline. Curiously, Francis barely mentions the Southern Agrarians, who wrote from the marrow of his own political tradition and who, well before Burnham, saw no fundamental difference between the government and corporate bureaucracies that in tandem form the new ruling elite.

The managerial elite that Francis criticizes consists primarily of the governmental, corporate, and institutional bureaucracies but includes the intellectuals in the media and universities. Its ideology rests on "manipulative, administrative social engineering," which, notwithstanding all good intentions, breathes a spirit of totalitarianism. Francis does well to begin with this depiction of our current situation, but he does not directly reply to Max Weber on the irresistibility of bureaucracy in modern society. Francis treats this extended bureaucracy as a class rather than as an unusually powerful stratum that bends to the will of other classes in essential matters. He assumes that modern bureaucracies, governmental and corporate, generate a discrete class interest. But the measure of truth in this insight identifies a tendency, not an inevitable outcome. He might here consider John Lukacs's distinction between bureaucracy and bureaucratic thinking, which is not as unrealistic as it might appear at first blush. For at issue is control of the managerial elite itself. An appropriate political movement could realistically set itself the task of disciplining the bureaucracy by forcing it to function as a stratum and thereby preventing it from controlling property and mobilizing itself as a social class.

In *Beautiful Losers* Francis ignores the early history of the managerial thesis. Perhaps that is just as well, for he provided an uncharacteristically error-ridden account in *Power and History*. The Marxist origins of the bureaucracy-as-a-class thesis are nevertheless worth recounting. Burnham began his political career as a prominent theorist in Max Schachtman's dissident Leninist movement, which rejected Trotsky's characterization of the Stalinist regime in the Soviet Union as a degenerate workers' state and instead characterized it as an original creation of a new bureaucratic class. In fact, the Burnham-Schachtman thesis, as it was widely called, emerged from the European Left with Bruno Ricci's *Bureaucratisation du monde,* and it forcibly challenged the American Left through Schachtman's influential *Struggle for the New Course.* If nothing else, attention to origins might have led Francis, as it might lead his readers, to pay more respectful attention to the Marxist theory of class power, which seems to have influenced his own thought, at least as filtered through Pareto, Gaetano Mosca, and Roberto Michels. The debate—or screaming match— on the Marxist Left highlighted the question of whether in fact the bureaucracy constituted a class-in-itself or a powerful stratum that constantly struggled to function as a class-for-itself while it nonetheless remained dependent upon an exterior social class.

Francis follows Machiavelli and Burnham in turning to history rather than metaphysics as the only sound basis for a viable conservatism, but he passes lightly over various historical matters. In moral philosophy he echoes the strands represented by the Southern Agrarians and other traditionalist conservatives. With mordant wit he writes, "The philosophical basis of contemporary American democracy is the Pelagian heresy of the natural goodness of man, and man is most obviously good where democracy has been the most 'developed.'" The logical foundation of contemporary American democracy, he notes, would be "unimaginable in a society that takes the idea of original sin seriously." Regrettably, these words do not comport well with his occasional sneers at those conservative intellectuals who, he alleges, slight practical politics for excursions into theology.

American conservatism, Francis insists, has failed to understand that a new ruling class of managers and bureaucrats has taken power and has been imposing an agenda based on its own class interests. Yet his own doubts about the managerial elite as a class-in-itself peep through his insights into the prospects for a new politics. He defends Edmund Burke's "little platoons" of family, neighborhood, and small town. He extols "traditional class identities and their relationships—as well as . . . authoritative and disciplinary institutions—the army, the police, parental authority, and the disciplines of school and church." Hence he opposes "the cosmopolitan ethic," with its promulgation of atomized human relations and its destructive if ultimately hopeless attempts to liberate us from the natural bonds of sex and from social stratification.

To the cosmopolitanism and universalism of managerial liberalism Francis counterpoises the ethos of Middle American Radicals: "the family, the neighborhood and the local community, the church, and the nation as the basic framework of values." Those values include "the duty of work rather than the right of welfare; the value of loyalty to concrete persons, symbols, and institutions rather than the cosmopolitan dispersion of loyalties; and the social and human necessity of sacrifice and deferral of gratification." To make the crooked straight he unabashedly—and refreshingly—endorses legislation to curb the moral degeneracy of our times.

I approve—emphatically. But when I remind myself of my youthful enthusiasm for Stalinism, I get nervous. Let me file a few caveats. (1) "Work," ran the great Soviet slogan, "is a matter of honor." Idleness was not popular in the socialist countries, which filled the jails and labor camps with "parasites." It was, as I recall, the countries guided by the ethos of the Roman Catholic Church in its heyday that insisted upon charity and graciousness toward beggars. (2) As Francis is fond of noting, the Communists piled up millions of corpses. Let us also note that they did so in the belief that they were delaying gratification in order to provide a better life for their children. (3) I wonder if Francis has read Comrade Zhdanov, Stalin's cultural commissar, who excoriated cosmopolitanism as a vicious imperialist stratagem and made a strong case for patriotic roots in one's Motherland. I would hope that those who legislate on morality for us first reflect on the nature and consequences of Comrade Zhdanov's glorious achievements. (4) Francis condemns universalism and defends the claims of Christianity against those who would promote a wholly secular society. Have I missed something? I thought that Christianity introduced universalism into Western civilization and would be unthinkable without it.

I do agree with Francis on the critical importance of the cultural front in today's political wars and on the need for measured repression, but we had better keep in mind that everything turns on "measured." To combine respect for basic freedoms with the reimposition of social discipline would require a tightrope act that no part of the political spectrum as yet seems capable of walking.

In protesting against the moral decadence of our times, Francis insists that the "life-style, values, and ideals" of the managerial elite and its mass media are opposed to those of Middle America. He stresses the interest of the managerial elite in destroying all traditional impediments to its own power, but he barely hints at the extent to which its course corresponds precisely to that of big capital and the extent to which the dissolution of time-honored moral values represents the logical outcome of capitalist development.

Francis slights the extraordinary power of the market, which perverts the principle of personal responsibility and promotes consumer choice as the arbiter of morals and even spiritual values. Here, he might recall his own invocation of original sin and human depravity. For without a collective decision to restrict personal choice, the lure of moral degeneracy becomes well nigh irresistible. The morality of Francis's Middle American Radicals can hardly be expected to withstand the onslaught of a managerial elite that is, in effect, driving forward the logic of the marketplace and thereby serving the interests of big capital as well as of itself.

The effectiveness of resistance to this creeping horror depends upon a willingness and ability to use force—to indulge in measured repression. But under present or foreseeable circumstances, who or what could impose such repression except a strong state drawn from the managerial elite itself? Francis constantly assaults the neoconservatives for supporting precisely such a state, accusing them of serving as rightwing spokesmen for the managerial elite. I would suggest that, however numerous their sins, the neoconservatives understand that the elite itself constitutes the essential terrain of social struggle and that we cannot do an end run around it.

The strongest parts of *Beautiful Losers* display little patience with the shibboleths of laissez faire and implicitly call into question Francis's insistence upon the autonomous character of the managerial elite. Francis sternly rebukes both the Old and New Right for their uncritical defense of the free market. Acknowledging the sociopolitical as well as economic necessity for a wide range of market freedoms, he wisely distinguishes between the exigencies of a sound economic policy and the exigencies of a sound sociopolitical policy. In the spirit of the Southern Agrarians as well as of Burnham, he supports as much of free-market economics as may prove not merely workable but socially constructive, and he repudiates the notion that social and cultural policies should reflect consumer choice.

In pursuing this theme, Francis makes fresh contributions to the development of the critique of equality and radical democracy. Consider, for example, his trenchant remarks on the effective use made of the egalitarian swindle by big capital:

> Equality is no less useful for large corporations, which require a nationally homogenized market of consumers that can be manipulated into buying their products and which find abhorrent and dysfunctional the persistence of local variations in

> their markets caused by smaller, localized competitors or class,
> ethnic, and regional diversities of taste and demand. . . . It is
> thus basic to the interests of the large corporations to erode
> social and cultural diversity and promote egalitarian uniformity,
> as well as to cooperate with and support political egalitarianism,
> the costs of which in increased unionization, protection of the
> labor force, regulation, civil rights legislation, and ecological
> environmentalism, are ruinous to the smaller competitors of the
> corporations but much less harmful to those larger economies
> that can absorb such costs and pass them on to consumers.

In economic policy Francis again reminds us of the Southern Agrarians he barely mentions. He insists that Middle American Radicals are justified in calling for a strong government to protect their interests: "The classical liberal idea of a night-watchman state is an illusion. . . . A MAR [Middle American Radical] elite would make use of the state for its own interests as willingly as the present managerial elite does." Reflecting on the 1960s, Francis recalls with approbation that the New Left attacked and exposed the new class and pilloried free-market economics, and that the supporters of George Wallace were concerned with social issues and cared little for market economics.

Under the circumstances, Francis's sustained attack on environmentalism raised hackles. Let us grant that a good deal of environmentalist propaganda disguises a design to foist every possible kind of government regulation on our private and corporate lives. Are we to pretend that we do not face serious environmental dangers to our health and safety? Were not conservatives among the first to sound the alarm a long time ago and make environmental conservation their very own cause? The Southern Agrarians relentlessly fought against the environmental effects of unbridled capitalism and socialism, denouncing big corporations and big government as the prime exponents of the devil-take-the-hindmost cult of economic growth.

Francis himself assails the cult of economic growth as destructive of human values, but he simultaneously pins his hopes precisely on economic growth as the sine qua non of social stability. There is no necessary contradiction here or in the comparable stance of Marxists who take similar ground, for policies to promote economic growth are one thing, and a fetishistic sacrifice of culture and society to the promotion of economic growth quite another. But Francis's one-sidedness plunges him toward a genuine contradiction. He wants to scotch most legal and administrative measures designed to protect the environment and, more broadly, scotch restraints on enterprise. Thus, in calling for the overthrow of the new managerial ruling class, he looks to the small and middling entrepreneurs of the heartland to mount an effective challenge to the corporate giants of Wall Street.

Government policies, ostensibly aimed at curbing entrenched big capital, usually do strengthen it. The strongest businesses can afford to pay for vast social programs, whereas small and middling businesses cannot easily afford the higher costs and often suffer erosion and bankruptcy. Francis ably exposes the managerial elite's promotion of social programs that squeeze out the entrepreneurs who most directly promote economic growth and job creation. Were he more interested in the Left as such, he might pay similar attention to the way in which its boundless enthusiasm for centralized and expensive social programs does the dirty work for the big capital it tirelessly denounces. He might then also ponder the encouraging implications of the beginnings of a reaction against that boundless enthusiasm within the Left itself.

Francis's love affair with new entrepreneurs nevertheless threatens to end in disillusionment and a political debacle. For he falls silent on capitalism's inherent tendency toward the concentration of capital in a ceaseless competitive struggle in which the most dynamic entrepreneurs are generally the most socially destructive. Raping the environment and brutally exploiting cheap labor are their stock in trade. If Francis does not wish to truck with Karl Marx, let him recall Joseph Schumpeter's alternate analysis. The Catholic corporatism of *Rerum Novarum*, which Schumpeter endorsed, was designed to discipline this very process and render it responsible to political control.

Francis accepts Schumpeter's thesis that the bourgeoisie has ruined itself by sloughing off the prebourgeois institutions that guaranteed the social stability required for its own hegemony. In view of Irving Kristol's regrettable declaration that the cultural war has already been won by the Left, Francis has some justification for accusing the neoconservatives of bourgeois complacency. Still, Kristol hardly speaks for all neoconservatives on this issue—certainly not for William Bennett or Michael Novak, at whom Francis takes a passing swipe. Francis responds by counterposing the "heroic" virtues of a bygone era. He is right to think that we need a dose of those heroic virtues and that, as the Communists were among the first to appreciate, their restoration would by no means be impossible in a modern society based on new social and property relations. But Francis does not explain how the new entrepreneurs could avoid a recapitulation of the rapacious experience of their predecessors unless subjected to the kind of state control he deeply distrusts.

The new entrepreneurs whom Francis courts are among the most vigorous promoters of the kind of cutthroat capitalism that, on his own showing, promotes the "consumerism, hedonism, and social dislocation" he condemns. And given their objective position in a highly competitive economy, what else should we expect of them, no matter how sincere they may be, as individuals, in endorsing family, church, and "traditional values"?

In pursuing his demand for a decisive split between the Buchananite Right and the Republican Center—and he seems to be demanding just that—he calls upon true conservatives to break decisively with the neoconservatives and other supporters of the managerial elite and its state. The neoconservatives, he charges, array themselves with the main enemies of community and civilized social structures. Francis ignores the tension in neoconservative politics—and in the politics of the healthier sections of the Left—and conflates the objective effects of some neoconservative and leftwing policies with their subjective intent. But that is not the main problem.

It is difficult to see how a political movement dedicated to the restoration of civilized life could hope to arrest the destructive cultural tendencies of our age without an economic policy that balances developmental and environmental concerns, balances

job creation with a decent standard of living for the poorest of
the working class, balances the imperatives of law and order with
social support for the poor and dispossessed. No one has yet
advanced a program that promises solutions, but nothing in Francis's generally acute analyses suggests that anything other than a
strong governmental hand in society and the economy would have
a prayer of success. And under the conditions Burnham so well
delineated and Francis acknowledges, a strong government hand
requires the hegemony of that detested managerial elite or, rather,
of a particular section of it.

These problems recur in Francis's illuminating discussion of
American foreign policy. For all his anticommunism, he excoriates ideological crusades and quixotic schemes to police the
world. His support for a hard line against the Soviet Union flowed
from his belief that communism was inherently expansionist and
therefore a threat to American national interests. Reflecting on
the Reagan years, he writes in his introduction, "It was the Right
of the 1980s that first seriously proposed official policy projects
for exporting democracy and intoned the imperative of spreading
the democratic gospel to the heathen." Nor does he spare Ronald
Reagan stiff criticism for his contribution to that gnostic heresy.
Not surprisingly, then, he and his leading colleagues at *Chronicles:
A Magazine of American Culture* outdid the Left in denouncing
President Bush's decision to wage war on Iraq as an imperialist
outrage.

Francis does not reject moral considerations in foreign policy.
To the contrary, he insists that foreign policy, like domestic, must
include "protection of the historic character and identity of the
community . . . [and] the whole range of intellectual, moral, and
social institutions that provide a common identity for, and identification of, a people." The contradiction in Francis's argument may
be only apparent, for the difference between its two sides could
be held in creative tension. But, as Francis readily acknowledges,
the working out of the specifics is a tall order. His suggestion that
economic nationalism is replacing anticommunism as the focus
of Middle American Radical foreign-policy concerns is plausible
but in itself offers little toward a solution. In fact, he and the

Buchananites have as yet not done nearly as well in balancing moral and national-state considerations as, say, the Republican "centrist" Richard Cheney.

Francis sees American foreign policy as largely an ideological projection of the managerial class's capitulation to a combination of imperialist aggression and supine abandonment of genuine national interests. But his critique betrays uncertainties. In berating the neoconservatives for seeking merely to temper and civilize the welfare state, he protests that they accept absorption of the American economy into a world economy and, *pari passu*, a world political system. He can hardly deny that the world economy is coming under the domination of corporate conglomerates, but he seems to believe that separate countries could somehow maneuver to protect their discrete national sectors. How this could be accomplished, if it could be accomplished at all, short of perpetual aggression and war remains unclear.

Francis's critique recalls that of Lenin's *Imperialism: The Highest Stage of Capitalism*, which argued that the cartelization of the international economy in a world of capitalist nation-states would inevitably lead not to world government but to ever escalating warfare. Thus Lenin foretold the First World War and, by extension, the Second. However powerful Lenin's argument in time and place, the onset of nuclear weapons has compelled sane political as well as economic leaders to consider options that previously could be scorned. A general war among competing capitalist powers is not likely, and what sane political movement would want to strengthen the slim possibility? And Lenin's political analysis rested upon an economic analysis that few Marxists adhere to any longer and that Francis shows no signs of crediting.

I do not suggest that we should yield to the siren calls of global theorists who would surrender American sovereignty to a world government dominated by a coalition of have-not powers. Buchanan's economic critique of NAFTA remains open to serious doubts, but his political critique, which Francis reinforces, retains disquieting force. A measure of neonationalism might well provide a strong corrective to the drift into a cosmopolitanism that gives every impression of being the grave digger for what is left of Western civilization. But surely, Wilsonian One-Worldism and Fortress-America nationalism do not exhaust the possibilities. The neoconservatives, of all people, can hardly be accused of being soft on One-Worldism. That charge could more reasonably be laid on the Left, which, as usual, has no foreign policy worthy of the name. And even the Left, if I understand its temperament aright, would be delighted to support anything from isolationism to military adventures against, say, a resurgent white-racist regime in South Africa, if foreign policy could be placed in the service of its domestic ideological agenda.

In short, Francis is good on the attack against the incoherence of American foreign policy and good in his strictures against plunges into a destructive cosmopolitanism, but, like the rest of us, he is having a great deal of trouble in coming up with an alternate program that takes full account of existing and emerging realities. For just that reason, one wishes he would temper his criticism and alter his tone in debate with others on the Right as well as with the sober elements on the Left.

Beyond the specifics of domestic and foreign policy, Francis despairs over the fate of republicanism and small government, for he no longer sees the kind of citizenry that could practice, defend, or even want them. He grimly but plausibly asserts that almost no one any longer knows what a republic is or wants to accept its burdens: "While every society is composed of groups that compete for special consideration, no reasonable determination of who should get what is possible unless all competing groups adhere to a consensus that affirms the values of some claims over others and establishes regular procedures for realizing these claims. It is precisely a consensus of this nature that America lacks at the present time."

These words again call into question his evaluation of class structure and attendant government power. To begin with, if he is right, as he may well be, how much faith can we place in the moral soundness of those Middle American Radicals? Francis tells us that, unlike leftwingers, Middle American Radicals do not see the government as favoring the rich, and that, unlike rightwingers, they do not see it as favoring the poor. Rather, they see it as favoring both against the middle and working classes, which have to pay the bills. That is, they see government as working for the rich and as co-opting the poor with a dole. Striking a hopeful note, he asserts that Middle American Radicals "form a sociopolitical force now coalescing into a class and perhaps into a new elite that will replace the managerial elite." They seek "the overthrow of the present elite and its replacement by themselves." He concludes an astute review of the shifting attitude of conservatives toward the relation of congressional to presidential power by calling for a "Caesarist tactic" to strengthen presidential power as an instrument to defeat the federal bureaucracy.

What remains unclear is how much the return of substantial power to state and local governments would matter, especially on his assumption of a loss of republican virtue. The transference of power from one bureaucratic level to another might indeed prove salutary but would hardly amount to a destruction of the bureaucracy, much less of the managerial elite as a whole. And the real shift in class power that Francis envisions implies a bureaucracy disciplined by a rebellious class that turns out to be his sainted heartland entrepreneurs. For no other class is on the horizon. To speak of Middle American Radicals as a "class" composed of small business owners, farmers, and workers is to risk incoherence. Francis, who admires Pareto, surely knows that these groups would necessarily provide the mass base for an elite with the economic power to impose its will. And the clearly capitalist elite to which Francis seems ready to turn does not look pretty.

The burden of *Beautiful Losers* belies the gloom and apparent hopelessness of its title: It calls for a coalition to assert the interests of a healthy Middle America and repel the welfare state. By no means is Francis ready to throw in the sponge:

> The strategic objective of the New Right must be the localization, privatization, and decentralization of the managerial apparatus of power. Concretely, this means a dismantling of the corporate, educational, labor, and media bureaucracies; a devolution to more modest-scale organizational units; and a reorientation of federal rewards from mass-scale units and hierarchies to smaller and more local ones.

There is much to applaud in these words, but their unmistakably utopian cast does not inspire confidence. Traditionalists, neoconservatives, leftwingers, and others are busily fighting the last war against each other. Meanwhile, each camp is wracked with internal struggles between those who deserve Francis's strictures and those who, whatever their weaknesses, are honestly determined to arrest the moral corruption that disgraces our society and to resist dogmatic adherence to one or another ideology and economic policy. That we need a new coalition to combat the reigning moral degeneracy and irresponsible individualism that are paraded as "alternate life-styles" is clear enough. That we can get anywhere by projecting imaginary new social classes to ground such a coalition is doubtful.

Francis's easy acceptance of the managerial elite as a class-in-itself threatens to undermine his best insights and defeat his hopes for a radical solution to the crisis through which we are living. An acute student of Machiavelli as well as Pareto and Burnham, he is properly chary of appeals to moral suasion. He insists that only power can check power and that power is the instrument of interests. If so, and if, as Burnham argued, the interests of a managerial elite that has crystallized in a social class correspond to the exigencies of modern life, then we are done. If, however, the managerial class is understood as a stratum that must reconcile its own interests and voracious appetite for power with the interests of those who, despite all checks by state bureaucracies, can exercise power from independent social bases, we have a way out.

Burnham began by admiring the managerial elite for its bold adaptation to the emerging economic realities of the twentieth century and by scorning the old bourgeois elite in both its liberal and conservative manifestations. He admired the new men of the emerging managerial elite for their readiness to take radical measures and to use force, ruthlessly if necessary. He ended by becoming disgusted with the managerial elite's increasing timidity, which has recapitulated the softness of the old bourgeoisie and lost the sense that anything is worth dying for. Under such conditions two alternatives are possible: a new and more vigorous class could overthrow the managerial elite, or we could be in for a prolonged period of social decomposition and virtual anarchy. The second alternative might be expected to follow the deadening paralysis of the managerial elite in a world in which no new class arises to challenge it. And no such class is in the cards.

Francis has himself suggested, although more clearly in *Power and History* than here, that the deepest interests of the managerial elite require a widespread popular support made difficult by its own efforts to undermine traditional authority and, indeed, any sense of legitimate authority. Thus, significant elements within it are compelled not merely to pay lip service to "traditional values" but to struggle to ground them in repositories of social power. That is, the continued hegemony of the managerial elite paradoxically depends upon its functioning in tension with forces of opposition.

Only power can check power. Very well. But no Middle American Radical class exists to wield such power. What do exist and can be strengthened are specific institutions—unions as well as corporations, churches as well as community associations—the leading elements of which inescapably constitute part of the managerial elite itself. It remains true that the managerial elite, despite all internal tensions or, as it were, contradictions, should be expected to close ranks on certain issues and under certain conditions. Although always dangerous, that common front would not always be a bad thing. More to the point, institutions and communities that retain considerable autonomy have the freedom of action to coalesce politically and impose their will. Francis, in his upbeat moments, says as much. Unfortunately, his obsession with the managerial elite as a class-in-itself keeps him from having many upbeat moments.

Marx believed that the proletariat had the historic opportunity and duty to replace the bourgeoisie as a ruling class, although, contrary to prevalent misconception, he knew it might fail: Recall, for example, his warning about the possibility of a "proslavery rebellion." He also insisted that, with rare exceptions, the state had to serve the interests of a specific ruling class. Marx did not prove a good prophet. Francis's analysis and the evidence all around us suggest that no class has the capacity to replace the old bourgeoisie and that the managerial elite has shown little sign that it can function as an autonomous ruling class.

A hegemonic elite we have always had with us, and no leftwing utopian dreams will change matters. For the foreseeable future that elite will be managerial and will doubtless pursue its discrete interests as a stratum. But the experience of fascism, national-socialism, communism, social democracy, and liberal bureaucratism casts doubts on the ability of the managerial elite to consolidate its rule. It cannot even consolidate itself. It splits, as all social classes now split, over visions of a civilized society as readily as it splits over the interests of its several components. And at such a historical moment, that moral suasion we realists are so quick to dismiss with contempt returns to mock us. Practical considerations, not idealistic projections, are teaching us that interests and moral vision are inextricably bound up within, rather than between, social classes. A political coalition that can arrest our national decline will have to cross class lines and bring a decisive section of the managerial elite to its service.

Francis's achievement, apart from the many insights he sprinkles throughout his essays, lies in his forceful reopening of the question of class power and critique of reigning illusions. Specifically, he challenges us to focus on the great underlying question of property relations: the consequences of the separation of ownership from control and the extent to which, and manner in which, private property can be defended and yet rendered socially responsible. It is no point against him that, along with everyone else, he has not yet found a blueprint to lead us out of the wilderness. The Left as well as the Right would profit greatly from a vigorous debate over his principal theses. It would be a shame if that debate were to be rendered politically impossible by a polemical stance that threatens a fratricidal war among those whose possible programmatic unity holds out the main hope for a radical change in our national fortunes.

Afterword

Francis has run into a problem that besets all who publish collections of essays—a problem I shall not be surprised to find that I have myself run into in this book. He has included material that seems to say one thing in the context of his book and yet might not well represent his views properly. Thus his harsh attack on the environmentalists does not necessarily mean that he is oblivious to environmental problems or that he is not prepared to support environmentalist measures of a certain kind. But by including one set of reflections without others, he has opened himself to a negative reading. On a broader theoretical matter: He has caviled at my suggestion that he implicitly embraces the rigid Marxist formula that one social class must replace another in power. I do not doubt that he could provide a much more flexible and sound exposition of his views than is suggested in his book. I do think, however, that his polemics have gotten him in a box, and I can only hope that he favors us with the superior formulation he is capable of providing.

22

The Southern Tradition and the Black Experience

I am, to say the least, honored to receive your Richard Weaver Award and to be invited to share some thoughts with you tonight.

Richard Weaver observed, in *Ideas Have Consequences:* "There is ground for declaring that modern man has become a moral idiot. . . . For four centuries every man has been not only his own priest but his own professor of ethics, and the consequence is an anarchy which threatens even that minimum of consensus of value necessary to the political state." Refusing to despair, Dr. Weaver fashioned his book as a weapon in a protracted war for spiritual renewal. Yet, reflecting on the ravages of what he called the "hysterical optimism" of modern man, he added, "Whether man any longer wants to live in society at all or is willing to accept an animal existence is a question that must be raised in all seriousness." With those words in mind, permit me some reflections on the deepening racial crisis in America and the constructive insights that may be brought to bear by the southern conservative tradition for which Dr. Weaver spoke.

About 50 percent of black teenagers do not attend school, and the black unemployment rate runs several times higher than that for whites. Plausible analyses project a substantial majority of black males dead, on drugs, or in jail by the age of twenty-five. Blacks may be pardoned for hyperbole in speaking of creeping genocide, for they are getting too close to the truth for comfort.

Behind the statistics lie not merely the unemployed and under-employed, but a growing number of unemployables. We may reasonably counter the implicit threat to our society by invoking the harshest of measures to put down riots, uprisings, and frontal assaults on our persons, homes, and political institutions. For self-preservation is the foremost "right" of any people. But we cannot reasonably leave it at that. For in resorting to what may become necessary measures, we shall risk the repudiation of our Judeo-Christian heritage, the defilement of our national soul, and the shredding of the very free political institutions we are trying to preserve.

The "drug culture," "crime in the streets," and the decline of "law and order," however much invoked as racist code words, gravely threaten all of us, especially the black people who constitute the principal victims. A debate on the Left was recently opened by the Reverend Eugene Rivers, the black Pentecostal pastor of the Azusa Christian Community, who has been leading the fight to restore civilized community life to the Dorchester ghetto outside Boston. His article in *Boston Review*, "On the Responsibility of Intellectuals in the Age of Crack," has created a storm that is now spreading to other parts of the country. Mr. Rivers, politically a man of the Left, has invoked what is generally perceived as a conservative theme and identified the root of the crisis as spiritual—as a catastrophic decline in Judeo-Christian moral values:

> As entry into the labor markets is increasingly dependent on education and high skills, we will see, perhaps, for the first time in the history of the United States, a generation of economically obsolete Americans.
>
> But remarkably, the tragedy we face is still worse. Unlike many of our ancestors, who came out of slavery and entered this century with strong backs, discipline, a thirst for literacy, deep religious faith, and hope in the face of monumental adversity, we have produced "a generation who [do] not know the ways of the Lord"—a "new jack" generation, ill-equipped to secure gainful employment even as productive slaves.

We should not be surprised to find that Mr. Rivers's superb essay evokes some of the essential values associated with Richard

Weaver and the luminaries of the southern conservative tradition. For a substantial portion of black America has long adhered to those values, notwithstanding deep disagreements over the ensuing politics. Mr. Rivers believes that America, black and white, must adhere to the moral baseline provided by the Ten Commandments and the Sermon on the Mount. And he insists that, so far as practicable in a world dominated by a global economy, political power must rest with the people of discrete communities, the historically evolved preferences and prejudices of which must be respected so long as they do not violate that moral baseline.

Thus he has forcefully opposed those who argue that the Cultural War has already been lost and that attention should be turned elsewhere. He has replied that if the cultural war is lost, all will be lost. In a response to Mr. Rivers's initiative, Glen Loury, the "black conservative" economist, made a critical distinction between the market economy, which he supports, and the improper extension of a free-market ideology to society as a whole. And in truth, it is hard to believe that we could expect to live as civilized human beings in a society that makes consumer choice the arbiter of our moral and spiritual life. Thus from across the political spectrum we are hearing calls for a reexamination of the relation of religion to society and long overdue challenges to the monstrous mendacity that interprets the constitutional separation of church and state as justification for the suppression of religion in our schools and from our political institutions.

Sadly, the primary obstacle to a critique of the relation of religion to American society arises within the mainstream churches themselves, significant sections of which have virtually repudiated the essentials of historic Christian doctrine and which undermine their own institutional autonomy by submission to prevalent political ideology. It is therefore especially heartening that black clergymen are raising their voices against these perversions of doctrine and attendant political opportunism.

But we dare not mince words on the lamentable stance long taken by southern conservatives on race relations. Tragically, southern resistance to national consolidation and totalitarian tendencies, combined with a discretely admirable defense of community autonomy, has historically served as a rationale for the defense of slavery, racial segregation, and manifold injustices. Here the intellectuals and community leaders failed miserably. It would have been one thing if southern conservatives had taken full account of the plainly irrational prejudices and vicious racial practices of their communities and worked calmly and steadily to bring their people to a higher standard of justice. Instead, they either fell silent or actually endorsed those prejudices and injustices.

Good Burkeans should not have to be told that an effective defense of historically evolved community prejudices and policies depends upon a willingness to effect needful reforms, especially in the face of blatant injustice. Those who today do not struggle against the enormity of racism in their own communities might at least spare us their whining when a federal government, with its own questionable and sometimes sinister agenda, imposes anti-discrimination measures from without. It serves no useful purpose to rail that consolidationist measures will, in the long run, do inestimable damage to black people as well as white. Black America is bleeding from every pore and can hardly be faulted if it gambles on a problematic federal intervention in the absence of effective alternatives.

At issue here is not this or that political or economic program, about which honorable men may disagree, but the context in which those battles are being fought out. Regardless of the political specifics, the American people, white as well as black, have poor prospects without that minimal moral consensus which Dr. Weaver insisted must rest on standards derived from the Judeo-Christian tradition and the piety inherent in what he called "the older religiousness of the South." And it is to that very piety which Mr. Rivers has appealed—as have countless unsung heroes in the ghettos, who selflessly struggle against a subculture of drugs, crime, and hopelessness.

There are, then, excellent prospects for a coalition across racial and inherited ideological lines to combat the moral degeneracy that now runs rampant throughout both white and black America. But the unspeakable misery that plagues black America cannot be cured by the resurrection of demonstrably inadequate integrationist formulas, whether of free-market, liberal, or socialistic varieties. So far, nothing has worked because, for different reasons, liberals, conservatives, and radicals alike obscure the essentials of the black experience in America. They all assimilate that experience to the experience of others—European and Asian immigrants, colonial peoples abroad, or the laboring classes in general. Yet its uniqueness emerges from the history of slavery and segregation, which confronted black people with a raw oppression and exploitation well beyond that experienced by European immigrants.

On this big subject permit me a few broad strokes. Other peoples contributed much to the development of an American national culture, but despite acute discrimination, they were not condemned as an inferior race, and they were able to progress and consolidate their gains through the steady accretion of political power. Not so for Africans and their descendants. Africans arrived with Europeans at the beginning of our history. Everything was done to separate them from their religions, languages, and general culture. Worse, unlike European immigrants, they were repeatedly driven backward and prevented from consolidating political and economic gains. Yes, they were offered the Christian religion, the English language, and the Anglo-Saxon political tradition, but they were simultaneously barred from full participation as equals and told to accept their place as menials and as, at best, second-class citizens.

In the event, by forging a distinct Afro-American culture, which should not be confused with the manifestations of moral decadence now celebrated by a cynical Academia and mass media, blacks survived the ordeal of slavery and segregation spiritually as well as physically. We need to understand the black experience as that of a people at once American and yet a people apart. Historically, it has been an experience that offers rational grounds for both integrationist and black-nationalist ideologies. For black people have constituted a nation-within-a-nation and have emerged as a people with—to borrow an expression from General de Gaulle—a "national personality" of their own.

I am suggesting that black people have good grounds for claim-ing a measure of autonomy to accommodate their simultaneous existence as Americans and as other. Emphatically, I am not sug-gesting that any other people can legitimately make such claims. To the contrary, nothing is more appalling than the current dema-gogy that proclaims the right of various ethnic groups to establish their own people's republics, with their own language and politi-cal principles.

All I ask is that whites of every political and ideological stripe consider the argument for a wide measure of black autonomy on its own merits. I do not much like self-quotation, but I shall ask your indulgence since I explored the political implications of this argument in my contribution to the debate in the leftwing *Boston Review* and do not wish to risk a shift in tone or content here. Thus I wrote:

> Any effort by the black community to combat spiritual and so-cial decay . . . depends upon that community's ability to impose considerable social discipline and to rein in antisocial elements. As Rivers has suggested, the struggle to restore a stable family life may well prove sine qua non, and, if so, the necessary measures may not comport well with the endless demands for individual rights and the arrogant pretensions to such newly invented constitutional protections as envisaged, for example, in the program of the gay and lesbian movement. Whites have no business in trying to tell the black community . . . how to resolve these problems and would do well to keep their preferences and prejudices to themselves. But to speak of "community" at all means to recognize as unavoidable the existence of prejudices, whether grounded in a historically or religiously developed sen-sibility or in response to an immediate threat to survival. Whites have a responsibility to support the efforts of black communities to solve all such problems in their own way and in accordance with their own preferences and prejudices, so long as standards of common decency prevail. . . .
>
> A government—any government—that cringes in the face of massive looting, rioting, and defiance of social order does not deserve to survive and probably will not long survive. If the American people are forced to choose between urban terrorism and authoritarian repression, it would be surprising if they did not choose the latter. And they would have every moral as well as

political sanction for doing so. For if any "right" is well grounded in human nature, historical experience, and common sense, it is the right of self-preservation.

The imposition of the law and order necessary for the survival of the black community cannot be effected from without. In a racist society such an imposition would take predictable forms with predictable results and would be bitterly and properly resisted. But if so, then black communities have good reason to demand considerable political autonomy and the power to deal with their antisocials in their own way. Community survival and healthy development require considerable discipline and, necessarily, considerable repression. The essential demand ought to be that these specific communities solve their own version of what is now a general problem for America in accordance with their own experience, traditions, and collective sense of imperatives. Must, for example, black communities, to say nothing of white, exclude the churches from their schools and affairs if they conclude that their inclusion and close cooperation with the polity are essential for the reestablishment of moral order? And if the churches, following scriptural and historical authority, declare homosexuality sinful and a threat to community reproduction, discipline, and good order, are they to be told that their autonomy stops there? If so, on what grounds? What, exactly, is the "self-evident truth" at issue here? To whom is it self-evident?

Let me elaborate on those remarks here tonight, as I expect to do in further discussions in leftwing circles. When Lani Guinier tried to raise urgent questions about the distribution of political power, she, in effect, raised the very questions forcefully posed by the political theory of John C. Calhoun and his proslavery compeers— most notably, the doctrine of concurrent majority. For in truth, racists or no, the southern conservatives were the first to raise most of the burning questions in the early days of the republic, and we have much to learn from their efforts. The question remains: Is it possible to separate the healthy core of that thought from the indefensible framework in which it was originally presented? I have no idea how Ms. Guinier would have responded to this challenge if she had been given her day in court. I do note, as no few others have, that the liberals who control the White House and Congress went to extraordinary lengths to suppress the issues.

We are today indeed engaged in a cultural war. To win that war will require a new and hitherto unimaginable coalition across political and racial lines. Richard Weaver's contributions to that effort, notwithstanding the political partisanship appropriate to his own day, remain indispensable. No less indispensable are the voices of a rising generation of blacks who have learned from the tragic history of their people the lessons that southern whites have learned from theirs. For the outcome of the Cultural War will decide everything else of importance, and that outcome will depend upon our common willingness to overcome ancient hostilities and hear each other's voices. It would be astonishing if white and black voices rose together, across long-standing ideological divides, to show the way to victory. May we live to be astonished.

Epilogue

"a decent respect to the opinions
of mankind"

23

The Question

As a university professor, I teach, participate in professional associations, lecture on various campuses, give papers at scholarly conferences, and review books for national journals and local newspapers: In short, I get around. For many years I have lived in dread of having to answer The Question. Curiously, no one has asked it.

At first I wondered if I had an ego problem. Did I feel bruised to learn that I am not important enough to be asked? Were not more visible and professionally celebrated chaps with similar backgrounds having to face the music? Apparently not. So far as I know, none of the others, whose number is legion, has been asked either.

The Question: "What did you know, and when did you know it?" For at the age of fifteen I became a Communist, and, although expelled from the Party in 1950 at the age of twenty, I remained a supporter of the international movement and of the Soviet Union until there was nothing left to support. Now, as everyone knows, in a noble effort to liberate the human race from violence and oppression we broke all records for mass slaughter, piling up tens of millions of corpses in less than three-quarters of a century. When the Asian figures are properly calculated, the aggregate to our credit may reach the seemingly incredible numbers widely claimed. Those who are big on multiculturalism might note that the great majority of our victims were nonwhite.

Never having been much good at math, I shy away from quibbles over statistics. Still, all quibbles aside, we have a disquieting number of corpses to account for.

Those of us who have preached the need to break eggs in order to make omelets might note the political complexion of some of the eggs. About twenty years ago, picking up on some passages in Roy Medvedev's *Let History Judge*, I wondered if Comrade Stalin had not killed more communists than were killed by all the bourgeois, imperialist, fascist, and Nazi regimes put together. "It can't be true," said I. "Has Comrade Medvedev taken up serious drinking?" So I sat down to do some rough arithmetic. (You do not have to be good at math to do that much arithmetic.) Alas, Comrade Medvedev had not taken up serious drinking.

Reflecting here on moral responsibility, I have referred to "we." For it has never occurred to me that the moral responsibility falls much less heavily on those of us on the American Left than it fell on Comrade Stalin and those who replicated his feats in one country after another. And I am afraid that some of that moral responsibility falls on the "democratic socialists," "radical democrats," and other leftwingers who endlessly denounced Stalinism but could usually be counted on to support—"critically," of course—the essentials of our political line on world and national affairs.[1]

Especially amusing has been the spectacle of those who pronounced themselves Anti-Stalinists and denounced the socialist countries at every turn and yet even today applaud each new revolution, although any damned fool has to know that most

---

1. In speaking of a measure of shared responsibility, I intend no equation of social democrats and liberals with Stalinists. I am concerned with a reexamination of concepts and values shared by the Left as a whole. One critic remarked that his preferred portion of the Left "refused to call socialist anything not truly democratic." Well, why not? Socialism, like capitalism, is a socioeconomic system, and I see no theoretical or historical reason to believe that socialism must be democratic. We need to reexamine our very understanding of "socialism" and of "democracy."

of them will end in the same place. For that matter, how could we have survived politically were it not for the countless liberals who, to one extent or another, supported us, apparently under the comforting delusion that we were social reformers in rather too much of a hurry—a delusion we ourselves never suffered from.

There are liberals and liberals, and a distinction would have to be made in a more leisurely presentation. Even in Academia there are indeed those who defend liberal principles tenaciously and honorably. But the countless opportunists and careerists who dominate the historical associations call themselves liberals as a matter of political convenience. They went with the McCarthyite flow in the 1950s and go with its leftwing variant today. In the unlikely prospect of a fascist or communist ascendancy tomorrow, they may be counted on to apply for party cards as soon as it looks like the smart move.

Many of my old comrades and almost all of those ostensibly independent radicals and high-minded liberals remain unruffled. After all, did we not often protest against some outrage or other in the Soviet Union or China, signing an indignant petition or open letter? I know I did. And does not that change everything? I am afraid not, but I have nothing to offer as critique other than that which may be found in *Galatians* 6:7.

On May 11, 1992, having been invited by the rightwing American Enterprise Institute to reflect on the collapse of the socialist countries, I summoned up whatever capacity I have for dissembling in an effort to deflect the one question I did not want to answer. I did not want to answer it before a rightwing audience because I feared I would unleash my Sicilian temper and counterattack with the litany of the crimes of the imperialists and their insufferable apologists. I began:

> It is a great pleasure to be with you today, although, since I claim expertise only as a historian of the Old South, I speak on current issues with trepidation. I do hope that your invitation carries no sadistic intent—that you do not expect an autobiographical *mea culpa*. For while it is true that I have been a Marxist and a bitter-end supporter of the Soviet Union, I dislike

autobiographies and admire the CIA's noble dictum, "Admit nothing, explain nothing, apologize for nothing."

The audience responded with good-natured laughter. Generally speaking, rightwingers are decidedly more courteous than we of the Left and would not think of abusing their guests, as I probably would have abused them if challenged. They laid some tough questions on me during the discussion period, but not The Question.

Recently, I remarked upon the corpses to a well-known leftwing journalist with whom my wife and I were having dinner. He looked disgusted: "You? You of all people are getting masochistic?" I reassured him as best I could. For, no, I am not getting masochistic in my old age. No, I am not about to cringe before rightwingers who supported numerous imperialist slaughters or social democrats whose responsible and moderate governments aided and abetted them. Yes, I do remember the glorious record of the bourgeoisie in the slave trade and the plantation colonies and the mass murders in Africa, Asia, and Latin America. I do recall that the Holocaust was not our doing. I still burn at the indifference with which virtually the whole American public received the reports of a quarter million Indonesian workers and peasants butchered in the 1960s, not in a civil war but in their beds. And I know the rest. No, I would not stand still for The Question from those people and would probably tell them what I have always told my classes, "Your side has had its mass murderers, and we have had ours."

Perhaps knowledge of the record of imperialist atrocities leads our liberal colleagues to refuse to single us out by asking The Question. But I am afraid not. After all, they never stop asking southern whites about their crimes, real and imagined, against blacks. And let's face it: All the combined crimes of white southerners, at least if we restrict ourselves to the period since emancipation, would be worth no more than a footnote in a casebook that starred us.

A few years ago there was a successful effort to get the Organization of American Historians to condemn apartheid in South

Africa.[2] In the OAH and other professional associations Professor Wilcomb Washburn resolutely opposed the politicization, and attempted to expose its hypocrisy by offering an amendment to condemn the "necklacing" of black South Africans, including children, by the militants of the African National Congress. (For those who have forgotten, "necklacing" was execution by burning the victim alive.) The ANC subsequently repudiated necklacing as not only wrong but barbarous. The OAH has yet to endorse that repudiation.

I laughed. Those bloody South African whites did kill a lot of blacks and ought to answer for it, but throughout their whole history they probably never equaled the numbers we put up in one of our more spirited month's work. I laughed even harder when our liberal colleagues poured out their wrath on the ghastly racists in South Africa while they remained silent about the immeasurably greater slaughters occasioned by the periodic ethnic cleansing that was—and is—going on in black Africa and every other part of the globe. The *New York Times* recently announced that the death toll in the latest round of ethnic cleansing in Burundi has reached 150,000, with the fate of a half million or so refugees in doubt. The historical associations have not been heard from. Nor should anyone expect that they will be.[3]

2. In 1969, I infuriated much of the Left by opposing the effort to commit the American Historical Association to opposition to the War in Vietnam. I had opposed that war from the beginning and came close to losing my job because of my outspoken support for the Vietcong. Indeed, I believe that I have the honor of being the only college professor whom Richard Nixon personally campaigned to get fired. But unlike most of my leftwing friends, I had sport with the notions that Ho Chi Minh was a latter-day Jeffersonian democrat and that the Vietnamese Communists were fighting for "freedom" and "democracy." The war, I insisted, was over national unification, socialism, and the balance of power in Asia—the rest was hogwash. I said plainly that the winning side would impose a harsh dictatorship and that the only question was who would do whom.

3. At the time this article saw print the much greater slaughter in Rwanda was making headlines, although not the slaughter in the Sudan, which has been going on for decades.

If we are to believe the worthies of the radical Left, to pose The Question means to engage in a reactionary ploy to deflect attention from the oppression of women, gays, and other beleaguered minorities. Scholars in our own ranks have shown precious little interest in reflecting seriously on the collapse of the socialist countries we supported to the bitter end or on any personal responsibilities we might have for the occasional unpleasantness that led to so sad a denouement.

And sad the denouement has been. For one might make a case of sorts to justify mass slaughters as the necessary price to be paid for a grand human liberation. Terrible as the sacrifices may have been, were they not justified by the beautiful world of equality, justice, and universal love we were creating for our children? During the communist revolution of 1919 in Hungary, Sigmund Freud startled his friends by announcing that he had become half a Bolshevik. One of his communist students explained that the revolution would mean oceans of blood out of which would come a just and humane society. Freud became half a Bolshevik: He declared his belief in every word of the first half.

In retrospect Freud looks good and we not so good. Our justification began to look seedy when the grand liberation featured hideous political regimes under which no sane person would want to live. It became preposterous when our project ended in the ignominious collapse of the social system that was supposed to undergird a brave new world and justify the staggering sacrifice of human life.

We easily forget the economic rationale that Marx taught us, namely, that socialism would have to provide unprecedented abundance if it were to sustain social liberation of any kind. With a few notable exceptions, leftists no longer find it fashionable to discuss economics at all beyond the now routine rejection of a "command economy" and some disingenuous mumbling about the necessity for markets. But where is there a serious attempt to determine the extent to which any socialism could function without a command economy or to show how a socialist economy could integrate markets? A few leftwing economists, most notably Louis Ferleger and Jay Mandle, tried to raise these questions long before the collapse of the socialist economies, but they were effectively shut out of the leftwing press and are still ignored. And we may doubt that the wry remark of Nancy Folbre and Samuel Bowles, two other respected leftwing economists, will cause a wrinkle: "Leftwing economists—among whom we count ourselves—have thus far failed to come up with a convincing alternative to capitalism."[4]

No one should be surprised that none of our leading historical associations have thought it intellectually challenging to devote sessions at their enormous annual meetings to frank discussions of the socialist debacle. We of the Left are regularly invited to give papers on just about any subject except this one. We are not asked to assess the achievements as well as the disasters, the heroism as well as the crimes, and the lessons we ourselves have learned from a tragic experience. No one need be surprised that we have never been called upon to explain ourselves. The *pezzonovanti* of our profession have more important things on their minds. When they can take time away from their primary concern (the distribution of jobs, prizes, and other forms of patronage), they are immersed in grave condemnations of the appalling violations of human rights by Christopher Columbus. I know that it is in bad taste to laugh, but I laugh anyway. I would rather be judged boorish than be seen throwing up.

We do not need guilt trips and breast-beating. We do need a sober reassessment of the ideological foundations of our political course. I am not sure that I am right to refuse to answer to our longtime political adversaries. But I am sure that we of the Left have to answer to ourselves, to each other, to the movement to which we have devoted our lives, and especially to the millions of our comrades who were themselves slaughtered in a heroic effort to make the world a better place. The Left sneers at Burke's

4. Nancy Folbre and Samuel Bowles, letter to *The Nation*, November 29, 1993; and see also, Louis Ferleger and Jay R. Mandle, *A New Mandate: Democratic Choices for a Prosperous Economy* (Columbia: University of Missouri Press, 1994).

great dictum that government—or, better, society—is a compact between the living, the dead, and the as yet unborn. But the truth of the dictum returns to haunt us again and again. If nothing else, we cannot escape the duty to see that the millions of our comrades who died in revolutionary struggles did not die in vain.

Am I crazy to think that if we do not understand why and how we did what we did, we shall certainly end by doing it again— and again? Crazy I may be, but I try not to be a fool. And only a fool would trust those who are now playing possum with even a modicum of political power.

What did we know, and when did we know it? We knew everything essential and knew it from the beginning. This short answer will doubtless be hotly contested by the substantial number of leftwingers now ensconced in the academic Establishment. I can hear them now: "Where does Genovese get off speaking for us? Yes, he himself always knew. He never even had the decency to pretend not to know. He thereby proved himself the cad we have always known him to be. But we ourselves never even imagined that we were hearing anything more than the usual stories circulated by imperialists and reactionaries. Honest."

I am prepared to accept those pleas of innocence, and I hope that everyone else exercises Christian charity and accepts them too. But I do worry about where pleas of innocence will land those who offer them. It occurs to me that it would be much safer to admit complicity. For Americans who honor the spirit and content of the Constitution would feel compelled to defend our academic freedom, including our right to have borne with equanimity the blood purges and mass executions. If, however, our innocents insist upon pleading ignorance rather than a complicity permitted by the Constitution, they ruin themselves. Especially the historians among them. For they thereby admit to a willful refusal to examine the evidence that had been piled high from the beginning. Thus they confess to professional incompetence. I counsel against such a plea, for it would constitute grounds for revocation of tenure. Safer to plead nolo contendere.

When someone gets around to asking me The Question I shall answer frankly, explaining as best I can our reasons for having gone along. But I shall insist upon doing so in a forum in which "democratic socialists," "radical democrats," and liberals are called upon to answer too. For it is our collective dirty linen that has to be washed. And besides, our rightwing adversaries already know the answer, even if they have no few hard questions to answer themselves.[5]

For the moment I shall settle for a few topic sentences. The horrors did not arise from perversions of radical ideology but from the ideology itself. We were led into complicity with mass murder and the desecration of our professed ideals not by Stalinist or other corruptions of high ideals, much less by unfortunate twists in some presumably objective course of historical development, but by a deep flaw in our very understanding of human nature— its frailty and its possibilities—and by our inability to replace the moral and ethical baseline long provided by the religion we have dismissed with indifference, not to say contempt.[6]

5. For shorthand: I supported the communist movement and the Soviet Union because I was convinced of the moral as well as material superiority of socialism over capitalism—convinced that the socialist countries could and would reform themselves and end their political brutality while preserving socialism itself. I was wrong. But I also argued that the American Left must engage in practices that would prepare us for a socialist America that respected freedom and diversity. Specifically, I always insisted that we could claim for ourselves no rights that we were not prepared to grant others and always staunchly defended the academic freedom of conservatives as well as of leftists. These themes were at the center of my book *In Red and Black: Marxian Explorations in Southern and Afro-American History* (first published in 1971; a new edition appeared in 1984 from the University of Tennessee Press).

6. I have been chided for identifying radical utopianism as the root of Stalinism. I should have been clearer. Usually, critics attack Marxist scientism and materialism and appeal to the early Marx. The roots of Stalinism do lie in both, and both, separately and in combination, need a stern reappraisal. If I singled out one side, I intended a corrective and have no wish to obscure the force of the other side. For an elaboration of my view of the doleful political effects of utopian ideology see my *The Future of Freedom in an International Civil War* (The Sol Feinstone Lecture, St. Lawrence University, 1975); "Critical Legal Studies as Radical Politics and Ideology," *Yale Journal of Law and the*

The question of moral responsibility has been raised within the Left, if gingerly and indirectly, by a few brave souls like Roberto Mangabeira Unger and Cornel West, who have drawn attention to the price we have paid for scouting Christian ethics while having nothing to substitute and who have, in effect, called for an end to the blind hatreds that confuse the sin with the sinner. Unger and West are justly revered figures on the Left and accorded at least formal respect. Yet their efforts toward a reassessment of the religious foundations of political ethics have not sparked the slightest discussion. It is fair to ask: What kind of respect is that? Are we supposed to believe that Unger and West have been kidding?

Our whole project of "human liberation" has rested on a series of gigantic illusions. The catastrophic consequences of our failure during this century—not merely the body count but the monotonous recurrence of despotism and wanton cruelty—cannot be dismissed as aberrations. Slimmed down to a technologically appropriate scale, they have followed in the wake of victories by radical egalitarian movements throughout history. We have yet to answer our rightwing critics' claims, which are regrettably well documented, that throughout history from ancient times to the peasant wars of the sixteenth century to the Reign of Terror and beyond social movements that have espoused radical egalitarianism and participatory democracy have begun with mass murder and ended in despotism.

Let us grant, *arguendo*, that the ruling classes have done worse. Whatever solace that thought may give us, our own problem remains: What kind of society could we build on a worldview marred by flagrant irrationalities paraded as self-evident truths, even if reinforced by sandbox cries of "You're another"?

The allegedly high ideals we placed at the center of our ideology and politics are precisely what need to be reexamined, but they

Humanities, 1991; and *The Southern Tradition: The Achievement and Limitations of an American Conservatism* (Cambridge: Harvard University Press, 1994).

can no longer even be made a subject for discussion in the mass media and our universities, to say nothing of within the Left itself.[7] They are givens: an unattainable equality of condition; a radical democracy that has always ended in the tyranny it is supposed to overcome; a celebration of human goodness or malleability, accompanied by the daily announcement of newly discovered "inalienable rights" to personal self-expression; destruction of all hierarchy and elites, as if ideological repudiation has ever prevented or ever could prevent the formation and re-formation of

---

7. The suppression of campus discussion and criticism by the Left is nothing new. Present practices recapitulate earlier ones. Elizabeth Fox-Genovese of Emory University presided over a Women's Studies program open to radicals, lesbians, liberals, conservatives, and all others. She was purged at the hands of our radical democrats, who have spread every kind of slander—right down to the droll charge that she (and I) try to force our graduate students to do our family laundry. For years I was under heavy assault for my pro-Communist views from the John Birch Society and other rightwingers, but, with rare exceptions, however ruthlessly they attacked, they attacked politically, never with wild inventions about my (and my wife's) alleged private life. On our campuses at least, only the radical Left practices character assassination and mendacity as a matter of course. It is worth noting, however, that campaigns of slander, no matter how vile or implausible, will always find a ready audience among academics, for whom gossip, fair or foul, seems to brighten up what must be dull lives. I have the sinking feeling that no sooner do these people announce their fantasies than they actually believe them. Now that is scary.

What continues to fascinate me is not the performance of the Mid-Atlantic Radical Historians' Association and the radical feminists, from whom I have learned to expect nothing better, but the active complicity or public silence of others on the Left and of professed liberals. I wrote that "we" knew everything essential about the communist countries from the beginning. But there are two kinds of knowing. Some of us knew, said we knew, and defended our positions one way or the other. Never, for example, did I hide the story of the great Soviet purges and the massive bloodletting from the students I taught in courses on Western civilization, Marxism, the communist movement, and the Third World. Others decided not to know what they damned well did know, and they transformed their lying into a higher truth. That kind of internalization of deceit was a hallmark of Stalinism, and we are inundated with it now.

hierarchies and elites; condemnation of "illegitimate" authority in the absence of any notion of what might constitute legitimate authority; and, at the root of all, a thorough secularization of society, bolstered by the monstrous lie that the constitutional separation of church and state was meant to separate religion from society. And we have yet to reassess the anti-Americanism— the self-hatred implicit in the attitude we have generally effected toward our country—that has led us into countless stupidities and worse.

Let us give ourselves some credit: Through it all we have preserved a rich sense of humor. The destruction of hierarchies, elites, and authority is to be effected through the concentration of power in a Leviathan state miraculously free of all such reactionary encumbrances.

No wonder liberals are ready to absolve us from our sins without first hearing our confession. No wonder we are witnessing the virtual fusion of left-liberalism and revolutionary radicalism in the wake of the collapse of the socialist countries. For most leftwing liberals share with radicals much the same ideology of personal liberation. Radicals and conservatives alike have always charged liberals with bad faith in refusing to carry out the logic of their own egalitarian and radical-democratic premises. They have been right about the refusal but not necessarily about the bad faith. There are more charitable explanations, including a healthy gut revulsion by humane liberals against the substitution of logical consistency for common decency and common sense.

I have been piling up assertions and may be wrong on all counts. But am I wrong in believing that unless the Left reopens these fundamental questions it will have no future and deserve none? The deepest trouble with "political correctness" arises from its thinly disguised invitation to an endless repetition of crimes, atrocities, and, worst of all, failures. Yes, worst of all the failures. For the deepening horror that black America faces, to speak of no other impending horror, cannot be arrested by a morally bankrupt movement with an appalling record of political and economic failure, no matter how many pyrrhic victories it piles up on deranged and degraded college campuses.

The Left has been right to fight for social justice. As Aleksandr Solzhenitsyn, no friend of ours, recently observed, "Although the earthly ideal of Socialism-Communism has collapsed, the problems it purported to solve remain: the brazen use of social advantage and the inordinate power of money, which often direct the very course of events" (*New York Times*, November 28, 1993.) Our indictment of class injustice, racism, and the denigration of women has not been rendered less urgent by the failure of socialism. The millions of our own martyred comrades who fought against those enormities need not have died in vain. But they will indeed have died in vain if we refuse to face our past squarely, subject our basic premises to stern review, own up to all that has gone wrong, and take the measures necessary to guarantee against the next round of the same old story.

Bibliographical Notes

"Marxism, Christianity, and Bias in the Study of Southern Slave Society" was presented at a conference on objectivity in history, sponsored by the Institute for the Study of American Evangelicals, at Wheaton College, in April 1994 and published in Daryl G. Hart and Bruce Kuklick, eds., *Religious Advocacy and History* (forthcoming).

"Hans Rosenberg at Brooklyn College: A Communist Student's Recollections of the Classroom as War Zone," recounts my experiences as a student at Brooklyn College in the late 1940s and early 1950s. Its political relevance need not, I trust, be belabored. It appeared in *Central European History* 24 (1991), the spring issue of which was devoted to the memory of Hans Rosenberg, the distinguished historian who left Nazi Germany for the United States and ended his academic career at the University of California, Berkeley.

"James Johnston Pettigrew," originally published as "A Representative Man" in *Chronicles: A Magazine of American Culture* 14, no. 10 (October 1990), reviews Clyde N. Wilson, *Carolina Cavalier: The Life and Mind of James Johnston Pettigrew* (Athens: University of Georgia Press, 1990).

"James Henley Thornwell" was originally published in *Southern Partisan* (1987). For more on the essentials of Thornwell's thought see John B. Adger and John L. Girardeau, eds., *The Collected Writings of James Henley Thornwell*, 4 vols. (Richmond, Va.: Presbyterian Committee of Publication, 1871–1873). A somewhat revised edition has been published by the Banner of Truth Trust (Edinburgh, 1986). See also Benjamin Morgan Palmer, *The Life and Letters of James Henley Thornwell* (Richmond: Whittet and Shepperson, 1875). We have no proper biography of Thornwell, but we do have a valuable book that reviews his thought and career at length and with insight: James Oscar Farmer, Jr., *The Metaphysical Confederacy: James Henley Thornwell and the Synthesis of Southern Values* (Macon, Ga.: Mercer University

Press, 1986), 77–121. See also William Freehling, *The Reintegration of American History* (New York: Oxford University Press, 1994), chap. 4.

"Thomas B. Chaplin," originally published in the *New York Times Book Review*, July 20, 1986, reviews Theodore Rosengarten, *Tombee: Portrait of a Cotton Planter, with the Journal of Thomas B. Chaplin (1822–1890)*, ed. Theodore Rosengarten and Susan W. Walker (William Morrow and Co., 1986). Copyright © 1986 by The New York Times Company. Reprinted by permission.

"The Culture of the Old South" was originally published as "The Cultural History of Southern Slave Society: Reflections on the Work of Lewis P. Simpson," in J. Gerald Kennedy and Daniel Mark Fogel, eds., *American Letters and the Historical Consciousness: Essays in Honor of Lewis P. Simpson* (Baton Rouge: Louisiana State University Press, 1987).

"Proslavery in Transatlantic Conservative Thought" was originally published as "Larry Tise's Proslavery: A Critique and an Appreciation," *Georgia Historical Quarterly* 72 (1988): 670–83. This brief review of Larry Tise, *Proslavery: A History of the Defense of Slavery in America, 1701–1840* (Athens: University of Georgia Press, 1988), necessarily compresses a good deal of argument and cannot begin to provide documentation. I must therefore refer to a number of papers by Elizabeth Fox-Genovese and me that develop various arguments and provide preliminary documentation. Essential from our point of view is Fox-Genovese, *Within the Plantation Household: Black and White Women of the Old South* (Chapel Hill: University of North Carolina Press, 1988), which includes a discussion of households that undergirds much of our own point of view on the discrete nature of southern slave society, and my *The Slaveholders' Dilemma: Southern Conservative Thought, 1820–1860* (Columbia: University of South Carolina Press, 1991). For the method we would contrast with that of Tise see Fox-Genovese and Genovese, "The Cultural History of Southern Slave Society," chapter 6, and the articles cited in its notes. On religious life and thought see Genovese, *"Slavery Ordained of God": The Southern Slaveholders' View of Biblical History and Modern Politics* (Gettysburg: "Fortenbaugh Memorial Lecture," Gettysburg College, 1985); Genovese and Fox-Genovese, "The Religious Ideals of Southern Slave Society," *Georgia Historical Quarterly* 70 (1986): 1–16; Fox-Genovese and Genovese, "The Divine Sanction of Social Order: Religious Foundations of the

Southern Slaveholders' World View," *Journal of the American Academy of Religion* 55 (1987): 211–33.

"Higher Education in the Defense of Slave Society" was an address to the Society of Historians of the Early American Republic, the University of North Carolina, February 1993. I wish to thank Robert Brugger, John Hope Franklin, and Anne C. Loveland for the valuable criticisms that they offered in response to this paper at the session of the SHEAR. Student papers referred to in the text may be found in the North Carolina Collection of the library of the University of North Carolina at Chapel Hill.

"The Poet as Social Critic" is the foreword to Richard J. Calhoun, ed., *Witness to Sorrow: The Antebellum Autobiography of William J. Grayson* (Columbia: University of South Carolina Press, 1990).

"The Slaveholders' Contribution to the American Constitution" was presented as the Ninth Clifford Lecture ("The Intellectual Foundations of Southern Republicanism: The Slaveholders' Contribution to the American Constitution"), delivered to the American Society for Eighteenth-Century Studies, Providence, Rhode Island, April 1993.

"Christendom under Siege," originally published as "The Arrogance of History," in *The New Republic*, August 13, 1990, reviews Forrest G. Wood, *The Arrogance of Faith: Christianity and Race in America from the Colonial Era to the Twentieth Century* (New York: Alfred A. Knopf, 1990).

"Religious Foundations of the Constitution," originally published in *Reviews of American History* 19 (1991), reviews Ellis Sandoz, *A Government of Laws: Political Theory, Religion, and the American Founding* (Baton Rouge: Louisiana State University Press, 1990).

"Abolitionism's Black Prophets" was submitted to *American Presbyterians: The Journal of Presbyterian History* at the request of the editors, but was not published. It reviews David E. Swift's *Black Prophets of Justice: Activist Clergy before the Civil War* (Baton Rouge: Louisiana State University Press, 1989).

"The Theology of Martin Luther King, Jr., and Its Political Implications" contains two reviews that focus on the religious thought of Martin Luther King, Jr., in relation to his politics. It necessarily includes a discussion of his academic career and the charges of plagiarism leveled against him. The first part reviews *The Papers of Martin Luther King, Jr.: Volume One, Called to Serve, January 1929–*

June 1951; senior editor, Clayborne Carson; volume editors, Ralph E. Luker and Penny A. Russell; advisory editor, Louis R. Harlan (Berkeley: University of California Press, 1991). An abbreviated version of this part appeared as "Pilgrim's Progress," *The New Republic*, May 11, 1992. The second part reviews *Volume Two: Rediscovering Precious Values, July 1951–November 1955*; senior editor, Clayborne Carson; volume editors, Ralph E. Luker, Penny A. Russell, and Peter Halloran; advisory editor, Louis R. Harlan (Berkeley: University of California Press, 1994). It appeared in slightly different form as "Martin Luther King, Jr.: Theology, Politics, Scholarship," *Reviews in American History*, March 1995. I am especially indebted to Jack Maddex for his searching criticism of the essay, the contents of which he should not be held responsible for.

An abbreviated version of "Does God Matter?" appeared in the *Boston Sunday Globe*, October 1993, as a review of Cornel West, *Keeping Faith: Philosophy and Race in America* (New York: Routledge, 1993).

The opening pages of "Herbert Aptheker" are from the introduction to the new edition of *In Red and Black: Marxian Explorations in Southern and Afro-American History* (Knoxville: University of Tennessee Press, 1984). The principal part appeared in Gary Y. Okihiro, ed., *In Resistance: Studies in African, Caribbean, and Afro-American History* (Amherst: University of Massachusetts Press, 1986, © 1986 by the University of Massachusetts Press), which grew out of a conference to commemorate the fortieth anniversary of Aptheker's *American Negro Slave Revolts*.

"Black Studies: Academic Discipline and Political Struggle" is reprinted from John Diggins, ed., *The Ordeal of American Liberalism: Essays in Honor of Arthur Schlesinger, Jr.* (forthcoming).

"Eugene Rivers's Challenge: A Response," from *Boston Review*, October/November 1993, was written as a contribution to a symposium initiated by Eugene Rivers, "On the Responsibility of Intellectuals in the Age of Crack," *Boston Review*, September/October 1992. The Reverend Mr. Rivers is pastor of the Azusa Christian Community in Dorchester, Massachusetts.

"John Shelton Reed" is the foreword to John Shelton Reed, *Whistling Dixie: Dispatches from the South* (Columbia: University of Missouri Press, 1990).

The section "In Memoriam" to "The Voice of Southern Conservatism" was first published in *Southern Partisan* (fourth quarter 1993).

"Southern Conservatism at the Political Crossroads" reviews Samuel Francis, *Beautiful Losers: Essays on the Failure of American Conservatism* (Columbia: University of Missouri Press, 1993). A briefer version appeared as "Class Power, Again: Assessing Samuel Francis" in *Crisis: A Journal of Catholic Opinion* (September 1994) and is reprinted with the permission of *Crisis*, P.O. Box 1006, Notre Dame, Indiana 46556.

"The Southern Tradition and the Black Experience" contains remarks given at the Rockford Institute dinner on the occasion of the presentation of the Richard M. Weaver Award for Contributions to Scholarly Letters, November 1993. The text appeared in *Chronicles: A Magazine of American Culture* 18, no. 8 (August 1994).

"The Question" was published in *Dissent* (August 1994), along with a number of responses by well-known leftwing academics and my reply. I have not altered the essay to include my reply, but I have added some notes to clarify my original intentions and the position from which I wrote.

Index

114–28; and fear of slave revolts,
208–10
Slave revolts, 202, 204–10, 216
Slavery: religion of slaves, 7–12;
Thornwell on, 10–11, 31, 33–39,
62, 111, 136, 139–40, 154,
156; defense of, based on
Christianity, 10–11, 31, 33–39,
62–63, 73, 85, 86–88, 94–95,
97, 106, 125, 131–41, 155, 156;
antislavery arguments based on
Christianity, 11, 34–35, 62, 131,
155; southern intellectuals on,
39, 56, 59, 61–64; defense of,
by southern intellectuals, 56, 68,
69, 71, 89–91, 105, 108, 110–13;
Randolph on, 56–57; Jefferson
on, 56–57, 75, 100, 118–19;
northerners' attacks on, 57–58; as
dark side of Self, 75–76; Simpson
on, 75–76; Tise on proslavery in
transatlantic conservative thought,
79–91; and Federalism, 80–83;
proslavery views of northerners,
81–82, 85–89; in West India,
84; proslavery views, in southern
higher education, 92–106;
antislavery views in southern
colleges, 95, 101; ubiquity of, in
world history, 105; proponents
of "slavery in the abstract," 111;
and Constitution, 115–16; and
Catholic Church, 138; Aristotle
on, 148; Elkins on infantilized
slaves, 205; black culture in, 223,
227–28, 230–31, 282. *See also*
Abolitionism
Slave society, definition of, 83
Slave trade, 138–39
Smith, Adam, 55
Smith, Theophus H., 187
Smith, William A., 62, 86
Sobel, Mechal, 10
Socialism, 98–99, 294–95, 297n
Sociology for the South (Fitzhugh),
110
Solzhenitsyn, Aleksandr, 301

Soul Theology (Cooper-Lewter and
Mitchell), 181
South. *See* Old South; Slaveholders;
Slavery
Southern Agrarians, 74, 76, 125,
168, 244, 248, 262, 263, 266, 267
Southern conservatives: and
Thornwell, 41; and states' rights,
116, 118, 124–26, 255; and strict
construction of Constitution,
116–18, 253; and community,
240–41; Reed as, 243–46;
Bradford as, 247–60; and racism,
248, 255, 257, 280–81; and
religion, 249, 250–51; versus
fundamentalists, 249, 250–51;
and charges of anti-Semitism and
fascism, 249–50; and capitalism,
251–53; and equality, 252; and
individuality, 254; Francis on,
261–77
*Southern Essays of Richard Weaver,
The* (Weaver), 258
Southern Institutes (Sawyer), 105
Southern Tradition, 25, 29–30,
243–46, 248, 253, 255, 278–84
Southern Tradition, The (Genovese),
126, 241
Southern Tradition at Bay, The
(Weaver), 258
Southern unionism, 84–85, 96, 97,
104, 110–13, 243
Spain and the Spaniards (Pettigrew),
29
Speech, freedom of, 124
Spirit of Modern Republicanism, The
(Pangle), 143, 146
Stace, W. T., 175
Stalin, Joseph, 290
Stalinism, 264–65, 297n, 299n
Stampp, Kenneth, 205
State and Revolution (Lenin), 214
States' rights, 102, 116, 118, 124–26,
255
Stephens, Alexander, 85
Stewart, Alexander, 102